Wrongfully Accused

Bob Ford

Blessings,
Bob Ford
Ps. 32:8 L.B.

His Voice Publishing
Everson, WA USA

Wrongfully Accused

Copyright ©2010 by Bob Ford

All rights reserved. No part of this book may be used or reproduced by any means, graphic, electronic, or mechanical, including photocopying, recording, taping or by any information storage retrieval system without the written permission of the publisher except in the case of brief quotations embodied in critical articles and reviews.

His Voice books may be ordered through booksellers or by contacting:

His Voice Publishing

7304 Goodwin Rd. Suite 102

Everson, WA 98247

www.hvpublishing.net

Because of the dynamic nature of the Internet, any Web addresses or links contained in this book may have changed since publication and may no longer be valid.

ISBN: 978-0-9825284-0-2 (pbk)

ISBN: 978-0-9825284-1-9 (ebk)

Library Of Congress No. 2010901970

Printed in the United States of America

Lightning Source, Inc., La Vergne, TN

His Voice Publishing rev. 2/05/2010

Wrongfully Accused,
a true life story of over-the-top,
supernatural, modern-day
miracles of God.

Acknowledgement

To my wife, Sue and our children,
Terri, Brenda, Robert Jr., Eric, and Michelle.

CONTENTS

Foreword

Preface

Chapter 1
    Bottoms Up   1

Chapter 2
    Seven Up, Seven Down   14

Chapter 3
    The Flip Side   29

Chapter 4
    Wrongfully Accused   42

Chapter 5
    God Is Our Real Estate Agent   53

Chapter 6
    Called By God   80

Chapter 7
    Miracles Galore   98

Chapter 8
    The God-Kind Of Faith   118

Chapter 9
    Moving On   137

Chapter 10
    The Mission, The Message, and The Means   163

Chapter 11
    Attacks, Obstacles, Challenges, Robbery,
    and Blessings, Too   189

Evangelistic Opportunities   220

Foreword

I first met Bob and Sue Ford in 1973. Our families were members of the same church in Riverside, California, and they had a large family just as Joni and I did. The church we attended, Trinity Christian Center, was on fire with the presence and power of the Holy Spirit at the height of the Charismatic Renewal. Miracles of healing and answered prayer occurring at all our gatherings.

Bob and I didn't get to know each other personally till we worked together in a weekend evangelistic outreach at Venice Beach along with several other brothers whose hearts burned to win others to Jesus.

I was struck by the depth of Bob's commitment to Christ right from the start of our acquaintance, but when Bob stood to teach our outreach team, I was amazed at the depth of his grasp of the Word of God as well as his ability to communicate what God had shown him from his study of the Scripture and he was just in the beginning stages of his walk with the Lord!

His Bible knowledge and teaching skills were remarkable, but even beyond that, what impressed me most about Bob Ford was his simple, childlike faith that there was nothing too hard for God in everyday life, and not just on Sundays while in church. It seemed to me that wherever Bob went, miracles followed him. Once we were in Mexico together on a missionary outreach, and it was Bob whom God used to light the fires of divine healing. He seemed to be on the cutting edge of supernatural manifestations that could convince unbelievers that we were serving a living God, not just trying to get people to join a religion.

Reading through this manuscript was like living a big part of my own life over again. God joined Bob and me together in the work of the Lord early in his journey of faith. I truly believe God is going to use Bob and Sue's testimony in this book to awaken a spark of faith in the hearts of many. The resulting fire will burn around the world as the church again prays the prayer of Acts 4:29–30. "And now Lord, behold their threats and grant to your servants that with all boldness we may speak your word by stretching forth your hand to heal, and that signs and wonders be done in the name of your Son, Jesus!"

Robert Fitts, Author, *The Church In The House*

Preface

I wrote this book to give glory to God for His grace and mercy in saving me and my family, and proving Himself through many signs, miracles and wonders in our life and ministry. The details of my testimony are not to give any place to the devil but to give thanks to God and our Lord Jesus Christ. Satan came to steal, kill and destroy me but Jesus came through and redeemed me and gave me life in abundance. I hope to convince the reader that no matter what kind of past you have, God can turn it around for good and use you to bless others in a mighty way, all for His glory.

    I have tried to make this book as accurate as possible. The entire text is presented in my own words (except for testimonials and quotes of others), and I take full responsibility for its clarity and factual truth. All named people, places, and times are real, and my prayer is that my writing will bring glory and praise to our Lord and Savior Jesus Christ. I hope that others will learn from my mistake and from my life that God can and does use anyone for His glory. I hope that after reading this book you will come to a saving knowledge of Jesus Christ, the Lord and Savior of us all.

    I am not proud of my past. I regret that I wasted years of my life in rebellion to God and man. I didn't take advantage of my time in school, and didn't learn what it could have taught me. Events that occurred before I was saved are set forth with great pain and remorse. What I say here is often embarrassing to me. I reveal my weaknesses and I am humbled, which God knows I need to be. Everything God has so graciously done in my life is shared here for the purpose of helping someone else find the true peace and joy of eternal life, and faith for miracles through Jesus, too.

    I had to go to jail before turning to God, but it was through that experience that He turned me around. Many have said to me that I have a good testimony, but the best testimony is the one in which the one who testifies has no stain. Such testimony requires dedication and obedience to moral uprightness and demonstrates a life of true sacrifice and Christian love. This is the testimony that stands head and shoulders above mine.

Looking back on my life, I can see that God was there all along, in the midst of the mess I was making. He took the broken pieces and used them to bring me to the point of either calling out to Him for help or thumbing my nose at Him and going my own way. Because He knows the end from the beginning, He heard my cry and chose to grant me the abundance of His grace. His plan all along was to "show Himself strong in my behalf" (2 Chron. 16:9) in hopes that others like you would believe and be an instrument of His love and power.

I, of myself, can do nothing. Anything good done in or through me is all done by the grace and power of God. This book, and my testimony, is not to bring glory or attention to me, but instead to the awesome love, grace, mercy and miracle-working power of God. He so loved us that He became the man Jesus and allowed man to ridicule, torment, and mock him. He allowed man to commit the greatest atrocity of all time, by crucifying Him. I am sure that, had I lived in the days of Jesus, I too would have been one of those in the crowd shouting, *Crucify him!*

My heart breaks with love and adoration for Jesus, who willingly died for me in spite of it all. When I think of the fact that through the fall of Adam all mankind owed a debt that we could not pay, and Jesus paid a debt that he did not owe, I am humbled beyond expression and indebted to Him for all eternity. Though he made everything that was ever made (Col. 1:16), he elected to redeem us from Satan with nothing less than his own sinless blood so that He, the Triune God, Father, Son and Holy Spirit, could love us and be with us throughout all eternity. What an awesome, loving God we have. Who could not but serve Him with their whole heart?

---------- *Chapter 1* ------------

Bottoms Up

God! I cried, *if there is a God in heaven, erase this thing I've done and I'll serve you the rest of my life!*

It was two o'clock in the morning and I was driving fast to get home, trying to get there before the cops did. If I can only get there first, I thought. I've got to see Sue and the kids one more time. I knew the prison term would be at least ten years. I can't go back there. I'll die in that place.

I had no faith in God, how could I, I never saw any proof that He existed, and like Santa Clause and the Easter Bunny, God was just a fairy tale, but if ever I hoped there was a God in heaven, it was now. My cry to him was a desperate one, but it was with deep remorse, high hopes, and a tone of respect.

The Browning 380 semiautomatic concealed in my waistband was loaded and ready. My wife, Sue, often pleaded with me to leave it home, but no way. It was my constant companion, the equalizer that converted a 148-lb., 5'7" reject into a Samson. Now it seemed awfully puny, but the thought of being a convict again left me no choice but to carry it. I'll fight for my life! I refuse to be taken prisoner! Thoughts such as these raced through my head like shooting stars.

My heart was pounding as I turned the corner toward home. There were no police cars anywhere. Man, am I lucky, I thought. It can't be fifteen miles between here and the scene of the burglary. Lady Luck stay with me, don't you leave me now!

I thought of the sawed-off sixteen-gauge shotgun hidden in the closet. I carried it during the Watts riots in the '60's, and I still had over half a box of double O buckshot. Thoughts continued to race through my head, No time to lose! Get ready quick! Don't forget the Smith & Wesson 41 Magnum and 200 rounds of ammo, the twelve and twenty-gauge shotgun, and the rifle, too.

Then a fearful thought came to me, You can't win, Bob! What if Sue or one of the kids gets hurt? With my heart in my throat and my stomach like a block of concrete, I broke out in a cold sweat. I drove up to the house, jumped out of the car, and ran in the house straight to our bedroom. Sue was in bed asleep. I felt as if I had already died. I slumped to my knees next to the bed sobbing. *I'm sorry, honey, I'm sorry, so sorry.*

Echoing in my mind were the all too familiar words of my father, *Haven't you got any brains in your head at all? Use your head for more than a hat rack! Can't you ever do anything right? You'll never amount to anything!* Deep depression began to choke out the last bit of life within me. No one could have convinced me that hell itself would bring more torment than I felt at this moment. I thought, How could I feel so completely dead and still be alive? I can't take this any longer! I'm such a total failure! I wish I were dead!

When I drank with my buddies we would say, "bottoms up" as we tipped the glass and drank it dry, but as I knelt beside the bed I felt that I was looking up at the bottom of the barrel. Life itself had gone bottoms up. I began to think, Sue, the kids? How will they make it? Sue was not a working woman. I had promised her she would never have to work unless she wanted to. Priding myself on being the sole provider, I'd support my family on my own or die trying! I had to prove to my dad and the world that I was a man.

I looked up and Sue was sitting on the bed slumped over with her head between her knees. Her face showed her pain as she asked, "Why honey? Why?" I had failed her again. I felt like a rat. I had been so selfish, thinking only of myself. What a slime ball. She was so hurt, so broken. I took her in my arms and we cried, knowing we would be separated soon. Between sobs she said, "I love you and I'll wait as long as it takes."

I was so thankful for her love. She was tender, compassionate, forgiving. She had always been faithful and dedicated to me, a perfect mother to our four children. She was the kind of wife and mother that stood head and shoulders above all the rest. Now her words made me even more aware of the scum that I was. How could I do such a thing to her and the kids? If only I could turn the clock back four hours.

I was startled by a noise outside, and an awful state of fear came over me. My breathing stopped and my heart beat like a bass drum. I stood up slowly. The lights were off, so no one could see into the house, but still I thought, With the house surrounded I can't escape. Maybe they'll just shoot me. How did I ever get into this mess? *Damn you, Bob, damn you!* I said under my breath.

As I stood there frozen with fear, my life began to flash before me. I was born in Detroit in September 1939. When I was two, I was diagnosed with severe asthma. The winters were hard on me, and Mom had to keep me inside most of the time. An asthma attack could put me on my back for weeks. Mother was very compassionate, a bit overprotective perhaps, but when I was sick she sat at my bedside and waited on me hand and foot.

My father was the exact opposite. He showed no empathy for the sick and he loathed what he saw as weakness. He was a hard, demanding, ultraconservative man with a quick temper. He was always right, critical and judgmental of just about everything. His attitude toward Blacks and Hispanics was contemptible. When I asked Dad about his family, he said there was nothing to tell. The only stories he ever told us were about him and his brother Robert, my Uncle Bob. They grew up in Toronto, and anyone who messed with them got the short end of the stick. Dad always said, "If they were bigger than us or outnumbered us, we'd pick up a club and beat the tar out of them."

How I wanted to be strong and brave like Dad. How I wanted to be loved and accepted by him. Huh, what a joke! We always wondered what kind of childhood he had had with his ten brothers and sisters. We did learn that he started smoking regularly at about nine and left home for good at about twelve. He was tough, self-sufficient, master of all trades, and never sick. Nothing kept him home from work. He only took a vacation once every five years or so, always the kind you spend at home working. He was definitely a workaholic.

By the time I was seven, my condition had become worse, and the doctors suggested that we move to a dry climate. Dad quit his job. He sold the house and almost everything we owned. It was "California here we come!" Off we went, Mom, Dad, and three kids, in a twenty-eight-foot travel trailer, the biggest one made back in the 40's.

California would surely be the miracle state where I would be well, we thought, but it was only a dream. I didn't improve, and five years later Mom came down with asthma as well. The doctors seemed helpless. Only rarely did any medication help us; the attacks just had to run their course. Grass, weeds and dust were our adversaries, and California seemed to have a million varieties.

When I was sick and home from school, Mom would do her best to fill in so that I wouldn't fall behind. Having my mother as a home teacher had advantages and disadvantages. Mom's zeal to teach me all she knew bit me like a rattlesnake during the fifth grade. In addition to the three R's, she had taught me how to sew, knit, and crochet. Yep, you heard it right! Disgusting you say? Exactly what Dad said. He was beginning to despise me and I became the target of his anger. To him I was turning into a girl.

Because of the asthma, I was weak and sickly; and I learned to obtain sympathy from anyone at any time. Well, after all, what did he expect? He never took us to a ball game or played ball or went fishing or camping or anywhere else with us. He was always too busy working, either on the job or around the house.

One day in the fifth grade I took some of my crocheted masterpieces to school. After all, the other kids were always showing off their hobbies. Wow! What an impression I made. I was a hit, the talk of the school. A group of girls begged me to show them how to do a popcorn stitch, and I didn't hesitate. A crowd gathered, and I was so caught up in showing off that I didn't notice the snickering. Then they all started to laughed at once.

First shock, then embarrassment, and finally anger welled up within me. This brought on an asthma attack, and their laughter became truly sadistic. One of the boys asked if I would show him how to crochet. Crying and wheezing, I made a vow to get even with them. The school nurse called Mom, and she took her little boy home, crying, wheezing, and heartbroken.

At school the situation kept getting worse and worse. At the bus stop, on the play ground, even in class, teasing was constant. Even some of the teachers thought it amusing. Bullies would steal my books and pick on me. I was so glad when the year was over. The summers were way too short for me, and the following year brought a whole new problem.

My name is Robert, nickname Bob, last name Ford. That's right, Bob Ford, same name as the guy who shot his train-robber partner, Jesse James Howard, in the back. Remember the song, "The dirty little coward that shot Mr. Howard, and laid poor Jesse in his grave?" Every day or so the school kids hurled those words at me. They exploded in my mind and brought with them a payload of hate. I abhorred being called a coward and vowed I'd get even with every one of them someday.

My brother, Dick, was fifteen months older than I was. It seemed that with Dad he could do no wrong. He was strong, healthy, intelligent, and popular. He didn't like me to hang around with him too much because he was older and had different friends. He was good at baseball, football, basketball, you name it.

With me it was a completely different story. As an asthmatic I wasn't very athletic. When the team captains selected their players, they never chose me. The teacher would always have to appoint me to a team, who would moan and say, "Oh, no! We'll lose for sure now!" I would beg the teacher to let me sit on the sidelines and watch, but she always persuaded me to play. I was mortified and nervous and consequently I would mess up.

One day in the eighth grade I bought the whole team ice cream cones just so I could be on the team. I was assigned center field. The first ball was hit. Guess where? That's right, center field. Now was my big chance. It was a high fly and I ran in to catch it, but instead it landed way behind me. The whole team called me names and ran me off the field. I hated them. I fantasized beating up every one of them.

Dick was in the ninth grade gymnastics class. How I envied him, bulging with muscles, stomach flat and tight as a drum. One day he set a new school record in rope climbing. It was twenty feet straight up, and you had to start by sitting on the floor with your legs straight out. You couldn't use your feet while climbing either. He did it in four and three-tenths seconds! He would do one-handed chin-ups to strengthen his arms so as to go up that rope quick as a monkey. I was determined to be strong like him. I'll do it if it kills me, I resolved.

When I reached the ninth grade, my first year in high school, Dick showed me around the campus. On registration day we both got there early. First thing we signed up for was gymnastics. I would be in ninth grade beginners, he in tenth grade intermediate. Both classes were in the gym at the same time during fourth period. Wow! Dick and I in the same class! Just the thought of it put me in seventh heaven.

The first day Coach Curtis called all the new students together in one line. He shouted,

"Okay, boys, we're all going to do some sit-ups and push-ups!"

I did zero and zero! He took me aside and said I wasn't strong enough to do gymnastics this year. I was shattered. My new life was ending before it had even begun. I wanted to work inside with my brother and the other guys. I begged and pleaded with the coach.

Finally he suggested that I take wrestling and boxing with Coach Billinger. Thank goodness, it was in the Gym during the same period as Gymnastics. I registered and started to work out. At night I did sit-ups before going to bed. Before long I could do one hundred without stopping. Sit-ups, push-ups, deep knee bends, you name it and I was doing it.

I found out that when I worked out my asthma actually got better. Once I had an attack right in the school gym. I immediately began to do some push-ups and sit-ups. Within a few minutes the attack was over.

I learned that often my asthma attacks were caused by a pinched nerve in my back that was connected to my bronchial tubes. It was right between my shoulder blades and I could feel a light pinch there at the beginning of an attack. Exercise could loosen up that area and the attack could end almost before it started.

I really liked the wrestling class and became quite good. The second semester I took boxing which was a lot harder for me. Every day I had to fight to get past a deep fear of getting hit. It was the desire for respect, strength, and getting even that drove me to overcome the fear that my father had planted deep within me.

Dad would smack me on the side of the head with a cupped hand over my ear, first the right side then the left, back and forth like a punching bag, over and over, until my ears rang, sometimes for hours. Once when I was about twelve or thirteen, my Dad was beating me like this, and my brother entered the room. In a voice of authority he said,

"Dad, don't hit him again!"

Deafening silence filled the room, and I think my heart stopped beating for a moment. Dad stopped, turned, and just stared at him for a few seconds. Then without a word, Dad left the room. I stood there speechless. I was not only shocked, but amazed, first that Dad actually did stop, and then that my brother would risk the wrath of Dad for me.

I always wanted to be away from home when Dad got home from work so as to give him some time to cool off and settle down. All too often when he got home, the first word out of his mouth, loud enough to be heard by the whole neighborhood, was "Robert!" That always meant that I was in for it. The minute I heard him holler my name I was terrified. My whole body would begin to shake and I was usually crying even before I entered the room. Many times just because I was crying he would throw accusations at me about being nothing but a baby. He would say,

"Stop your crying or I'll give you something to cry about."

Because of his anger, his yelling, and his raised hand ready to strike me, I would often cry even more. If Mom was close she might step in and try to calm him down, but that usually made matters worse.

Bang! On the side of the head with a cupped hand, and my ears would be ringing like mad again. I was lucky if it ended there. Often he would take off his belt, fold it in half, and start beating me with it while holding me by the arm. If I tried to break away I'd get it even worse.

I began to despise my name, because every time I heard Dad say it, it meant I was in trouble. It didn't matter whether I had done whatever it was or not, my crying, denial, or excuses would set him off and I'd get it again. So, to everyone else I went by Bob, and never mind the guy who shot Jesse James. It wasn't a name that my Dad used, so it suited me just fine.

Later in life I began to put two and two together. I could see why my Dad thought so little of me. It had to do with his older brother, my uncle Bob. Although I don't remember meeting him, Dad idolized his brother Bob. He never said a negative thing about him, not that he ever said very much about his family anyway. We all knew that Dad thought higher of Uncle Bob than he did of anyone else in the whole world, and, apparently Uncle Bob was everything that I was not.

As I grew older, because of this kind of treatment from my Dad, I learned to lie and make up excuses in order to get out of trouble. I was defensive and always tried to push the blame off on others. These emotional problems created habits and reactions that were hard to detect and extremely difficult to overcome later in life.

From sophomore to senior year it was gymnastics all out. Many nights before going to bed I would do a hundred full sit-ups without stopping, all with my hands behind my head, and thirty or forty push-ups. Now *my* stomach was flat and tight as a drum, and my chest and arms were really something. I was on the school gymnastics team with my brother, and competed with other schools. Parallel bars and rings were my favorites.

As a grocery stock clerk I would often go into the produce department back room and use a hundred-pound sack of potatoes to work out with. Holding that gunnysack by its corners I would curl it as many times as I could, then rest for a moment and do it again and again until I couldn't do it any more. In my senior year I could press that sack of potatoes over my head three times with one hand. All this strength and hate, plus a huge chip on my shoulder, made a dangerous combination. I did a little getting even along the way, but now I was really ready.

Mom and Dad had not been getting along for some time, and the word *divorce* was heard more and more frequently. When I was about seventeen, the inevitable finally happened. I had already had all I could take from Dad and was thinking about leaving home. He had said on more than one occasion that much of the trouble in the family was my fault. One night I entered the living room in the middle of an argument he was having with Mom. When he made a derogatory remark about her, I got angry and said,

"You better apologize to her right now!"
He looked me up and down and said,
"I won't apologize for nothing!"
I stood my ground.

"Dad, I'm going to give you one more chance. You either apologize or I'm going to beat the crap out of you!"

He was sitting in his chair and I was standing about four feet in front of him. He gave me a look I had never seen from him before. He was afraid of me, and furthermore, he knew I meant exactly what I said. He knew he didn't have much time to either apologize or get up and defend himself. Because of his stubborn pride, he chose the latter.

Dad was no slouch; he was lean and mean through and through. In a single bound he came out of that chair and at me with fists blazing. Now was my chance to get even. Before this I had never raised my hand against him, or my voice either, for that matter. I had always feared him like a cat fears a dog, but there was no fear in me now, just hate and an overwhelming urge to get even. He had beaten me to the ground with his hand and his belt, but now the score was going to be settled.

With a confident smirk on my face I motioned with my hands for him to step toward me.

"Come on, Dad. Let's see just how tough you really are!"
Instead of landing a single punch, he ran into a brick wall of angry flesh and tense muscle. I plowed into him swinging, and down he went. While trying to keep his distance, he was holding his side and working hard at breathing. Now it was my turn to hold him with one hand and beat him with the other.

Just as I was about to plow into him again, I came to a stop.

I could see that Dad realized that I was more than a match for him, and he just stood there with a pathetic look of defeat on his face. But strangely, and slowly, as I looked into his eyes, my anger and hate turned into pity. I began to feel sorry for him.

I thought, I can't hurt him anymore. He ... he's my father. Deep down in my heart I loved my Dad and respected him, too. Respected? I can't explain it, but it was true. I dropped my guard, backed off, and he sat down, still holding his side, hardly able to breathe. I learned later that he had a couple of broken ribs.

He called the police and they talked with me for some time. Mom stuck up for me, of course, but I decided it was time to leave home for good. Just as I was going out the door, Dad said,

"You can't make it on your own! You're a failure! And don't come crawling back begging to live here again!"
I never did return, and I did make it on my own.

Later I realized that Dad had some good qualities as well. He was totally committed to providing for his family of five. Never did he go out with the boys to a bar or a card game. He did all his drinking at home and never laid a hand on Mom. Although he drank often, he never got drunk, nor did he gamble. He was busy from early morning to late at night, weekdays and weekends. Everyone knew there wasn't a lethargic bone in his body.

Dad was true blue to Mom. After she divorced him and even after she died, he wouldn't date another woman. He was a one-woman man. With Dad, our food, shelter, clothes, and care always came first. He could get more wear out of clothing and shoes than anyone I ever knew. He was an honest man, and his word was as good as gold.

As I stood at the window, looking for the cops I knew were coming, the video of my life rolled on and on.

In high school I never had any time for girls and I didn't know anything about drugs. Gymnastics, drag racing, and scuba diving took up all of my time. My brother and I were good buddies and went scuba diving with our friends every chance we got. Even though we got hungry, we would spend all day in the ocean and not come in until evening. Then, as soon as we could see food it was gone. Now that's a real *sea-food* diet.

Like most siblings, we tormented each other just for the fun of it. One day I was watching a huge black and yellow spider in his web, teasing it with a stick. Dick sneaked up behind me and ran a little twig down my neck. I came unglued and jumped back, slapping my neck to get the imagined tarantula off of me, but when I saw that it was just him, I could have sent him to the moon. I chased him all around the yard until neither of us could run any longer. I got even, of course, one way and another, starting the cycle all over again. You know, these are called, *family bonding* times. We just laugh about them now. I really respected and looked up to my brother and was so grateful for the good relationship that we had.

As a kid I did a lot of dreaming about being strong, healthy, popular, happy, wealthy, successful, a hero. You know, the same kind of stuff most kids dream of. Like many kids, and maybe some adults for that matter, I often thought, I'm going to show the world that I can make it. I'm going to make a mark and be somebody, you'll see.

But dreaming and reality are two different things, and deep down inside I knew it. I felt that I had nothing going for me except a big false front. My outward show made me look like a strong, self-reliant, confident person, but inside I was a scared guy trying to be something that he was not. But the show was all I had to hang my hat on. In fact, it was like a drug; it eased the pain, but brought no permanent cure.

I was thoroughly addicted to the drug of fantasy and outward show. I was living a lie and I knew it, but I couldn't let anybody else even suspect it. If it hadn't been for this lie I was living, I wouldn't have fit in anywhere at all. Living a lie takes a lot of energy; it takes a lot out of you. I had to win! I had to show them all, especially my dad that I was somebody, even if it killed me.

In high school I took four years of auto mechanics. I could build a motor from the ground up, which I did with my '57 Chevy pickup. The small 265 cubic inch, 135 horsepower stock engine came out. I bored the cylinders out past the safety zone to a total 292 cubic inches. I milled the heads forty thousandths. The biggest valves possible went in the fully ported, relieved and polished heads that sported a set of Headman Headers.

Three Rochester two-throat carburetors went on top of an Offenhauser manifold. The list included a radical racing cam with solid lifters, chopped flywheel, special heavy duty racing clutch, and racing slick tires on the rear. The compression ratio was 11 to 1 with a magneto type ignition and somewhere around 300 horsepower.

The rev of the engine was music to my ears, and the sound of the dual glass-pack mufflers was sweeter than a symphony. This is not a car club magazine, so here's the bottom line. All-out top speed wasn't that great, but zero to seventy-five was like a shot out of a gun, and back then the standard gasoline octane was 103.

The traffic tickets began to stack up. I was kicked out of my car club because of my bad driving record. Fighting, racing, and now drinking, I was getting deeper and deeper into trouble. My license was suspended, but I drove anyway. I just couldn't pass up a race.

Once I was in downtown Long Beach, the light was red and a guy in a hot-sounding Ford pulled up next to me. He revved his motor a couple of times and looked my way. I revved back. I looked around for the police, everywhere except right behind me. The light turned green and our tires squealed.

All of a sudden there were red lights flashing in my mirror. I pulled over and the motorcycle officer walked up to my window and stood there brushing tire dust and soot off of his uniform. Shaking his head and looking at me with disgust he said,

"Where's your head, boy? I was sitting right behind you at that signal! Didn't you see me?"

I didn't say anything, just swallowed hard.

"Let me see your license, son!"

This was it. Now what do I do?

"Um ... well ... I ... I don't have my license, officer."

"Well, where did you leave it?"

"I ... um ... it's been suspended."

"Suspended?" His voice got stony. "Do you know that I could take you to jail right now?"

I proceeded to give him some phony song and dance, and I could see that he was beginning to show some sympathy. He lectured me, wrote out a ticket, and let me go, saying,

"Son, you look like a nice clean-cut kid. Do yourself a favor and take this thing straight home, park it, and hide the key until your license is returned, okay?"

"Yes sir!" I said. "I really appreciate it! You have my word, officer!"

In those days my word wasn't worth much. I took my truck home; after all, I was headed there in the first place. Park it? Of course I parked it. Hiding the key was something else. After all, how can anyone hide a thing from themselves? I kept on driving. I even drove myself to the courthouse to take care of the ticket. I'll never forget it.

Holding my ticket in his hand, the judge called me up before him and said,

"Mr. Ford, Do you know what the word *suspended* means?"

"Yes, Your Honor, but ... but ... I have to drive to get around."

It was a dumb, dumb thing to say, and I knew it instantly. The judge rose up from his chair and leaned toward me with his eyes filled with rage. He pointed his quivering finger at me and said,

"Young man, you *don't* have to drive anywhere! And you *won't* drive anywhere! Do I make myself clear?"

"Y ... Y ... Yes, sir!"

He sat down. Except for my pounding heart, you could have heard a pin drop. He looked hard at me for a moment and said,

"I'm extending the suspension for a full year and fining you $150 plus court costs. Do you have the money to pay the fine today, Mr. Ford?"

"Yes, sir, I do."

My answer seemed to disappoint him; $150 was a lot of money then. Grinding his teeth, he said firmly,

"Step up to the bailiff and I'd better not see you in my courtroom again!"

Little did I know that I was on a collision course with the law and that in a very short time I would know, from experience, the awesome power that I was up against.

Chapter 2

Seven Up, Seven Down

My encounter with that raging judge scared me half to death, but it didn't change me in the least. Things went from bad to worse. The more the authorities pressed down on me, the more I rebelled. On a number of occasions I drove while intoxicated. It was a miracle, back then I called it luck, that I never had an accident or killed someone.

About a week before Sue and I were to get married, I got another ticket. I knew for sure I'd go straight to jail this time, so I told the officer that I was my brother, John Richard Ford, and that I had misplaced my license. He asked me all sorts of questions. Of course, I knew all the right answers: his birthday, height, weight, hair color, employer, everything. About the only real physical difference between us was the color of his eyes, and he was about an inch taller.

The officer wrote up the ticket and I signed my brother's name to it. I put the ticket in my pocket and planned to take care of it after our honeymoon. I also planned to tell my brother about the ticket right after the wedding. I didn't want him to be angry with me and mess up our wedding plans. Instead, I waited until after our honeymoon, and then you would have thought I had loosed a wild grizzly.

He told me that I had done a foolish thing and I'm sure that he wanted to punch my lights out. I pleaded with him to accept my money and pay the fine for me so that no one would be the wiser. But his only response, no matter how much I begged him, was to refuse. He said that maybe it would teach me a lesson. Wow! He hit the nail right on the head.

I met Sue at a birthday party some of my friends and I were having for another friend who was turning twenty-one. Five of us would get a date, do some dancing, drink some beer, and celebrate.

As it turned out, all of us were stood up, except me. I didn't even try to get a date. So it was just five guys, no girls. Then somebody I didn't even know named Patrick—we called him Pat—showed up with Sue, his date. Wow! I took one look at her and thought, She's mine! It was love at first sight.

I approached Pat and asked about his date. When he said they weren't going steady and that Sue was just a friend, I asked for her name and permission to ask her out, and he said it was fine with him.

Sue and I dated for two years and then got married. She was everything I ever dreamed of: blonde, 5'1", 101 pounds, the face and voice of an angel, and the body of a movie star. But most of all, she had a heart of gold. Boy oh boy, was I fortunate to find a girl like her. She was kind and patient and I felt lucky to have her.

On June 18, 1960, Sue and I were married and spent a glorious week in Yosemite and Sequoia National Parks. I was twenty, she was eighteen, and off we went on our honeymoon with a rented camper on my pickup truck.

What a glorious time it was! I was in seventh heaven. I found out that Sue was not real fond of camping, though. As we settled in at our campsite that first night she made me scotch tape our marriage license to the camper window so that everyone could see we were married and not just kids trying to get away with something out in the wide open spaces.

She was nervous because, she said, there were lions, tigers, bears, snakes, and man-eating spiders out there! I thought it was comical, but she believed it, mostly. I tried to convince her that it was safe at the campsite, and then a small black bear came strolling by and rummaged through the garbage. That did it! Her fear of the wild made her stick to me like glue. I must admit, I liked that part of it.

We were so much in love and made the most of every

moment. We laughed and played like children and had so much fun together while drinking in the fantastic scenery. I was the comedian, and she loved every silly thing I did. She was all the audience I needed. I loved her and she loved me, like no other couple ever loved each other.

Her approval of me and my humor fed my ego and built a strong bond between us. She was the only girl ever in my life. I did go on a date once or twice in high school, but that was it. I had such low self-confidence that I couldn't run the risk, and, although the same hormones were exploding in me as in every other guy my age, I already had more problems protecting my ego than I knew what to do with. The last thing I needed was to be the talk of the whole school like some guys I knew. Talk like, He's a bad date, or, He kisses like a wet fish. No, I decided it was better to play it safe and stay away from girls as much as possible.

At the campsite I did all the cooking, thanks to Mom, who had taught me how to cook. The other reason was that Sue didn't know much about cooking, especially out in the open. So here we were, cooking over an open wood fire. Oh yes, the food contained some ashes and maybe a twig or two, but good eatin' anyway. And In Sue's eyes I could do no wrong, and she encouraged me and praised me all the way.

Being with Sue during this time was like seven days in heaven. I was high as a kite and walking on air, but like the saying goes, What goes up must come down. Little did I know that after spending seven days in heaven, I would later spend seven days in hell.

Sue didn't know how to drive, so after we got home I drove alone to the courthouse to deal with the ticket. We had saved $300 to pay this fine, it was all the money we had. As I walked into the courtroom and sat down, I had a feeling that I was facing more than just a fine. When the judge called for "John Richard Ford," I stood up.

"Are you John Richard Ford?"

"No, your Honor, I ... "

He interrupted,

"Well then, sit back down, please. Will John Richard Ford please come forward."

I hadn't even fully sat down and I stood back up again and said,

"Your Honor, I'm John Richard Ford's brother. And he's not here because he didn't get the ticket, I did, and … "

He interrupted me again, this time with irritation,

"Don't tell me *he* didn't get the ticket, son, when I have a copy of it right here in my hand! What's your name?"

"I'm Robert Ford, Your Honor, and …"

"Well, Robert, you are excused, and we will put out a warrant for your brother's arrest."

Stammering I said,

"But … but … Your Honor … I got the ticket and signed his name to it."

"You *what*!" He shouted. "Are you trying to cover for your brother?"

"No, Your Honor! I really did get the ticket and sign his name to it. I was afraid that if I told the officer who I really was I might go right to jail."

Leaning forward on the bench the judge yelled out,

"I ought to put you in jail right now for forgery!"

Hesitating and looking me in the eye he began to ponder the whole matter. Then he said suspiciously,

"Robert … I don't believe you. I think you are trying to pull something over on me and I'm getting very upset with it all."

Suddenly it dawned upon me that if I couldn't convince the judge of my story there would be *big, big* trouble with big brother, so I blurted out,

"Your Honor, I have everything to lose and nothing to gain in telling you the truth."

The judge was quiet for a moment. Then, after some more conversation back and forth, he ordered my driving record to be brought to him. Meanwhile, he had me sign my brother's name twenty-five times to verify whether I really did sign the ticket. After comparing my signature with the ticket and reviewing my bad driving record, he sent me to a higher court down the hall. Now I was answering a charge of forgery as well as driving on a suspended license.

The second judge read the report given to him and my entire driving record. He looked up from the papers several times and looked straight into my eyes. I could see that he was getting very angry. He asked me to tell him the whole story and I spared no details. Finally he said,

"Robert Ford, how do you plead to the charge of driving on a suspended license?"

"Guilty, Your Honor."

"How do you plead to the charge of forging your brother's name?"

"Guilty, Your Honor."

"Mr. Ford, you've had a hard time learning what it means to obey the law, haven't you?"

As hard as it was to admit, I knew there was only one answer to that question. Embarrassed, ashamed, and scared, I answered,

"Yes, sir!"

He went on,

"Well then, Robert, I think we can make it a little easier for you. I'm going to sentence you to *ninety* days in jail! You won't be able to drive in there, will you?"

My head felt numb and my legs got weak. It was like some drug had caused me to lose my equilibrium and I almost fell over. For the first time in my life I knew I was really in *big* trouble. Feeling light headed and a bit weak, I sputtered,

"But … sir … Your Honor … I just got married seven days ago! My … wife doesn't work! I'll … I'll lose my job! Please, your Honor, I promise I won't drive without my license any more!"

He said sternly,

"Mr. Ford, you should have thought of that a long time ago. Your record proves you refuse to obey the law."

I felt like my life was about to come to an end. I was desperate. Every cell in my body said, I just can't go to jail and leave Sue all alone! I continued to beg him,

"Please, Your Honor! Please give me one last chance! I promise! I promise!"

He took a deep breath and paused for a moment. Then he said firmly,

"Robert, I will suspend eighty-three of the ninety days and put you on probation for one year, during which time if you get so much as a parking ticket you will serve the eighty-three remaining days. Also, your driving privileges are *revoked* for one year. Your seven days will begin as of *today*! Take him away, Bailiff!"

The eighty-three-day suspension gave me some relief but I still had to spend seven days in jail. Oh well, I thought, jail can't be all that bad, maybe a lousy bed and some bad food, but it surely can't be all that bad. The worst part, I was thinking, is being separated from Sue for seven days. But having never spent a night in jail before, I was in for a gigantic surprise.

The bailiff ushered me into a room where two officers took custody of me. I had to empty all my pockets on the table. I took out my comb, pocket knife, watch, new wedding band, change, wallet, and the $300 in cash and put it all on the table.

One of the officers said that my things would be kept in a large envelope. He handed it to me and told me to sign it. I wrote my name on it and left it on the table along with my belongings. Then they took me to what they call a holding tank, a cell just outside the courtroom for new prisoners to wait before they're taken to jail.

About four hours had passed since I left home, and all I could think about was Sue. She would worry when I didn't return. I thought, How can I get a message to her? What about the $300? She'll need it for food and bills. I mentioned all this to another prisoner, telling him about signing the empty envelope. Shaking his head in disbelief, he huffed,

"Well kid, you can kiss your three hundred bucks goodbye. You'll never see that money again."
I blurted out,
"But my wife needs that money! It's all the money we have!"
As a feeling of desperation engulfed me, I shouted in fear,
"She has to have that money!"
Disgustingly he snapped,
"Well forget it, kid! You're stupid, you know!"
My Dad's voice played in my mind as my cellmate continued,
"What were you thinking, kid? Do you think that because they're cops they're honest?"

Sheepishly I replied,

"Well ... yeah ... I thought so. I've never been in jail before, so I just did as they told me to."

In disgust he said,

"Yeah, right!"

Then, shaking his head, he looked at me in pity and said,

"Well, kid, I don't know if they'll listen to us, but let's see what we can do."

Then he began to yell for the sergeant, saying that the cops were stealing my money. I was so desperate I said along with him,

"The police are stealing my money! The police are stealing my money!"

The bailiff barged through the door from the courtroom yelling,

"What the hell is going on in here? Pipe down, all of you, we can hear you clear out in the courtroom! And, nobody's stealing anything, kid!"

From behind the bars I fearfully and quickly told him my story. While I was explaining the other inmates kept yelling,

"Let him see his envelope! Let him see his envelope!"

Finally the guard opened the door and took me into the room where I had emptied my pockets. My envelope was opened and everything was there *except* the $300. The police sergeant called in the two officers who signed the envelope and said,

"This young man says he came in here with $300 cash in his wallet. Does anyone know anything about it?"

*S*ilence filled the room. The two other officers just looked at each other. It seemed that the sergeant hadn't believed me up to this point, but then one of the officers said,

"Oh yeah, I almost forgot!"

Reaching into his shirt pocket he pulled out a roll of money: $300 exactly!

The sergeant gave the officer a look that could kill. He turned to me and asked

"Why did you sign the envelope without this recorded?"

Innocently, I replied,

"They told me to sign it and they'd record everything later."

The sergeant looked at the two officers in disgust and said,

"Be in my office when I get there!"

The sergeant let me make one phone call. It was hard to tell Sue that I was going to jail. She called Dick, who drove her to the jail to get the money. I only got to hand the money to her and tell her I would be in jail for seven days. They wouldn't even let me hug or kiss her. Shocked, she took the money, turned, and slowly walked away fearful and confused. We were devastated at what was happening to us right at the beginning of our lives together.

The ride from the courtroom to the LA County Jail seemed to last for hours. We were all handcuffed and chained together. I had a window seat in the paddy wagon. Repulsive looks were cast at us by onlookers. I was humiliated, and what little pride I did have, was shattered. I had been breaking the law for years, and now I would pay for it. All I could think of was how I had failed my wonderful, innocent wife.

Upon arrival at the huge jail we were stripped naked and examined by a doctor for communicable diseases and such. Then they ran us through the showers like animals. Next we were sprayed with a disinfectant, given prison clothing and a few of our possessions, and taken to our cells.

The cells were in a long line of about ten with an attached hall on one side similar to a large dog run. When the individual cell doors were opened, the prisoners could mingle with each other in the run, about forty men altogether.

Every night we returned to our own cells and the doors were locked until morning. Three or four men shared a two-bunk cell with one or two men sleeping on the floor. I discovered that the prisoners in my cell block were not minor violators like me. They were murderers, bank robbers, arsonists, pimps, gangsters, counterfeiters, pushers, and addicts.

I hadn't been there an hour when an inmate trustee tried to get me to make a one-dollar bet on a sure thing. I refused. He insisted. I said,

"I don't even have one cent on me."

"Oh, that's all right, kid, I'll front you the money and you can pay me out of your winnings."

Something told me to stay away from it and he gave up on me. I soon saw what had almost happened to me.

A new prisoner was added to our block and approached by the same guy about the bet. They were betting that one of the inmates couldn't lift five men all at one time. The trustee said that this man had just barely lifted four men yesterday, and they knew he wouldn't be able to lift five men today.

The new inmate wanted in on the action. Although it would only cost him a dollar, they said, they'd need his help. He would need to be one of the five men to be lifted. He agreed, and as soon as the other men got into position on the floor with him in the middle, they grabbed him. Four men held his arms and legs and the other prisoners moved toward them. The new guy was face down on the floor and they pulled the back of his shirt up over his head. Then they all took off their belts and one by one they beat him. The guards just turned their backs.

I wish I could turn off the memory of that scene. I felt so sorry for this guy, I thought I would cry. They just kept on whipping him. When they finally quit, he could hardly move. His back was covered with welts and bruises. It looked like it had been plowed.

For the remaining three days I was there, this man was silent, often with tears running down his face. He couldn't sleep on his back and hardly ever sat down. Even to bend his legs was painful; he was so swollen and bruised from shoulders to feet. I would have thought the guards wouldn't allow such a thing, but they turned their backs and pretended it never happened.

There was a large black man in our cell block, about 6'6" and 300 lbs. of solid muscle. He was on his way to the penitentiary for killing his wife. His hands were huge; he could palm a basketball easily. I was told that he squeezed his wife's neck with one hand until her neck broke.

I was terrified every time he came close to me. Although he never said a word to anyone, he walked around grinding his teeth and glaring at us, glassy-eyed. I was already walking scared but he really put fear into me. Oh, how I wanted to see my wife. If I could only wake up and find I had been dreaming.

The next day, sometime before noon, there was a hassle in the next cell block. It wasn't real noisy, but it was a fight and everybody knew it. Within fifteen minutes or so we saw a stretcher go by toward the fight, now quieted down. Then it came back with a prisoner on it, covered with a blanket. He didn't move or make a sound. It was said that he had stolen a candy bar from one of his cellmates and was stabbed with a spoon handle that had been sharpened like a knife.

I began to ask myself some questions, What are you doing in a place like this? Where's your head at anyway? Have you lost the sense you were born with? Then my mind began to replay my father's voice in living audio, "Can't you ever do anything right? Use your head boy! You'll never amount to anything! You're stupid! You don't even have the sense you were born with!" On and on it went.

It was a very familiar recording to me. Every time I heard it, more and more anger and hate welled up within me. I began to think that all the things my father said about me must be true after all, and the realization of this was sheer torture. I was convinced now that I was absolutely no good to anyone. I was a professional failure with no hope for the future.

Having suffered all my life from a low self-esteem and self-worth, I tried to cover it up with arrogance, pride, and being a wise guy. Everyone else in life seemed to fit in, but I was always the black sheep, the misfit. This all-too-often feeling of depression weighed heavily on me. Like a big clamp was around my chest and was being tightened more and more all the time. I was just a walking empty shell of a man with no hope.

I couldn't understand why Sue hadn't come to visit me. I longed to see her, to hold her, to hear her gentle voice. Besides Mom, she was the only person who believed in me. Sue told me later that she had called the courthouse looking for me, but they wouldn't give her any information, and she was terribly worried. She had kept my going to jail a secret from everyone except her best friend, Linda, who stayed with her so she wouldn't be alone.

On the third day I was transferred to a minimum security prison in Palmdale. These cell-mates were nonviolent offenders like me. But the first night I was caught talking after the lights were turned out. A guard was secretly listening through the slightly opened door of the large sleeping room. On went the lights and the officer shouted,

"All right! Who's doing the talking?"

Nobody responded. In the silence all you could hear was the hum of the florescent lights overhead. Again he demanded,

"I said who's the blankety-blank that's doing the talking?"

In fear I raised my hand and said,

"I was, sir."

Why I did this, I'll never know. It was two other guys that were talking and I had only reminded them we weren't supposed to talk after the lights were out. In anger the guard shouted,

"Get your butt up and over here right now."

I climbed out of bed and cautiously moved toward him. With his nightstick in hand he grabbed me by my right wrist, pulled me into the hall, and slammed the door shut with his foot. He slung me around like a wet rag, beating me with that stick while he spewed out vile curses at me. My legs, shoulders, back and arms were his targets, just like my Dad used to whip me with his belt when I was a kid.

When the guard released me I went straight to my bed, and from then on I kept my mouth shut. I spoke only when someone in authority spoke to me expecting an answer.

Following this seven-day education in jail, I didn't drive again until my license was reinstated over a year later.

Back in my dark bedroom with Sue, I couldn't understand why the police hadn't come to take me to jail. I directed my attention back to the noise I had heard outside the window. The silence had a chilling effect. I began to feel cold and clammy. Goose bumps covered my whole body and I was shaking all over. Minute by minute went by in utter silence. I began to think, Maybe the noise was just in my head. In fear and frustration I squeezed my head between my hands and tried to clear my thoughts. I was an emotional wreck.

Then I began to reason, Get rid of the guns. Do something smart for a change and surrender. Maybe lady luck will be on my side once again.

I moved closer to the window and peered out through the

glass, but I couldn't see anything. Puzzled, I thought, No police? No police cars? My mind began to imagine the worst. Maybe they're waiting around the corner. They could have the whole block surrounded. Are they waiting for me to come out? I won't go! It's dark and they might shoot me before I can surrender!

My past prison experience exploded within my mind and I just couldn't trust them. Then my thinking made a one hundred-eighty degree turn, and I calmed down a little. I thought, Only a murderer would shoot into a house with a family in it. Surely they'll call me outside to surrender. I cautiously re-examined the yard, the patio, and the street, but I didn't see a moving thing.

Fully clothed, I climbed into bed with Sue. We talked, but I was preoccupied with the sequence of events that led up to this awful moment.

It all started about a year earlier. I was employed by a large Southern California food store chain. I was approached by Bob, my boss, to consider working for him at a new food store chain that he and a man named Neeley, were starting. Bob told me of their plans to open several new stores and he wanted me to be one of their future store managers. I would be getting in on the ground floor.

After a few days of considerable discussion with Sue, I decided to make the move. I would soon have my own store with Sundays and holidays off and much better pay. We had been told that most of the profits would go back into the business and there was a profit sharing program. I joined the team. I worked there for about nine months and then my dream fell all apart.

As usual, I came to work about an hour before the store opened. I always worked at least two hours without pay every day. When I approached the front door, it was opened by a stranger from inside. I hesitated to enter. My first thought was, It's a robbery. My gun was concealed within my waistband, but I made no move for it.

"Are you Bob Ford?" the man asked.
Without moving an inch I reservedly answered,
"Yes!"
"Bob, Mr. Neely would like to see you in his office."
I slowly stepped inside and paused, keeping my eyes on him

and my hand ready to draw my gun if needed. Something was wrong, but what was it? Looking around I saw two employees talking. My eyes beckoned to them for some sign of what was going on but to no avail. They didn't look scared, so I relaxed a little. Then the man who let me in closed and locked the door behind me. His attitude was casual; therefore I didn't feel too threatened. I dismissed the thoughts about my gun and followed the stranger to the office, where Mr. Neeley was sitting behind his desk.

Upon entering I noticed two other unidentified men were present also. I tensed up again but thought, If this is a holdup where are their guns? What is going on here? I looked around in confusion as Mr. Neely began to say,

"Bob, I'm sorry to have to tell you this, but, we are bankrupt." Stunned, it felt like someone had hit me on the side of the head with a bat. Mr. Neeley paused, then pointing at the man who had let me in, said,

"From now on ... Mr. Wilson ... and these men are in complete charge of everything."

Gasping and staring at him, I was speechless. He continued,

"I'm sorry, Bob ..."

In fierce anger I interrupted,

"Bankrupt! How could that be? What happened to all the money we were saving? Where has all the profit gone?"

He just sat there and stared at his desk.

"You don't understand, Bob ..."

I interrupted again,

"Oh, I think I understand perfectly! The rumors are true, aren't they? You've been spending the money on yourself, haven't you? That mountain cabin and your new boat were all bought with our money, right?"

I was mad enough to kill him. Thoughts of harm and getting even ran through my mind like striking bolts of lightning, I won't let him get away with this. But for the moment, frozen in a state of shock, I did nothing but stand there. Then, Mr. Wilson escorted me from the office and began to tell me the cold facts.

Everything in the store including the fixtures was to be sold. I was owed a week and a half of pay, and I might have to settle for twenty-five to fifty cents on the dollar. It might be months before we were paid; there would be a legal battle between the creditors and the corporation. To top it all off, we were asked to remain there as employees until everything was sold, at full pay of course. Because most of us didn't have any place else to go, we stayed.

Everything was discounted 10 percent, then 20 percent. In the end some items were reduced 50 percent. We could see that our past wages were as good as gone. Mr. Wilson and the trustees were like policemen, there every minute, watching every move. Everything had to be sold within a week or two. With the bigger and bigger discounts the customers had a heyday, and as the days went by, the employees got madder and madder.

One day at closing time, Joe, the manager, said,

"Hey, Bob! Let's go have a few drinks."

With anticipation I said,

"Why not? I need to drown this anger in a good stiff drink or two. I'll even buy the first round."

We arrived at the bar about 10:30 PM. We made quick work of it; drinking fast and talking stupid. Instead of burying our problem, we pumped life into it. Joe suggested we make up for our losses by robbing the store. We figured that since the owner had been stealing from us all along, it was now time to get our investment back. So we made some quick plans and went right into action.

Joe borrowed a one-ton stake bed truck and then met me back at the store around 12:30 AM. We turned the alarm off, entered the building and decided to take only what we could sell fast. We took liquor, wine, beer, cigarettes, and of course a few hams and steaks for our freezers.

Everything was stacked neatly by the big freight door. We opened it as quietly as we could and loaded the truck. All the lights remained off. The whole thing was too good to be true–cases upon cases of things we could get good money for.

Cautiously Joe whispered,

"All set, Bob?"

I whispered back,

"Ready when you are, pal!"

Joe started up the truck and headed for a friend's empty

garage where we'd stash the goods. I started my car and left in a different direction to meet him there by another route. As we left the parking lot, we discovered that we weren't alone. Man, you talk about panic. You never saw two guys split so fast in your life, but it was hopeless. Joe was immediately surrounded and arrested and I was making tracks like a scared rabbit.

Somehow I managed to race out of the parking lot without a cop on my tail. I credited that to my driving ability, a fast vehicle, and lady luck. I went through alleys and down side streets, heading for home like a rocket. Then the thought came to me that it's a federal offense to steal liquor and cigarettes. That means the penitentiary for sure.

In desperation I cried out,

God! If there is a God in heaven, erase this thing I've done and I'll serve you the rest of my life!

My words didn't even make any sense. How can something be erased that's already been done? It was an impossible request, but I meant every word of it.

Arriving home, I pulled into the garage, looking all around for any sign of the police. I ran in the house, locked the door, and went directly to our bedroom where Sue was sleeping. We waited in the dark, but the police never came.

I was puzzled to say the least. Coping with the suspense of this moment was difficult enough, but nothing could have prepared me for tomorrow.

---------- *Chapter 3* ----------

The Flip side

I woke with a start. It was early, night still wrestling with the break of day. By 7:00 AM the sun had conquered the sky, but the dead silence destroyed every hint of peace. I was a wreck, I had jerked awake so many times that Sue hadn't slept either. We didn't know what to do, and hiding under the covers was so absolutely futile and would only delay the inevitable.

Sue lay quietly beside me. We discussed my alternatives for some time. I could go into hiding, turn myself in, or go to work and take my chances there with the police waiting to arrest me anywhere along the way. We both agreed I should get up and go to work, knowing that I might not even get to the end of the block before they stopped me

After a cup of coffee and a piece of toast it was time to go. Walking out the front door was like entering directly into a prison cell. It took more courage than I thought I had, and kissing Sue and the kids good-by was much different than ever before. Was it the last kiss? The last hug? The last tender touch? I wanted it to last forever, but time was my enemy now. Time had run out for me and I had to get on with the plan before I did something stupid.

The kids wondered why Mom was crying and what was so bad about my leaving for work. We hadn't told them that I wouldn't be returning home. Although it was chilly and damp outside, I didn't wear a coat. I wanted the police to see that I wasn't carrying a gun.

I opened the front door and examined the front yard, the

flower beds, and all around the hedge. All seemed to be clear. I looked at the garage door. It was open. Could there be anyone inside? Last night I must not have closed it. Oh well, there's only one way to find out. Carefully, I entered the garage, but no one was there.

How could this be? I got into the car and backed out to the street, scanning the neighborhood. I studied every yard, every bush, and every tree on both sides of the street. My heart was pounding and the palms of my hands were sweating like dripping rain. Every fiber of my being wanted to go back inside with Sue and the kids, but I knew that I had to go back to the scene of the crime and face the music.

Every inch I drove was frightening as paranoia over sirens and police cars gripped me. They seemed to be everywhere. At a stop light about halfway to work, a police car pulled up behind me. I couldn't look in the rear view mirror. I was sure that if he wasn't already following me, he would recognize my car and license number from his wanted list. I hoped he'd just disappear. But when the light turned green he was still there. I was so nervous I could hardly drive.

He followed me. I turned at the next corner. He continued to follow. My whole body began to shake and my teeth began to chatter like I was out in frigid cold. I turned again a few blocks further on. He turned also. That settles it, I thought, I'm going to give myself up.

I pulled over to the curb, but he went right on by. Dumbfounded I watched him drive off. I thought, What's going on here? Am I just imagining all this? Quickly I looked around for other cops, but there weren't any anywhere. Emotionally raped by fear, I was sweating and shaking uncontrollably. I slumped over the steering wheel and just hung on trying to reconstruct my sanity. It took some time, and everything within me wanted to go back home.

I thought for a while about going into hiding, but I knew that would never work, not with a wife and kids. I had been had. There was no way out and the thought of having to go and face the music made me think of taking my own life. I wish I was dead, I thought, but then I took it back. I may have felt more dead than alive, but I feared death too much to make it happen. Deciding to stay alive no matter how bad I felt, I thought about something that happened in high school.

When I was about sixteen I had a good friend, Dean, a year younger. He was clean-cut, well liked by everyone, good looking. He was a fun guy with good moral character and smart, too. One day he didn't show up for work, and I was told that he was killed in a hunting accident. I just couldn't accept that he was gone. I thought, Gone? Gone where? You can't just be here one day and gone the next, and besides, only old people are supposed to die.

It would be a closed-casket funeral. You see, Dean was shot in the face and chest with a twelve gauge shotgun at close range. Hearing this, I wilted feeling as if all the life within me just evaporated. It felt like my heart had been ripped right out of me. I was such a wreck that I couldn't even attend the funeral.

A few years later, after Sue and I were married, my younger sister, Patsy, committed suicide. Somehow she had gotten mixed up with drugs and some people on a ranch in California. After moving off the ranch and in with Dad, to try to get her life straightened out, she took her own life. She was in her twenties, just beginning to live, now gone.

One night at about 1 AM, I got a frantic phone call from Dad. I raced to his house and found him sitting in his chair with his head in his hands, rocking back and forth. He was crying so hard I could hardly understand him. He repeated over and over, "It's my fault! It's all my fault!" A policeman was talking softly to him, trying to calm him and bring him back to reality, but Dad didn't even hear him. In a panic I asked the policeman where my sister was. He said that she was out in the backyard, covered with a blanket. I asked,

"Why? What is she doing out there?"
Cocking his head in sympathy, he said softly,
"That's where we found her!"
I started for the back yard but the officer stopped me. I tried to go around him, saying,
"I have to see her!"

He blocked my way and said,

"I don't think that's a good idea. I think you'd better just sit down for a minute."

Insistent, I said,

"I don't want to sit down; I want to see my sister! Maybe she is alright! Maybe I can help her! Maybe ... maybe ..." I broke into sobs,

"Please don't say she's dead. Please, please don't say she's dead!"

In a calm, authoritative voice, the officer told me to pull myself together. He didn't need me to freak out like my dad had.

All I could do was stand there and listen as he explained things to me. She found my dad's .22 caliber pistol and shot herself in the head. I only heard about ten percent of what he was saying– it just wouldn't compute. But Patsy was dead. She had given up because things were too horrible to bear, and I would never see her again.

I hated and feared death. I thought, Death? What is this awful thing called death? It just can't be! But it was, and I felt so helpless.

At the funeral, I couldn't stand to see her casket go down into the ground. I wanted so much for her to be alive that the sight of it was tearing me apart. She was in that casket and they were putting her down in the ground. I couldn't stand it, and my heart ached like never before. I was so confused, so full of questions. This is why I feared death so much that I couldn't even take my own life.

Seeing no police cars and feeling I might be safe after all, I inched my way out from the curb and drove to the store. Upon my arrival, I began to scan everything in sight. There they were, two black and whites parked around the side of the building. I knew the cops were inside waiting for me, and it started all over again. Trembling and scared to death, I wanted to run for it. I actually began feeling sick to my stomach and was afraid I'd vomit.

I swallowed hard, took a deep breath, and straightened up. Then I literally spoke out loud and said, "Bob, get a grip on yourself!" Slowly the nauseous feeling began to subside. I drove around in the parking lot while telling myself that I had to stop stalling.

I began to realize that my surrender and arrest would soon be all over with, and to my surprise that brought a small degree of relief. After all, I didn't see how I could feel any more depressed or fearful than I was now. In that short moment of time I quit fighting it; I gave up. I had come this far and I wasn't going to quit now.

I parked the car and sat there for a few moments trying to gather my courage and strength. I was so exhausted that I felt like I had run a marathon. Finally, I got out of the car and headed for the store entrance. As I walked my legs felt like they weighted a hundred pounds each.

Entering the store it seemed that everyone was looking directly at me. It was all I could do to keep from collapsing from fear and exhaustion.

I walked in a little further along the front of the store to see where the police were. All of a sudden Mary, one of the cashiers, looked at me and said,

"Bob, what are you doing out of jail?"

"Huh? Ah …" I choked.

Just then I saw the policemen in the back of the store talking to Mr. Wilson. They hadn't seen me yet. Without saying another word, I began to slowly, cautiously walk toward them. Believe me it took a lot of effort to put one foot in front of the other. When I got within about ten feet of them, Mr. Wilson turned my way and said,

"Bob, you're late! Get your apron on and fill the front freezer with those Banquet chicken and beef pies! Mark them ten for a dollar—we've got to get rid of them soon!" Bewildered, I stuttered,

"Y … Y … Yes sir!"

"Oh, and Bob, could you work late tonight to make up for the lost time this morning?"

"I guess so … sure, Mr. Wilson … I can."

"Thanks, Bob, I appreciate it. We have a lot to do and I need everyone I can get to help."

I walked into the back room so stunned that I literally thought I was dreaming. I actually pinched myself to see for sure. I wasn't; I was fully awake. But, It was all too incredible to be true. And everything was spinning around in my head like a whirlwind.

My imagination went into passing gear. Could this be some

plot to trick me? Why didn't the police arrest me? If Mary knows I was involved, why haven't they arrested me? Why don't they at least question me? Then I thought, All the employees know that I carry a gun. If they told the police, then they must think I'm armed, but surely they can tell by looking that I'm not. With my mind going off in all directions, I needed to focus.

I decided to confront them and said,

"Excuse me, officer ... is anything wrong?"

He looked at me casually and said,

"No, we're just getting a few facts for our report."

I paused for a moment, taking in what he said and how he looked.

"Oh ... okay, good. Thanks. Sorry to bother you!"

As I spoke, I almost gave myself up to be arrested, but something within me wouldn't let me do it. I felt a glimmer of hope that I might remain free. Free? How? I didn't know, but I allowed myself to consider that it might be true. I went into the back room, willing myself to act casual. Running on pure nervous energy, I wheeled out a stack of pies and started filling the freezer.

Just then Mary left her empty checkstand and approached me. Looking grim, she asked,

"How did you get out of jail?"

Startled I said,

"Shhh! Do you want everyone in the store to hear you?"

Leaning close to her I whispered,

"I was never in jail."

Jerking back, she said,

"What! You mean they didn't arrest you along with Joe?"

"No, I've been home all this time."

Puzzled and suspicious she asked,

"Why didn't they arrest you? Everyone in the bar heard you and Joe planning the burglary!"

Stunned to the core I said,

"I don't want to talk about it. Please, just leave me alone!"

I stood there in a daze and began thinking, Wow! So that's how the cops got tipped off. A few other employees went to the bar, too. What fools we were to let anyone overhear us planning this thing. As Mary walked away she said sternly,

"Bob, don't let Joe take this rap alone!"

I decided to work, keep my mouth shut, and let the chips fall where they may. My emotions were tapped out, but the ray of hope was still there. Despair hadn't won out after all. At the same time, my heart would race at the smallest thought of fear, or of a suspicious move by someone around me, and my ears would flex and strain at the slightest sound. I expected at any moment to be arrested.

Reader, if you've ever been like this, a complete emotional wreck, along with a little glimmer of hope, then you know exactly what I mean. This emotional back-and-forth battle tried to consume every bit of strength and energy that I had.

Every minute seemed like an hour. At lunchtime I called Sue and told her what had happened. At the end of the day, I was able to leave the store and go home to my family. Happily waiting for me was one gorgeous wife and four beautiful children. Crying, we embraced. Crying, we kissed. Crying, we looked deep into each other's eyes and ran our fingers through each other's hair. With burning passion we said to each other, "I love you! I love you! I love you so much!"

Then, as a family, we talked and just loved on each other for a good long time. Slowly, but ever so strongly, I could feel something happening in my heart that was effecting my whole being. I began to feel so happy that I thought I would pop. And I was starting to get a warm, fuzzy feeling all over me. It's hard to explain, but let me put it in these words of rhyme,

> *It was something strange, something new;*
> *something different, it was true;*
> *something soft, something like love;*
> *something surely from above.*

I didn't know it at the time, but God was giving me a ticker tune-up. And believe me no one needed this more than I did. At this very moment I welcomed this heart transplant, even though I didn't understand it at all. All of a sudden I felt like there was some real hope for me. Hope? Where did that come from? And, it wasn't that

I was just thinking it, but I really felt it in my heart. I had a strange, but welcome feeling, that all would be okay, and believe me, reader, I can't even start to explain it to you; it's more felt than told. I vowed to change and to make up for every ounce of hurt I had caused my wife and family.

But Joe was in jail, and I was free. This is wrong, I said to myself. For once in my life I've got to do what's right. I just can't let him take all the blame.

Before I got a chance to do anything, Joe got out on bail and called me. We met and talked the whole thing over. As far as my involvement went he said they must have made a mistake somewhere, that something had gone wrong. Shaking my head, I said,

"A mistake? I drove right by the cops! They saw the make and color of my car, the license number, and even got a good look at me. And don't forget that someone squealed on both of us! What do you mean something went wrong?"

Just then I remembered my prayer and thought, Wow! Could it really be true! Did God really hear and answer the prayer I prayed the night of the robbery? I remembered my prayer word for word *God, if there is a God in heaven, erase this thing I have done and I'll serve you the rest of my life.* Now I was sure of it–it just had to be. There wasn't any other explanation for it, and with great excitement, I told Joe about the prayer.

"Nonsense, Bob! Don't start freak'n out on religion. It was just your lucky day. Something went wrong and you made out big time, that's all, and just leave things alone. My old man's loaded and he's got me a good attorney. He said things don't look all that bad for me anyway."

Joe seemed confident he would beat the rap, but I couldn't leave it alone and blurted out,

"But how can you say that? How can you say that something went wrong?"

I couldn't understand how he could ignore what I had just told him. I was looking at a miracle, but Joe was on a different page altogether.

"You're all freaked out, Bob! You're losing it, man. So go ahead and believe whatever you want. But I'm telling you, don't mess with things or you'll make things a whole lot worse for me than what they are."

Reservedly I said,

"Well, okay, but it all seems so weird, but don't worry, I won't mess anything up. I won't say anything you don't want me to. So you'd better tell me exactly what you told them so we both have the same story."

After telling me everything, he went home. Now, more than forty years later, I have not seen or heard from him again, nor have I heard a word from the police about it, either.

The more I thought about the whole ordeal, the more convinced I was that God heard and answered my prayer. From that time on my life did a complete flip-flop. It was kind of like an old 45 rpm record. They had one song on each side. Sometimes side one wasn't that good, but side two, the flip side, would be terrific. The first twenty-four years of my life was the bad side, but the flip side has been a song worth singing, one that gets sweeter and sweeter as the years go by. Here's another rhyme the Lord gave me,

The Lord gave me a special song; a song I can't but sing.
Do I sing because I'm happy? Or happy because I sing?
I find that both of these are true; and peace they always bring.
Yes, I sing because I'm happy; but, I'm happy because I sing.

Sue and I began to think about what was missing from our lives. We figured it was religion. Huh? Religion? Where do you start? Neither of us was raised in the church. It's not that we never attended church, but we were never active or regular because our parents weren't. When Sue was a little girl her mailman would sometimes come by on Sunday on his mail bike. He would put her in the big basket over the front wheel, and off to church they would go.

She doesn't remember much of what went on there. She enjoyed going, though, mostly because the mailman was like a father figure to her. Sue's father was in the Navy and was away from home for long periods at a time, so she was basically raised by her mother. As Sue grew older, however, church was not a part of her life.

As for me, I also went to church occasionally with my parents, but Dad was raised Baptist and Mom was raised Catholic, and they couldn't agree on religious things. Therefore, they thought it best to pretty much stay away from church. I do remember once when I was young, our whole family was baptized at one of the Christian churches we attended once or twice.

As I reflected on my recent experience, I began to wonder just how much God had intervened in my life.

As a kid I used to climb the steel high-voltage wire poles with my brother and our friends. Like a foolish kid, I always had to pass the sign that said, *Go No Further, 18,000 Volts*. We could actually feel the magnetic field of all that voltage around us. We thought that was pretty cool.

On a number of other occasions, I drove my 1950 Ford convertible at top speed over a local road we called Airplane Hill. The whole car would leave the ground and the passengers would fly off their seats six or twelve inches. The front bumper would scrape when the car landed.

I was in a motorcycle accident on the Los Angeles Freeway. I was thrown over the handle bars onto the highway right in front of a Volkswagen bug that was directly in front of a semi. Somehow, everyone got stopped without running over me. I always thought that I was just lucky.

These are only a few of the things that crossed my mind. I began to think that maybe I hadn't been alone, that God was with me all the time. I began to ask myself, Why? What have I ever done for God to deserve anything from Him? The answer to that question, I gradually realized, is *absolutely nothing!* As I pondered that thought, I began to realize that God loved me all along in spite of what I was. This was too much for me to understand at the time, but I couldn't deny that it was obviously true.

My prayer of desperation on the night of the robbery went through my mind again and again. The thing that stood out to me the most was that I hadn't had any faith in God. In my prayer I said, *IF there is a God in heaven*. What I couldn't understand was why God would answer me when I didn't believe. Granted, I did truly hope, but genuine faith, I didn't have.

Sometime later I learned that what I received from God was *grace*. Grace is defined as *unmerited favor*. Wow! Unmerited favor! You see, *grace,* is God giving us what we don't deserve (e.g. love, forgiveness, heaven, etc.) Whereas, *mercy*, is God withholding from us what we do deserve (e.g. judgment).

Wow! What a God! What a loving, forgiving, understanding God! Now, I've known some people over the years that just took the blessing from God and ran with it, never even looking back with so much as a thank you. Not me, I not only wanted to know more about God, I wanted, if at all possible, to be best friends, too.

The next thing that impacted me about my prayer was the words, *I'll serve you the rest of my life.* Serve you? I thought, How do you serve God? So, Sue and I began to discuss this at length. We both thought, Surely it can't mean to be a minister, can it? No way! It probably just means to go to church. Okay, church it is. Just then, Sue asked if I had one in mind.

"Well ... um ... I don't know, Honey, what do you think?"

"Gosh, I don't know, I went with my aunt to a Catholic church once. I was always standing when they were sitting or sitting when they were kneeling. I felt dumb not knowing what was going on and the Priest spoke in some strange language that I couldn't understand."

"Well, that's not for me," I said. "How about some of your girlfriends, do any of them go to church?"
Sue jerked back and thought for a moment, then said,

"I don't think so. In fact, I don't think we know anyone that goes to church, do we?"

"I don't think so either. None of the guys at work do, that I know of anyway. Our parents don't. None of your brothers do, and my brother doesn't either. Man, I can't think of anyone that goes to church. What about some of our neighbors? Maybe you could ask some of them?"

"Look Bob, if you think I'm going to start asking that question you're crazy! We only know two families on the whole block and we *know* they don't go!"

This discussion was going nowhere, so I said softly,

"Well, Honey, let's drop it for now. Something will come up. It's not like we have to do something right now. Let's give it some time and think about it." Sue persisted.

"What about the minister that married us? He has a little church in Norwalk. We could try it!"

I didn't feel comfortable with that,

"Honey … I don't know. I'm not ready to put on a suit and tie. Besides, we don't know anybody there. Let's think about it for a while."

Suddenly she jumped to her feet and blurted,

"Hay! I just remembered! Where's yesterday's Newspaper? There was an ad in there about a new church starting up. It's some kind of drive-in church."

"What did you say? A drive-in church? Come on, Sue, I think you must have read it wrong. I've never heard of such a thing!"

She was insistent,

"No I didn't! It's a drive-in church that … here … here's the paper. I know it's in here … here it is! Look! It says *Come as you are and worship in your car*."

Running to her side I said,

"Let me see that!"

As I read the ad I said,

"Wow … that's weird! I never heard of a church where you could stay in your car and still be in church! Don't they have a building? And how can anyone hear what's going on?"

"Well, Bob, it's like a drive-in movie. You hook the speaker in the window and, yes, they have a building, so you can go inside or stay in your car."

Absolutely amazed I said,

"Well, if that don't beat all! Heck … I'm game if you are, Honey. What do you say, shall we give it a try?"

"Sounds good to me! And just think, you won't have to wear

a suit and tie if you don't want to. It says, *Come as you are!*"

Now, you'd think this going to church thing would be easy, but we had no idea what we were in for.

---------- *Chapter 4* -----------

Wrongfully Accused

There we were on Sunday morning, sitting in our car, speaker in the window, having church. They had some special music and a prayer or two and then the ushers started going from car to car collecting the offering. Zing! This was something I hadn't planned on, but the usher just stood there at my car door with two things–the offering plate, and a *big* smile.

I was going to put in some pocket change but all of a sudden I began to feel real generous. It was the motivating power of his *smile*, I'm sure. Out came my wallet. Out came a bill, into the plate it went, and the plate disappeared. I watched my money go down the row and up to the front, never to be seen again.

Sue kindly asked,
"How much did you put in, Honey?"
I whispered,
"A dollar!"
Covering her mouth a bit with her hand she said,
"A dollar, is that all?"
"Can I put in some money, Dad?" came a yell from the back seat.
"No you can't put any money in. I put in all that we can afford."
Lovingly, Sue said,
"Honey, you spend more than that on beer!"
That was *zinger* number two, and I was beginning to wonder if this

"church" thing was going to work out. The pastor was not there for some reason and the assistant pastor gave the message. Two things stood out to us. He prayed too long and he talked too long, but, on the way home we decided to give it another try next week when the pastor would be there.

During this week we decided that we had better get a Bible and familiarize ourselves with it. That way perhaps we could understand the sermon a little better. I was anxious to dig in and planned to read it from cover to cover as fast as possible. I have always been rather impatient so I figured I could do it within the week. Huh! Not only did that never happen, but I was in for a big surprise.

I thought that the Bible was just like any other book, with a simple beginning, a middle, and an end. I opened it and began to thumb through it. I saw all the chapters and their strange titles and I thought Genesis was the first chapter and Revelation was the last chapter. Then I saw that Genesis had fifty chapters in itself, but I forged ahead anyway.

Starting in Genesis 1:1, "In the beginning, God..." sounded like a child's storybook—"Once upon a time," but the more I read, the more questions I had. When I read, "And God said, let there be light: and there was light." I thought, Huh? You mean to tell me that he just spoke and light appeared? I read further on to see if there were any more details, but all I could see was that God had just spoken or used the dust of the ground, and things appeared. Wow! This was exciting!

The interesting thing was that I had no reason to doubt it and, therefore, just believed it. It wasn't—blind faith—,which is nothing but a leap in the dark. It believes in something that has no foundation to it, no real substance, but my new-found faith had real substance to it.

I had a genuine heartfelt, settled assurance that what it said was, in fact, true. I couldn't explain it, and my head didn't understand it, but I was sure in my heart that it was so. This was the first time I had ever experienced anything like this. Later on I learned that my faith was grounded upon a *revelation* that God had put in my heart. I'll talk more about this later on.

As I read on in Genesis, I was beginning to have a pile of questions about many things. My questions were legitimate though, not questions of doubt, but real curiosity. I just wanted answers and I began to wonder how I would get them. As I thought about the Bible, I thought that maybe all my questions would be answered further on. On the contrary, by the time I had finished chapter nine, I had so many questions written down that I thought I would run out of paper. Being the impatient person that I was, I decided to check out the middle of the Bible and see if any of the answers I needed were there.

It opened in the book of Ezekiel, so I turned to the beginning of it and started reading. "Now it came to pass in the thirtieth year, in the fourth month, in the fifth day of the month…" and so on. I read ten or twelve verses and thought, Holy cow, what's all this?

So I moved to the next book, Daniel. "In the third year of the reign of Jehoiakim, king of Judah…" Again I thought, Man, this sounds like one of my high school English literature classes. I began to wonder if I was ever going to get any answers to my questions. I checked the front and back of the Bible for instructions, but I came up empty. It didn't have any notes or directions or anything. It just said, *Holy Bible, King James Version.*

I began to think that because the front of the Bible told how things began, perhaps the back of it will tell how things end. Man, did I ever hit the nail on the head! Off to the book of Revelation I went. Just the name intrigued me. I thought, Revelation—everybody knows what that means. This has got to be it. Surely I'll get some answers now. I probably should have started here in the first place!

I read the first three verses of Chapter 1 and something leaped inside my heart. I had surely struck gold. Not that I had any answers yet, but somehow I knew that I was onto something. Now this was a stronger, deeper feeling than the one I mentioned earlier. When I looked back over the three verses, I didn't see anything that could explain why I had this feeling.

I read those three verses over and over and over again. But still I didn't understand why they impacted my heart with such a sense of peace, victory, satisfaction, and sort of oneness with the words.

My eyes kept taking me back to that name, Jesus, and I sensed that something, or someone, was guiding me, like talking to me through those words. It was a strange experience, one like never before, but it was refreshing. I felt more alive now than I had ever felt in my life.

As a child I had heard the stories about Jesus as a baby in the manger, but I never gave it any thought. Now, as I read these first three verses in Revelation, I felt (yes, dear reader, I said felt) deep down in my heart, my soul, that there was something real, something alive, something powerful, about this man, Jesus. So, like a miner seeing the vein of gold he's been searching for, an excitement of discovery detonated in my soul that motivated me to dig up every bit of treasure I could find.

I read the entire twenty-two chapters of Revelation without stopping. I read right through all the symbols and types, the beasts, plagues, suffering, wrath of God, Satan, the False Prophet, and so on.

I didn't understand one percent of it, but I kept on reading. In fact, I couldn't stop reading. In some places it was so scary that my heart pounded. It was like reading science fiction, but I knew this was anything but fiction.

I knew I was in *big* trouble. In fact, I could see that the whole human race was in trouble. I could see that God was not one to mess with or take for granted. He obviously had a plan for man and a set of rules to live by, and I was completely in the dark as to it all.

Reading Revelation woke me up out of a stupor and had me shaking in my boots. In fact, to be perfectly candid with you, it literally scared the hell right out of me. But don't take me wrong, this was a good thing.

Now I was really searching for answers. All my other questions faded away in comparison to the ones I had now. This was serious. I was looking for answers like a drowning man fights for air. I was drawn back to Chapter 20, verses 14–15, where I had read that whoever didn't have their name written in the Book of Life would be cast into the lake of fire. But I couldn't find any place where it explained how to get your name into this book, and that frustrated me greatly.

As I pondered this, all I could think of was the mess I had made of my life. The lies, cheating, stealing, hate, fighting, name-calling, deception, rebellion, drunken parties, disrespect, and on and on, plagued me now like a rotting cancer. The words of my father once again played ever so loudly in my head, "You'll never make it! You're a loser! A failure! You're stupid and don't even have the sense you were born with!"

I couldn't take it any longer. I drove to the Christian bookstore and unloaded on the sales clerk about some of my questions. I could tell I must have overloaded her with it all. In obvious frustration as to where to start with it all, she went from one area to another pointing out different books.

Then she asked me,

"How long have you been a Christian?"

Curiously I said,

"A Christian?"

Not understanding the question, I asked exactly what she meant. After a lengthy discussion about it she took me over to the books for new believers. I bought three or four, two of which I still have: *How To Begin The Christian Life* and *Now That I Believe.*

In the course of reading these booklets and following their steps, I became a Christian. I checked the verses they had listed with my own Bible and found that all my sins were forgiven through my faith in the sacrifice of Christ at Calvary. Through the death of Jesus, I had been redeemed from the curse, or punishment, for my disobedience to the Commandments.

Now, as a believer, I was a new creation, justified, sanctified, an heir of God, and joint heir with Jesus. I was now a saint and no longer considered a sinner; now I was a child of God and a friend of Jesus! Reader, this was real, as real as it gets.

Wow! All of a sudden I felt like I was finally a—somebody. For the first time in my life I was *chosen* to be on a team, God's team. I had some real value now, and I was loved with an unconditional, unchanging love. Now there was hope for me. And, best of all, I was useful and needed.

I began to realize that in the light of the Bible all those

accusations in my past were lies fashioned and fabricated by the devil and hurled at me by man. It was as Jesus said in John 10:10: "The devil came to steal, kill, and destroy, but Jesus came to give us life in abundance."

For the first time in my life I could see that by man I had been judged, condemned, and wrongfully accused, for God's Word says everything to the contrary. I shouted, "I'm free, I'm free, praise God, I'm free!"

Another thing, I had a strong, settled peace within me, a peace that passes understanding, and it wasn't in my head, but in my heart. This peace wasn't connected to anything earthly or physical, and it had more life to it than anything I had ever known. It wasn't just a knowing in my heart but an overflowing emotion of joy unspeakable. In fact, I thought it was going to come right out of me and fill the whole room.

I began to sense a drawing from above, and as I looked up, I fully expected to see right through the sky and into heaven itself. Let me put it this way, I actually felt out of place down here on earth, and one last thing, I was no longer afraid of the undertaker—for now I know the Upper-taker.

This song, by Mosie Lister, conveys exactly how I felt at the time, and still do:

> There were so many others, that He might have chosen,
> to follow Him.
> Others with learning, and greater distinction,
> to follow Him.
> Men with authority, and forceful ability,
> who know how to speak and be heard.
> I don't know exactly why I'm here at all,
> but today I follow my Lord.
>
> It was business as usual, till I heard Him say,
> come follow Me.
> I left all behind me when I heard Jesus say,
> come follow me.
> I emptied myself of my old life completely,

with no thought that this could be wrong.
And as long as I follow the steps of the Master,
I know I'm where I belong.

For He chose me, He chose me.
I could not say no when He said follow Me,
and you'll be a fisher of men.
And from now on, and from now on,
I will not look back on the things left behind,
He chose me to follow Him.

The following Sunday at church was much better. We liked the pastor's style, and his message was practical. After a few months we began to go inside to worship. Yep, you guessed it—suit and tie. The whole family had to have new clothes. This—church—thing was already becoming quite expensive, but did we ever look sharp and snappy. Somehow those nice clothes made us feel better about the Lord, and ourselves as well.

It was a Reformed Church. Obviously, many of the members were well off, and here we were, poor, as naive as they come, but hungry for God. We drank in every word of the message. Every message seemed to be just for us. Now Bible reading as a family was a regular thing.

After about six months I was approached to help in the fifth-grade boys Sunday school class, about ten or twelve boys in all. The teacher needed a helper to take attendance and help control the class. It seemed easy enough to me.

"Sure," I said. "I think I can handle that! Glad to help out."

What a surprise. This class was a real circus. Spit wads, airplanes, pinching, kicking, you name it. I had to be a sergeant-at-arms, and then came the real bomb. Two weeks later the teacher quit, and the Superintendent asked me to take over the class.

"I can't teach!" I blurted. "I don't know the first thing about it."

"Now, don't worry, Bob. Read the story at home during the week and look up the Scriptures and it will go just fine. The teacher's manual tells you everything to do."

Hesitantly I said,

"I don't know ... I'm just a brand-new Christian myself."

"We know that, Bob, but you and Sue have a love and excitement for God that many other people don't. Besides, we don't have anybody else. Would you try it? If it doesn't work we'll find someone else."

Reluctantly conceding, I replied,

"Well ... okay. I guess I could give it a try."

Well, reader, as it turned out, I loved every minute of it, but I did less teaching than I did learning. I would start studying the teacher's manual on Monday, and by Wednesday I was ready for Sunday. In fact, Sundays couldn't come fast enough for me.

During the week I dug up illustrations that added to the lesson. And because Sue and I started out with a miracle-working God, our faith in him brought about miracles in our life on a regular basis.

Almost every week I had at least one miraculous real-life experience to share with the kids, and they ate it up like candy. They were on the edges of their chairs and never forgot to bring their Bibles. It was easy to teach them. They just drew it out of me like a pump drawing from a well. Soon they were testifying about answers to their own prayers.

One thing was really lacking:—weekly memory verses. They just wouldn't learn them through the week. So the Lord gave me an idea as to how to get them to do it. It was quite simple.

I would get to class early and print the scripture on the blackboard with its reference at the bottom. Then I put numbers one through twelve, or as many students as I had that week, plus two more for growth, on small pieces of paper folded up and put in a small basket. After the lesson I would have the entire class read out loud, in unison, the verse with the reference. Then, if needed, I would explain the verse using the teacher's manual.

At that point one of the students would pick out one piece of paper and read the number on it out loud. The student sitting in that numbered chair would then come up front and pick out one word of the scripture, erase it, and go back and sit down. Then the whole class would read the verse again, including the reference, while inserting the missing word (or words) from memory.

This process would continue until the entire verse was erased, the reference being the last to go. Then the entire class would recite the verse and reference, all from memory. And, praise God, it worked! Just another one of those miracles I had come to know and expect from God.

When the boys got out of class they often went to their parents and recited the verse to them. Many of the parents commented on how their child had changed, and showed enthusiasm about coming to class and learning the Bible. One parent reported that on Sunday morning their son was the first one up just to make sure that everyone else in the family was up in time for church. God gave me this idea and everyone was giving me the credit. All I could say was God was doing it–give Him all the glory.

Within a few months the class had doubled. One Sunday, Sharon, one of the other teachers, said to me,

"What are you doing with those boys? That class used to be the worst in the church but now they're like little angels. All they can talk about is you and your lessons. How did you do it?"

"I don't know what you mean Sharon, I'm just teaching the lesson from the lesson book."

I figured that the rest of the teachers were surely doing much more than I was; unlike me, they were experienced teachers. What Sue and I didn't know was, that most of these people didn't really believe in modern-day miracles and showed little, enthusiasm for God. But I was sharing miracle after miracle with my class, and I was so excited about the Lord I couldn't sit still.

We were very naive back then. In fact, when we told some of the adults about these miracles of ours, the majority of them would graciously slip away. We always thought it was either because we talked too much or because our miracles must have been so commonplace in comparison to theirs that they weren't worth listening to. We soon learned different.

I loved my class more and more every week. We were in church twice on Sunday and again on Wednesday night. We wouldn't miss a service for anything. Soon the congregation grew to around five hundred, and it required two morning services.

The head usher asked me to be an usher, and I jumped at it. This was almost too good to be true. Not only were we going to church every Sunday, but me, Bob Ford, a Sunday school teacher and now an usher too? Who would have believed it?

I was ecstatic. Could it be that now I was serving God like I promised Him? Along with the satisfaction of serving God, this "religion" thing was real, and our lives had really changed. Let me clarify that. It wasn't that we had religion. What we had was a living, personal relationship with God through Jesus Christ His Son. And, most everyone else couldn't figure this out.

Our friends and family members were watching us like a hawk. It was like living in a fish-bowl, where everyone could see us. They thought that this was just a new fad and that this church thing would soon get old and come to an end. But it didn't, our commitment to God and our relationship with Him grew and grew.

As I grew in faith, I remained conscious of my promise to serve God the rest of my life. That's why I put on the cover of this book that I'm *Serving A Life Sentence For Christ*. Of my own free will I am a bond-servant of Christ.

Back in the New Testament days, a bond-servant, once a slave, was one who was freed from serving his master but chose, of his own free will, to remain as a servant to his master for life. So, as the apostle Paul said that he was a bond-servant of Christ, so do I.

Every message Pastor Bill preached got better and better. It was like he was living right in our house. Everything he said was just for us. So one day, at the conclusion of the morning service, I approached the sound man and gave him a standing order for every sermon. He said,

"Bob, this is ridiculous! Do you have any idea how long it takes to duplicate these tapes?" They were six-inch reel-to-reel tapes, not cassettes.

"No Frank, but I'll pay you whatever it costs."

"Bob, you're the only person in the whole church that wants them. What are you doing with them?"

"Sue and I listen to them every chance we get. Sometimes we invite people over to listen as well."

Looking at me in amazement, he asked,

"Does anyone come?"

"Of course, a few of our friends and neighbors have."

I couldn't understand this haranguing over such a simple thing. Had Frank's toast burned this morning? But as he continued, the light began to shine.

"I can't believe this, Bob. Hearing the sermon once is enough for me."

"Frank, I'd really appreciate you doing this for us. Is there any way I can help you?"

"No, Bob, ... but ... oh, never mind, I'll have the tapes ready for you next Sunday."

"Thanks, Frank. I know the Lord will bless you for this."

"Huh? Oh ... sure, Bob, sure."

Everything was going so fantastic. My life was filled with joy and now had real meaning to it. If anyone had said it could get any better, I would have said they were dreaming. But in a few days I would receive an unexpected phone call that would be the beginning of a new dimension of God's supernatural miracle-working power in our life.

Chapter 5

God Is Our Real Estate Agent

Up until now we've ploughed through quite a bit of detail, and the pace has been slow, but from here on the pace picks up, and the miracles get bigger and better. So hold on to your seats, and your hats, too, because you are about to be blessed right out of your socks.

Our theology was simple. Since God blessed us so much when we did absolutely nothing for Him, surely He would bless us even more now that we believed in Him and were serving Him. And, by the way, this is scriptural, for in John 15:7 Jesus said that if we abide in him and his words abide in us, we can ask what we will and he will do it for us.

This seemed too simple for some of our friends, but it worked for us. Just for the record, our main focus wasn't on God's blessings and trying to get something from Him, but on His love and forgiveness. This developed a genuine heart-felt debt of gratitude that ignited our love for Him, and a determined desire to obey His Word.

Here's another thing of importance. We didn't have a bunch of old half-truth doctrine or traditions of men to have to weed through and unlearn. We just took the Bible as God's Word of truth to be applied to our lives and acted upon in faith. Where the Bible says whosoever, that includes us; where it says he that believeth, that includes us, too. Where it said, "These signs shall follow them that believe," that also includes us, because we are believers! Glory to God in the highest!

Dealing with my pride was a lengthy process, oops; I mean it's still in progress. It was somewhere around this time in my life that God showed me there was no good thing in and of myself. I began to realize that without His grace, without His Spirit, I was rotten to the core, but by means of His Spirit and grace, He was changing me into the image of His son, Jesus, as stated in Romans 8:29. In contrast to the old Bob Ford, now I had a healthy self-esteem, due to the work of the Holy Spirit within me.

When I realized that God created me and all of us in His image (Gen.1:26), and that He really did love me, my whole attitude and outlook on life changed. That, my friend, birthed a spirit of love within me for others, something I never had before.

Now the arrogant pride, the blatant raw humor, the life of the party, the class clown, was all being dealt with through the Cross of Christ. Little by little I could see and feel the Holy Spirit changing me. The feeling was joy unspeakable and full of glory.

I no longer had to live the lie of trying to prove that I was someone or something that I was not. I had been delivered from my home-made drug of hypocrisy. Now my smile was genuine and my joy was full. What you see is what you get, is the real me now, and it comes from God's Spirit within me. Let me put it in these words of little rhyme the Lord gave me.

Up to this point there's been too much; of I, myself, and me.
But from now on all credit goes, to the Holy Trinity.

One evening the phone rang. I answered and heard,
"Hello, Bob, this is Pastor Bill."
It was Bill Medema, our pastor from Community Reformed Church. I was surprised; he had never called me before.
"Hi, Pastor, how are you?"
"Fine, Bob, just fine. Say, Bob, I have some good news for you. You've been nominated to be a deacon!"
"A deacon?" I gasped.
"That's right, Bob. What do you think about that?"
"Well … Pastor, I don't know the first thing about being a

deacon."

"Now don't you worry about that, Bob. You'll make a fine deacon."

"I don't know, Pastor. I'm not sure that I could do the job."

"Bob, I'm confident that you would make a fine deacon. In fact, I would be very pleased if you were a member of my deacon board."

"Well ... if you think so, I'd be honored to be considered a nominee."

"Very good, Bob, I'll put your name down as approved. See you at the business meeting a week from Wednesday, okay?"

"Okay, I'll be sure to be there! And, thank you and, God bless you."

"God bless you, too, Bob. Good night."

Well, was I flying high. Sunday School teacher, usher, and now perhaps a deacon? This was too much to contain. Immediately I called my brother, who had just started going to church. He was almost as excited as I was and after our short conversation he congratulated me.

On election night, while walking toward the fellowship hall, I overheard some men talking to another nominee. The part of the discussion that surprised me was when one of the men said to the nominee, "Don't worry about being elected, Jim, you're a shoo-in." At this time in my Christian walk I didn't understand religious politics; in fact, I didn't even know it existed.

Consequently, I wasn't voted in, but I wasn't disappointed, because I wasn't sure I could do the job anyway. Pastor Bill was disappointed, and that moved me. This was still all part of God's plan because, unknown to us at the time, he had something for us that was out of this world.

Let me bring you up to date. It's 1970 and we have five children now, three girls and two boys—Terri, Brenda, Robert Jr., Eric and Michelle. They were growing in faith as Sue and I were. Every time we went to church we got filled to the brim. We were overflowing with the joy of the Lord and our permanent smiles were real. We loved to sing with everything that was in us and couldn't understand why many of the others didn't. As I sang the hymns along with the congregation, it was as if the words were bathing me in God's love and forgiveness. His presence was almost as real to me as the one standing next to me was.

One day after the morning service Pastor Bill and I were talking.

"Bob, it's good to see you today! How are you and Sue doing?"

"Just fine, Pastor, just fine. Say … um … when I listen to you preaching, I sure wish I could be up there. I think I'd like to do that someday."

"What? You can't be serious! You may as well forget all about that. You're too old and have too many kids. By the time you finished the schooling you would need you'd be way too old."

"Oh? How much schooling do you need?"

"Well, Bob, what with your family and all, it would probably take about eight to ten years."

"Oh, really? Wow! That's a long time for sure. Yeah, I guess you're right, Pastor."

"You see, Bob, there's a lot more to being a pastor than just preaching. I've got to run. You have a good day now. Will I see you guys at the service tonight?"

"Sure thing, we wouldn't miss it for anything."

I wasn't angry or hurt, but I had an unexplainable feeling of disappointment. I began to realize that I had a desire to preach and a confidence that I could do it. But I was thirty years old, way too old to be thinking about being a preacher. So I promptly discounted the whole thing and removed it from my mind.

About six months later Sue and I had a desire to move out to the country, but we didn't want anything that wasn't of God. So we made a deal with God. We learned later that in the Bible this is called a fleece. This word has a negative connotation, but it has a different meaning in the Bible. It means to test, to see what the will of God is. Now I know what that sounds like, but notice that I didn't say we'd be tempting God. After much prayer, Sue and I had true peace from God to do what I'm about to explain.

Here was our test: we would put our house on the market at a little above market price. If the first person who looked at it bought it at that price, then we would accept that our plan to move was the will of God. We told the real estate salesman that we wanted a one-day listing for our house and explained why. He thought we were crazy and told us the shortest listing contract they could give us was for thirty days.

We said that we were committed to our agreement with God no matter what. Therefore, we couldn't sell it at all, if the first person who looked at it didn't buy it. He had a tizzy-fit over it and said that we were out of our minds. No matter, we signed the thirty day contract. The house was listed on a Monday and scheduled to be shown the following Sunday.

During the week we did some general clean-up, and on Saturday we tore into it. With sleeves rolled up, off came the screen door. The kitchen furniture went out in the front yard. Sue was shampooing the carpets and I was scraping old paint off the fascia boards in the front of the house. Everything was topsy-turvy.

Somewhere around noon a nice white Lincoln parked out front. A lady got out and came to the front door. Sue answered the doorbell.

"Pardon me, Mrs. Ford, I'm Mrs. Johnson with Star Real Estate Co. Would you mind if I took a look at your house?"

"Well, I don't know, Mrs. Johnson, the house isn't supposed to be shown until tomorrow at the open house."

"I realize that, but I want to get an idea of the floor plan and the property. It will only take me a minute, and I promise not to bother you."

"Well … I guess so. Sure, go ahead."

Mrs. Johnson was there about five minutes. As she went out the door she said,

"Thank you very much, Mr. and Mrs. Ford. Have a good day now!"

We said goodbye and went back to work. About two hours later, the white Lincoln showed up again. Out popped Mrs. Johnson and a middle-aged couple. I was up the ladder painting, and Sue was inside cleaning the living room.

Before I could climb down the ladder, Mrs. Johnson said,

"Mr. Ford, I know that the house is not to be shown until tomorrow, but these folks are only in town for the day. May I please show them your house?"

By this time, Sue was out of the house and standing at the bottom of the ladder. She looked at me with that "you'd better not do this to me" look in her eye. Sue always prided herself on a clean, tidy house and with things in such disarray I knew the answer to that question was a flat no.

"No, Mrs. Johnson, I'm sorry but our contract says that showings start tomorrow during the open house!"

"But, Mr. Ford, it would only take a minute."

"Mrs. Johnson, the house is not ready. Everything is out of order; the living room carpet is still wet and ..."
She interrupted,

"Mr. Ford, that doesn't matter to us, we only need a few minutes to look it over and we won't walk on the wet carpet, I promise!"

While still up on the ladder, I began to remember our deal with the Lord. It *must* sell to the first people who look at it or we don't move. Now I was convinced they wouldn't look at it. I came down the ladder and told Mrs. Johnson that Sue and I needed a moment together, alone.

As we talked about it, we both agreed that it was out of the question. Then, all of a sudden, the thought came to us that if we were going to trust God in this then we had no right to screen out anyone.

Because of that, we felt compelled to say yes. We were disappointed and our hearts weren't in it, but the answer had to be yes.

"Okay ..., Mrs. Johnson. Go ahead."

"Thank you, Mr. Ford! We'll only be a few minutes, I promise!"
With our heads hung over, we sat on the lawn picking blades of grass. Sure enough, five or ten minutes later they were out of there.

"Thank you, Mr. and Mrs. Ford, have a good day now!"

Speechless, all we could do was watch them drive away. We began to talk about it and decided that since they were one day early, maybe we didn't have to count them. But our hearts condemned us and we knew God was requiring otherwise. Disappointed, we puttered around a while longer with no hope of moving. Then we decided that we might as well go ahead and finish the work we had started. At least the house would look a little better and be a little cleaner, too.

About two hours later the phone rang. Sue answered it, I couldn't tell who it was, but she seemed excited. I came inside and waited for her to hang up. Then she blurted out,

"They bought the house! They bought the house!"

"What? Who bought the house?"

"The people who were just here, and Mrs. Johnson is on her way over with the offer."

"She is? Did she say what the offer was?"

"Yes, she said it was a full price offer!"

"Full price! Glory to God, Honey! Praise the Lord! Praise the Lord!"

We were so excited we danced around the room like little kids.

We signed the papers and had to be out in fifteen days. Now what do we do? We needed a place to live and we needed it quick, but we didn't want to buy, we wanted to build. To rent an apartment required signing a lease, and the minimum we could find was for twelve months.

So we packed up everything and moved in with Sue's parents. They lived in a small two bedroom house. Were we close? Like canned sardines! That lasted for three and a half months. Sue and I were in the second bedroom and all five kids were sharing the family room. Within these few months we began to think that the house was shrinking, but we thanked God for it, and everything worked out well.

We paid our own way and Sue cleaned the house and cooked most of the meals. I cooked a few myself; people seem to like my spaghetti. We shared Jesus as often as the atmosphere permitted. We saw no immediate fruit, but Sue's family did get to witness first-hand that our religion was real. I'm a no-compromise kind of guy.

When I set out to do something, it's all out or nothing.

My mouth used to run like a sewer; now it was too clean for their comfort. Sue's folks often admitted that we had changed and they were happy for us, but you could tell they couldn't understand it all.

Jim, Sue's dad, was a thirty year Navy man. He'd seen it all, heard it all, said it all, and done it all—or most of it anyway. Jim and I didn't have much in common, but we got along well, and he was supportive of all we were doing. Then, about a year or so later, he accepted Jesus as his personal Lord and Savior. Hallelujah! Sue was so thrilled that God allowed her to be the one to lead him in the sinner's prayer

We bought a three-quarter acre lot in Norco, California, on Three Bar Lane. We had a twenty-five-hundred square foot, four-bedroom, three-bath, air-conditioned ranch house built on it–with a three-car garage. The total cost was $42,000. I could afford that now that I was working for Mother's Cookies.

As a route salesman I earned $18,000 to $20,000 a year. That was a very good income in the early 1970s and it was fantastic for a guy who barely made it through high school. Moving into this home took many trips, 30 miles each way, in our station wagon and a friend's pick-up truck. The whole thing was joy unspeakable and full of glory.

A few months after we moved into this little ranch of ours, we bought two horses, two ponies, three pigs, twelve baby chicks, a couple of ducks, and a dog. Wow! What a life! It was everything we ever dreamed of and more. The air was clean out here, and the freeway was never crowded. This area was the wide open spaces.

Next door to us lived an elderly couple named Peeler who belonged to the Mormon Church. Their son lived across the street and he was the Bishop of their church. We knew nothing about Mormons at the time and thought nothing of allowing our children to attend Primary, summer mid-week classes, with the Peelers at their Mormon church. Then our children began to talk to us about the Mormon prophet Joseph Smith, and a few other things. Sue and I became alarmed and I began to investigate their beliefs. We stopped letting our children go to Primary.

I bought some of their books, including, *Book of Mormon, Doctrines and Covenants* and *Pearl of Great Price* and set out to know exactly what they believed. This took a great deal of time. When I learned that they actually believe that the Mormon men will become Gods with a capitol *G,* I was shocked, (see *Millennial Star*, Volume 54, by Lorenzo Snow, former president of the Mormon Church, and *The Gospel Through the Ages* by Milton R Hunter, pp. 105–106). They also believe that Mary, the mother of Jesus, had sexual relations with Michael the Archangel to produce Jesus (see *Journal of Discourses* pp. 50–51).

Also, they believe that you must belong to the Mormon Church in order to go to heaven, (*Journal of Discourses* p. 159). It stunned me to learn that Adam, the first man, is actually their God (*Journal of Discourses*, Volume 1, p. 50). These are just a few of the things I discovered, and that was already too much for me.

Unknown to us at the time, the two years of research and study about Mormonism was all part of God's plan for us down the road. God placed us on the exact piece of real estate where we needed to be so as to be exposed to Mormonism and the need to research their beliefs. These few years of training paid big dividends in the ministry that God had planned for us.

The Peelers tried many times to get us to join their church, but we refused. We always showed the scriptural reasons. As time went by, the Peelers were witnesses to a number of miracles God was doing for us. Because of this they were sure we were supposed to be Mormons, but every time I tried to discuss the Bible or their beliefs, they said that we would have to talk to the Mormon missionaries about it.

It became quite clear to me that the Peelers, like the majority of Mormons, didn't know the Bible at all. Therefore, they had no answers to our questions. Later I discovered that most Mormons don't even know what their own church really believes.

Mrs. Peeler was a retired nurse, and a very sweet, gentle lady. She saw our daughter Michelle's fever go from 103 to normal in an instant when I laid my hand on her forehead in the name of Jesus. The lady was flabbergasted. There was another miracle that was almost too much for them to believe, even though they saw it with their own eyes.

We returned home from church one Sunday and discovered that our mallard duck had been attacked by our dog, Ginger. The duck was huddled in a corner on the other side of the fence, and clumps of feathers and flesh were missing from his back and neck.

He was covered with dried blood mixed with dirt and loose feathers. He had been there for some time; the poor creature was traumatized. Apparently he had stuck his head through the chain-link fence and the dog got hold of him. I picked up the duck and took it into the house. We all looked at it in deep sadness, contemplating what to do. We washed it off as best we could, and then discovered the horrifying result of the attack.

The large gaping hole of missing flesh allowed me to look into the bird's chest cavity and see his heart beating. My heart sank. With my eyes closed, my head fell forward and I gasped,

"Oh, Lord!"

All the children had to look at it, and Sue and I stood there shaking our heads. I thought, How could this duck still be alive? It looked utterly hopeless. We all looked at each other wondering what to do.

We talked about sewing him up but that was out of the question because of the missing flesh. Sue came up with the idea of applying some first-aid spray and covering him with an infant tee-shirt. She got the shirt, and we stuck his head and neck out one hole and his bottom out of the other. We sewed up the shirt to keep his wings from flapping so he would be constrained, as well as to keep out as much dirt as possible.

What a sight. Here was this mallard duck, one of God's most beautiful creatures, with their glistening green, black and brown feathers all perfectly placed around their neck and body. His head stuck out of the neck hole and his tail stuck out of the waist opening and his feet stuck out of the arm holes. It looked like grave clothes to me. Something like Lazarus was wrapped in.

We agreed that we would believe God for a miracle. All seven of us put a hand somewhere on the duck's body and said a part of the prayer for healing. We took authority over the injury and spoke complete healing to him. We asked God to restore him to perfect health, and then we took him back outside and put him with his mate.

I could just imagine what was going through her little duck mind. She backed off and cocked her head to the side, looking at him like something from outer space had landed in her pen. He tried to approach her but she backed off. Finally he sat down and we went back inside.

We checked on the duck a number of times each day. One day Mr. Peeler said to me,

"Why don't you just shoot the poor little thing?"
In response I said,

"We're expecting a miracle from God."
He shook his head in disbelief, huffed, and then he turned and went into his house.

There were a number of times we all had our doubts, and we had to constantly reaffirm our faith in God's Word. You see, our minds were working against what we believed in our hearts, but, then again, every day the duck remained alive, was a miracle to us.

After a few days we decided to exchange the tee-shirt for a clean one. As I approached the duck's pen, Mr. Peeler came over to the fence and asked what I was going to do with him. I said that we were going to remove the shirt, check him out, and put a clean one on him. He rolled his eyes and shook his head and said that it was cruel to let the duck suffer. I said nothing more and picked up the duck.

Into the house I went, and up on the kitchen counter went the duck. The kids gathered round watching eagerly. I held the duck and Sue started to remove the shirt, cutting carefully and being careful not to nick him. Finally, she peeled off the shirt. Gasp! Both of us had to catch our breath in amazement.

"Let me see! Let me see!" came from each one of the kids as they fought their way in closer.

"What's this?" I said. "Where is the wound? It's all healed up! Praise the Lord!" I shouted. "God has done it just like we prayed!"

Every feather that was missing had been replaced with a *full sized* new one. You couldn't tell he had ever been wounded. It was a miracle like never before, and we had a Praise the Lord party right there and then.

I suppose the duck was wondering what the racket was all about. He was obviously glad to get out of that strait-jacket of a shirt. He stretched his wings like someone who just got out of bed and stood up straight with his head high in the air. He quacked a few times, shook his tail feathers, and started exploring the kitchen like nothing had ever happened.

I took the duck outside and called Mr. Peeler over to the fence. He was floored, and said he would not have believed it was the same duck had he not seen it with his own eyes.

Right then a revelation hit me like a ton of bricks. If God would do this for a duck, what on earth would He do for us whom He had suffered and died for? Reader, the answer to that question is *all things*, for the Bible says in Romans 8:32, "He that spared not His own Son, but delivered him up for us all, how shall He not with him also *freely* give us *all things*," emphasis mine. Think about that: *freely give us all things.* This is fantastic! Thank you, Jesus!

Since then I've often wondered how long that duck had been healed before we finally got that confounded shirt off him. What if we had prayed before we put the shirt on him? Would we have seen each feather replaced and the wound closed up right there and then?

Although we will never in this lifetime know for sure, I do believe it could have been just like that, for God, who cannot lie, said to Mary through His angel Gabriel, "For with God, nothing shall be impossible" (Luke 1:37). Jesus said the same thing in Mark 9:23, "If you can believe, all things are possible to him that believes."

Shamrock, one of our ponies, came down with a bad case of colic. She was about twenty-five years old. She had to be fed only hay cubes so as to be able to digest her food. One day she got into the fresh alfalfa, and by the middle of the day she was laying on her side in agonizing pain. If you have ever heard a horse cry, you can imagine how agonizing this was for all of us.

We called the vet, and she examined Shamrock. After many futile attempts to get her on her feet the vet finally said that we needed to put the pony out of her misery. She offered to do it but we couldn't agree. Mr. Peeler was watching all this through the chain-link fence.

Sue and I discussed the situation with the kids, and we gathered around Shamrock. We laid hands on her and prayed our hearts out. While we were praying that old pony got up all on her own and started walking around like nothing had happened. The vet said,

"I don't believe it! It's a miracle!"

Once again, in amazement, Mr. Peeler stood there looking through the fence.

Miracles like these are a fulfillment of Jesus' promise to his disciples in Matt. 28:19–20 concerning the supernatural things that would happen as they obeyed his command. Jesus had told them to go into the whole world and teach converts to "observe all things whatsoever I have commanded you." The word observe, literally means *put into practice.*

The disciples were commanded by Jesus not only to preach the gospel of salvation but to teach other ethnic groups and generations to put into practice everything he had taught them. Therefore, they were to teach others such things as healing, casting out devils, and raising the dead. How long was this to go on? It was to continue "even unto the end of the world," until the second coming of Christ. Glory to God in the highest!

It was now forty miles one way to church but we never missed a service. After about six months of country living, we felt as if we had gone to heaven. Although we were happy with our church, we felt that God wanted us to find one closer to home.

We looked in the phone book and found the address and service times of the Reformed Church in Corona, a few miles from our home in Norco. On Sunday morning we were all there with high hopes. We didn't know a soul, and that made us a little uncomfortable but we forged ahead.

When the Pastor began his message, we sensed a distance, a separation from him. The longer he spoke the worse it got. Toward the end of his sermon he made a remark that struck us as very unbecoming of a man of God, and we left there disappointed, never to return.

We continued to look around, and one day we passed a building up on a hill and Sue said,

"See that mortuary up there?"

"Yes, what about it?"

She continued,

"Charlie and Linda go to church there."

Startled, I replied,

"They what? Did you say they go to church in a mortuary?"

"Yep! That's what Linda told me the other day. She said they rent it on Sunday and hold services there."

Thinking over what Sue had just said, I replied,

"Well Honey, we did get married in a mortuary, and that worked. Why not try going to church in one?"

We actually did get married in a combination mortuary/wedding chapel, the Chapel of Memories in Norwalk, California, on June 18, 1960.

The following Sunday, there we were inside a mortuary, having church. The name of the church was Trinity Christian Center, (TCC). It was different. These people were very excited about being in church, and another thing, we could actually hear the people turning the pages of their Bibles as they followed along with the sermon. This was new, and it excited me.

When it came to worship, they sang like they really meant it. And to top the whole thing off, they hugged each other too. Did you say—hugged—Bob? Yep! You heard me right! I mean they hugged big time, but it was genuine, and it was pure and holy.

Obviously these people really loved Jesus, and each other. With their eyes closed, they raised their hands in the air while they sang. We had never experienced anything like this before, but it didn't bother us; for we could see that these people clearly had a deep relationship with the Lord. To make a long story short, we fit in with this new-found fellowship like we had been born there.

All during this time I was devouring material on the Spirit filled life by Campus Crusade for Christ. One day while at work, I asked Ed Plains, a coworker and fellow Christian, about all this.

"Ed, what do you know about the Spirit filled life?"

"What is it that you want to know?"

"Well, these books say that all I have to do to be Spirit filled is to breathe out my sins and then breathe in the Spirit. I do that every day, but when I read the Bible I feel in my heart that I'm still missing something."

"What do you mean?"

"Well ... it's kind of hard to explain, but when I read the Bible about the baptism in the Holy Spirit, I can see that back then they had the gifts of the Spirit. But these books say the gifts of the Spirit, such as miracles and healings, ended with the apostles. They also say that the baptism of the Holy Spirit is given at salvation and, even my Scofield Bible footnotes say that!"

"Well, what do you think, Bob? Did all the miracles and gifts end with the apostles?"

"No way! Sue and I have seen many miracles."

"Bob, are you Spirit filled?"

"Well ... I think so."

"Are you saved?"

In utter amazement and with raised voice I said,

"What? I can't believe you asked me that! Of course I'm saved! You know I'm saved!"

Ed stood there for a moment or two and let me ponder what I had said. Soon I was asking him a few more questions.

"How come I know I'm saved but I don't know if I'm filled with the Spirit?"

"Well, Bob, I think you've answered your own question."

I thought about that for a moment, then asked,

"Are you filled with the Holy Spirit?"

A big smile appeared on Ed's face.

"Yes, I've been Spirit filled now for thirty-eight years."

"You have? Well then, how can I get filled with the Spirit?"

"Well, Bob, why don't you ask your church about that?"

"Oh, do they know how to get me filled with the Holy Spirit?"

"Yes, I'm sure they do. Why don't you ask them?"

I paused for a moment and began wondering who I would ask. Then it came to me.

"Say, what if I ask Bill Castleman? He's a deacon or something there. Do you think he could help me?"

"Yes, I'm sure he can."

"Hey, Ed, I just remembered. They have a meeting tonight. Do you think they could do it then?"

"I don't see why not. Why don't you call Bill and see?"

"I'll just do that! Thanks, you've really helped me."

I couldn't wait to get home from work. Linda and Sue were in the front yard talking. I went right up to Linda and began asking what she knew about the baptism in the Holy Spirit. After answering a number of my questions she mentioned that she and Charles were going to the Bible Study tonight. She offered to pick me up and take me along, so as to learn more about it. I said I would be ready and waiting.

I went inside and called Bill Castleman to ask him about being filled with the Holy Spirit at the Bible Study. He encouraged me to be there and when I asked if he would arrange it all for me with Pastor Stout, he said he'd be glad to. It was the Wednesday night Bible Study meeting that TCC held at a Lutheran church.

The Bible Study seemed to take forever. Every minute I waited in great expectation for some word about the baptism in the Holy Spirit and my request. Pastor Stout was teaching, and after an hour it was time to wind up the meeting. He had everyone join hands in a circle and then said,

"Let's close in prayer."

I thought, Close in prayer? I thought Bill was going to set everything up for me? They can't close in prayer yet. I came to be filled with the Holy Spirit!

First one person prayed and then another. It was very gentle and smooth, nothing emotional, just short prayers by a few different people. During this time, all I could think of was the possibility of missing the opportunity to be baptized with the Holy Spirit.

Then, all of a sudden, I felt like I was going to pray. I had never prayed out loud in a public meeting before. In fact, two weeks before this, Pastor Stout had asked me to pray over the offering. I felt like throwing the plate down and running out of the church.

Pastor saw the panic on my face and got someone else to say the prayer.

Here I stood in this prayer circle, wondering what would happen next. I was surprised and frightened—and determined! I kept waiting for Bill to say something—anything. I wanted the baptism in the Holy Spirit now more than anything in the world, but I was afraid I would miss out on it.

Then, gradually, that prayer of mine moved from my heart to my throat. I tried to swallow it but it wouldn't go back down. My prayer had overcome every obstacle. Having bounced off my palate it slid over my tongue, then pried open my lips and came flowing from my mouth like honey from a jar. With a supernatural balance of authority and humility, I said,

"Lord Jesus, I came to be baptized with the Holy Spirit and I'm not going home without it!"

My ears seemed to ask, *Did you say that, Bob?* My heart nodded with a big, *yes!* I could hardly believe I had spoken up. But what was about to happen was even more profound. I began to feel something warm in my feet, moving up through my ankles and my legs. I began to feel tipsy. I was still holding hands with the people on each side of me and my eyes were still closed after the prayer. I didn't know if I was still standing or not. I felt weightless.

I opened my eyes and saw the most magnificent illuminating glow imaginable, greater by far than anything I had ever seen in real life. Then I was compelled to close my eyes. This light had filled the room, and it had filled me. I was saturated with an indescribable holy presence.

I would have sworn I was seeing Jesus as a bright light, but it wasn't exactly a bodily figure; it was more a holy and divine presence of living light, almost liquid light. It radiated from a central point and seemed to occupy the entire room. The light seemed to be an intelligent spirit being of love and holiness.

I could still see and recognize other figures and objects in the room, but the light made everything else slightly obscure. It had no recognizable shape or distinguishing features, but I knew in my heart and soul that it was Jesus. How is that possible? I don't know, but it looked like Jesus to me.

My body was overcome with a feeling I can't put into words, but what was happening in my heart was even more powerful. In that divine moment it seemed that I died to every possession, every worldly thing, and every aspiration. All I wanted was all of Jesus. More correctly, I wanted to *go and be with Jesus.*

Not a single thought crossed my mind to say I might want to stay here on earth. And, I didn't have the slightest feeling or thought that this was wrong; in fact, it felt perfectly right. I was utterly *homesick* for a home in heaven; I felt summoned to be there. This homesick feeling was as genuine an emotion as I have ever felt. My only explanation is that the Holy Spirit had so saturated my being that I felt one with the Lord as never before.

I opened my eyes again. Wow! It must be Jesus! It couldn't be anything but Jesus, but I couldn't continue to behold his glory. I felt unworthy and it seemed irreverent to keep my eyes open, so I closed them again. I knew I was standing in the presence of Jesus, and his holiness completely exposed my unholiness. The words of the prophet Isaiah explain how I felt: "Woe is me! For I am undone." (Isa. 6:5).

My eyes flew open for the third time and it started all over again; so beautiful, and magnificent, and loving, so forgiving, understanding, and giving. The reality shone without a word spoken. I knew He was not just offering, but giving me, pouring into me, everything. Everything I wanted, everything I needed, and much, much more.

Then my entire body was filled with this supernatural warmth and love as if with warm oil starting at my feet and moving slowly up my body and into my head. I was filled with His divine love and supernatural faith. If I couldn't have seen the others in the room I would have thought I had been translated to heaven.

Pastor Stout called to me.

"Bob, come here. I can see the Holy Spirit all over you."

When I looked across the circle toward him, I could see that the glorious penetrating light filled the entire room. I went over to him, and he laid hands on me and began to pray for me along with everyone else. I had been baptized with the Holy Spirit, with the Biblical evidence of speaking in tongues.

I must confess, I've done the best I can here, but words fall far short. There are no words that can do justice to such an experience. And another thing, when I prayed my prayer I was only expecting Bill Castleman or Pastor Stout to respond to my request to be baptized with the Holy Spirit, whatever that meant. But, in my innocence I asked Jesus directly, and Jesus did it right there and then. You see, dear friend, as I learned here, Jesus is the baptizer with the Holy Spirit.

When I arrived home that night, I must have floated into the house. Sue stared at me and said I looked different. I was different. We sat on the sofa as I told her all about it. It took a good thirty minutes to explain it all, and then I sat down at the dining room table and opened my Bible. It fell open to John 14.

I started reading from verse one. Verse twelve reads, "Verily, verily I say unto you, He that believeth on me, the works that I do shall he do also; and greater works than these shall he do because I go unto my Father." My faith took a giant leap. It was as if Jesus himself was standing in front of me, saying these words directly to me. That verse had my name written all over it. My faith soared. God birthed a supernatural faith in me and I knew I could believe for anything and everything now.

Okay, so exactly what happened here? I've read this verse many times, but this was a more powerful reaction than ever before. What's the explanation of this? Another thing, how can two people read the same Bible verse and only one come away with tangible insight and strengthened faith? The answer is revelation.

The word revelation means to uncover or unveil, to make manifest, or to make known. God and only God, by the Holy Spirit, can give this revelation, as recorded in the Bible, and it's according to His will, not ours.

Once again my friend, this was the grace of God, grace meaning *gift*. This gift of God was not by positive thinking or positive confession, not by the abundance of sacrifice nor any other works nor power of my own. This gift of revelation is given, as the Bible says, by the Spirit of God to "them that love Him."

If you truly love God with all your heart, this is for you too.

Just expect it! God has promised it and that settles it. Once I heard someone say, "God said it and that makes it so!" I say a big Amen to that.

This profound abundance of faith made me wish I was standing in the presence of a dead person. I knew in my heart that through my prayer of faith, God would raise the dead to life again. I told Sue I believed I could walk on water. I wasn't kidding, and I meant it in a most reverential way. In fact, I almost filled the bathtub with water and tried it, but because I didn't want to tempt God, I didn't. I wish now that I had.

From that time on I was so full of God's explosive combination of love and faith that nothing bothered me. I so thoroughly loved everything and everybody that no one could do anything to upset or offend me. Because of all this, Sue began to get concerned. I was giving away money like water, and all I could see everywhere was love, love, love.

God knew that His love was my biggest need, so He gave me a double portion of it. That old chip on my shoulder was completely gone. All my hurt, unforgiveness, and anger were washed away by His precious love. The load was lifted, now I was even freer than before. I couldn't do enough for Sue, the kids, and others. All I wanted to do now was to love others as Jesus loved me.

All my life I had been taking whatever I could from wherever I could get it, all because of a lack of love. Now I was learning the difference between lust and love. The word *love* is a word of action, seen more in what we do than in what we say. *God is love* isn't just a figure of speech; it's a fact. The Bible says that "God so *loved* the world that he *gave* his only begotten Son" (John 3:16, emphasis mine).

In reference to the difference between love and lust, somewhere along the line I picked up this nugget of wisdom.

> *"Love gives at the cost of self to benefit others*
> *because love desires to give.*
> *Whereas, lust takes at the cost of others to benefit self*
> *because lust desires to take."*

God had so turned me around with this truth that I couldn't give enough. In every area of my life I could see God moving on me to be a *giver* and not a *taker*. I believe that if a husband and wife will apply these words to their marriage relationship, they will surely experience a greater degree of harmony and joy and reap the blessings of God as well.

The Holy Spirit, through study of God's Word, began to reveal to me how closely faith and love are connected. The apostle Paul revealed this truth to the early Church when he said in Galatians 5:6, "Faith which works by means of love." As my love for God grows deeper and stronger, my faith grows in proportion to it. You see, you can't really have faith in God without loving God, and you can't really love God without having faith in God.

My faith and love can't help but grow stronger when I think that out of God's love for us He gave us His Son, Jesus Christ. Out of His love for us He has saved us from the guilt and punishment for our sins. Out of His love for us He has saved us from an eternal burning hell! Out of His love for us He gives us everything. Our faith, our love, our spiritual gifts, our talents, our abilities, all comes from God. Yes, the more I consider all of this, the greater my love for Him, and the stronger my faith in Him.

A few days after being baptized with the Holy Spirit, I noticed something very profound. I was reading the Bible with a new understanding, a new insight. The Bible was alive! It was more real, more meaningful.

Jesus became more and more personal. The devil did put up a fight, and my flesh cried out for a truce, but the Spirit wouldn't have it. The fight ended up in a blood bath—the precious blood of Jesus. Sin lost. The flesh surrendered, and I was being washed daily in the precious blood of Christ.

My faith continued to grow as I read God's Word and put it to practice in my life. I would jot down scripture references that I wanted to memorize and my mother, bless her heart, would type these scriptures on pocket sized cards that I carried with me everywhere. Fantastic! Memorizing scripture was a piece of cake now, two, three, as many as six scriptures a day. Wow! Was there no end to this glorious new relationship with God? No! No! A thousand times, No!

My mother began attending the weekly Bible study that Sue and I held in our home. During one of these Bible studies I was teaching on witnessing to the lost and leading them through the scriptures on salvation. I was explaining the necessity of a person confessing that they were a sinner, repenting, asking forgiveness for their sins and accepting Jesus into their heart as their Lord and Savior to guide them and to change them. I talked about Nicodemus, who was a religious leader, but Jesus told him that he needed to be born again.

Just then my mother said,

"Son, I've never done any of this!"

I was surprised and said,

"Mom, surely you're saved, aren't you?"

Earnestly and lovingly she said,

"All I know is that I've never done what you said and, I don't believe that I'm saved. I've always believed in God, and I believe that Jesus died for our sins, but I never knew that I had to accept Jesus as my Savior and surrender my life to his Lordship. So I don't know for sure that I would go to heaven."

Since Mom had been raised as a Catholic, I assumed she was saved, but she said that all these scriptures we were reading were new to her, and she felt a great need to follow them. Without any further ado I said,

"Well then, Mom, how about if we pray right now and settle this matter once and for all?"

We prayed and she was gloriously saved with the full assurance of the Holy Spirit in her heart that she was now a child of God and was heaven-bound.

This was a great lesson to me. All my life my mother demonstrated genuine love, kindness, generosity, forgiveness, respect, and compassion to everyone. She didn't have a critical bone in her body or a harsh word for anyone. If anyone looked like a Christian to me, she did. But from then on, it didn't matter to me if you were born in a church building and had preachers for parents, I asked the critical questions necessary to prove for sure if a person was saved or not.

During another one of these home Bible studies I was teaching on how to receive healing by faith. About half-way through the lesson Mom jumped up from her chair shouting,
"I'm healed! I'm healed! Praise God, I'm healed!"
For years she had a severe case of sciatic nerve disorder that often made it hard for her to walk or sit. She would visit the doctor about twice a week for this but received little or no relief. What had happened to her is a good example where faith works without prayer, but don't expect prayer to work without faith. Mom started running around the room with her hands in the air, then skipping, then jumping all the time shouting,
"I'm healed! I'm healed!"
It was a marvelous sight reminding me of the lame man in Acts 3:8 who went "walking and leaping and praising God."

I want to make it clear that I do not focus solely on miracles, signs and wonders, or the gifts of the Spirit. My focus is on the sacrificial work of Christ on the Cross of Calvary. But, I don't limit this all-sufficient work of Christ to salvation only, for that would be denying the *complete* work of the atonement wrought by Christ. All the miracles in the Bible (especially in the Old Testament) pointed to Jesus and the Cross; and so do the miracles we have experienced, and are privileged to tell you about in this book.

Miracles of healing are no greater than the miracle of salvation; both are gifts of God's love to us. Both are a result of the all sufficient sacrifice of Christ on the Cross of Calvary. The shedding of Christ's blood *bought* and *paid* for, in full, everything and anything we receive from God, both in this world and in the world to come.

Everything we receive from God is by means of the promises of God through faith in Christ. All God's promises have been offered to us with a guaranteed yes, not maybe, or sometimes, or I'll think about it, or if you're good enough to earn it, or if God feels like it, but Yes! The Bible says in 2 Corinthians 1:20, "For all the promises of God in Christ are yes."

I began to notice an insatiable hunger for the Word of God. The Holy Spirit was saying to me, *"He that reads give strict heed to what the Spirit is saying. Read the Word! Meditate on the Word! Study the Word! Devour the Word! Obey the Word, and there will be no end to your glorious relationship with the Lord."*

He reminded me of Psalms 1:2, speaking of the true believer, "But his delight is in the law of the Lord, and in His law does he meditate day and night." God's Word is truth and he wanted me to learn and memorize his Word. The Holy Spirit was constantly reminding me of the words of Jesus in John 8:32, "And you shall know the truth, and the truth shall make you free" and of the Psalmist in 119:11, "Thy Word have I hid in my heart, that I might not sin against thee."

This burning desire to read, meditate, study and practice God's Word came from a deep love for the Lord, from my heart and not my head. It was not motivated by a desire for favors, repayment for salvation, or blessings. No, it was just the plain and simple love for God and his grace and mercy.

What I received from God was *grace*, unmerited favor. Grace is God giving us what we don't deserve: love, forgiveness, heaven, and more. Mercy is God withholding from us what we deserve: being called to account and receiving judgment and punishment, hell.

I experienced what King David spoke of in the Psalms: loving God and his Word. The Word brought him joy, peace, strength, faith, courage, healing, and victory over sin as well as victory in battle. I was having the time of my life in a heart-felt relationship with the creator of the universe. Wow! Who'd a thunk it!

Here's something the Holy Spirit showed me early on, and kept reminding me of almost daily. The word Christian means Christ-like. That doesn't mean that I, or anyone else, will be a savior, but it does mean that we should strive to act and work as Jesus did, (1 Jn.2:6). How did Jesus act? He always pleased the Father in righteousness in thought, word, and deed and resisted the devil with all his might. How did Jesus work? He preached the gospel of salvation, healed the sick, raised the dead, restored sight to the blind and hearing to the deaf, speech to the mute, and cast out devils.

Reading Mark 4:22–25, the Holy Spirit shone a light on my understanding. In plain, simple terms it's saying use it or lose it. When we apply God's Word to our life by practicing it, he will give us more and more faith, insight, revelation, and understanding of his Word, which will produce more anointing and power for righteousness, and for miracles. Simply put, *do* it and we'll find that next time we'll have more power to *keep on doing* it.

When I read the Bible, I look to see how I can apply its words to my life. Of course, some things I thought I had already accomplished, I find that I need to relearn. My old nature is stubborn and needs to be constantly dealt with. I have to cooperate with the Holy Spirit, and allow God to change me. Just like you, I want the victory over sin right now, but it doesn't always happen overnight. In the Old Testament it was one thing for God to get the children of Israel *out* of Egypt, and quite another to get the Egypt out of the children of Israel. So it is with me, and it is the work of the Holy Spirit, not the work of the flesh.

It was time for the family vacation, and the station wagon was packed inside and out. By the looks of it you would have thought we were going for a month or two. All seven of us (eight counting our dog Ginger) were packed in along with all the camping gear and food. We were off for a week to Zion National Park in Utah, about eight hours north.

It was beautiful! God's creation is breathtaking, and we were enjoying our time of relaxation. Suddenly a car speeding through the campsite ran over Ginger, and the driver never even stopped to see what happened. Ginger just lay there bleeding from both ends.

The children were all crying and dared not touch her; she was barely alive. I gently removed her from the road and called the family to prayer. We laid hands on her and took authority over the injury and death, speaking healing into her body as the people in the campsite watched.

Once again God demonstrated His love, grace, and mercy.

God is so good. Within a matter of minutes Ginger was up and running around as if nothing had happened. Glory to God! He is worthy of praise!

The onlookers were flabbergasted. They seemed to be waiting for Ginger to fall over dead any minute. She returned home with us in fine health, with never any problems from the accident. In fact, I can't even remember her ever being sick after that.

We had a great time at Zion National Park and we came home and enjoyed our little ranch more and more. We bought three baby turkeys, about five or six inches tall. We knew nothing about raising turkeys; we played it by ear.

Sue came home one day and found that one of the turkeys was dead. It had been laying dead on the bottom of the cage for some time, with others stepping on it and pecking at it. She picked up the dead bird and, without giving it a thought, threw it into the trash barrel. Right away she sensed that she should have prayed for it, but she thought that was a bit silly. After all, it was just a turkey.

But the impression became stronger and stronger to the point that she prayed saying,

"Lord, are you telling me to pray for that turkey?"

She returned to the trash barrel and looked at the dead turkey, unable to shake the words of the scripture: "Nothing is impossible with God." After all, she thought, God created that turkey, so he can raise it from the dead. She removed it from the barrel. It was dead, dead, dead, no doubt about it.

Her faith took a dive as she stood there looking at it in her hand. She shook her head, shrugged, and laid it back in the cage. When the other turkeys began to pick at it again this upset her. Immediately she said with a loud voice,

"In the name of Jesus I command you to come back to life!"

Well, reader, what do you think? Sounds a little foolish, right? I can almost hear someone saying, *"A little foolish? Come on, Bob, be realistic. This is way out there."* Well, you're right. It was foolish, and, she felt rather foolish about it. But remember the Scripture says God uses foolish things to bring Him glory, "But God has chosen the foolish things of the world to put to shame the wise and God has chosen the weak things of the world to put to shame the things which are mighty" (1 Cor. 1:27).

Also, Jesus said in John 15:7, "If you abide in me, and my words abide in you, you shall ask what you will and it shall be done unto you." The words "what you will" in that verse pretty much means anything, right? That is, anything that is not harmful to others and will glorify God. So, Reader, what do you think about all this?

Well, here we go again. Yep! You guessed it! That turkey bounced up off the cage floor pronto, full of life like nothing had ever happened to it. Nope! I ain't pulling your leg either. I mean, that turkey flat got up and moved. He had gotten a new lease on life and he knew it. What do you want to bet he had a few things to tell the other turkeys, too? For the record, he lived to weigh over thirty Thanksgiving pounds. *You mean you ate him?* Of course we ate him. He wasn't going to live forever.

Now, I'm going to close this chapter with a little poem I made up just for you, hopefully this will prepare you for what's coming up.

> I've shared with you these miracles,
> and do hope you believe.
> That God would like to give us more,
> than what we have received.
> But if right now you have some doubt,
> then stop and let us pray.
> Cause what I'm about to share with you,
> just might blow you away.

---------- Chapter 6 ----------

Called By God

Things progressed rather quickly. There never was a dull moment. Living for Jesus is the most exciting life there is. TCC moved into a new building and grew to around 250, and the Holy Spirit impressed Pastor Stout to take me under his wing. He gave me hands-on training and required that I take courses at Melodyland School of Theology. Melodyland, a former amusement park, was purchased by Dr. Ralph Wilkerson and turned into a school of Theology that had an on-campus full-gospel, Spirit-filled church.

This was a real step in faith for a guy who hated school and passed by the skin of his teeth. But I wanted so much to serve Jesus and learn all I could about him and the Bible that I was compelled to take the plunge. I never was very good in English, and I'm not all that good at spelling and grammar, so learning New Testament Greek kept me praying constantly. Many nights and weekends were given solely to study.

During this time I asked Pastor Stout if I could start an adult New Believers Class on Sunday mornings, but he said there wasn't an available classroom. Even the sanctuary was being used for an adult class. Determined, I asked if I could use the small kitchen, with room for about eight people. He asked me who would come, and I suggested we announce it in the morning service for the following week. Reluctantly, he went along with it. He didn't think it would work. He made the announcement, and the following Sunday there were three of us.

The attendance went from three to twelve in the first month. We moved into the book room, managed by Eldon and Nancy Heaton. It held about thirty people with all the book racks and tables moved to the side. After two months in this room, we had thirty-eight adults inside and another five or so out in the hall. Credit where credit is due: It was "all God." His grace and anointing were evident. As I taught the Word, God confirmed it with the signs and wonders He promised in Mark 16:20.

Then I asked if we could share the sanctuary with the other class, but Pastor Stout said no. The other class was being taught by an outside minister and former Seminary professor who, unknown to me, was not Spirit Filled.

I had never met him, but one Sunday morning after class he approached me and challenged my teaching on miracles and the gifts of the Spirit. He proceeded to strongly rebuke me concerning my doctrines. He gave me a book he had written on the basic doctrines of the Bible and told me to study it. I did, and, although it was good, it lacked any teaching on the baptism with the Holy Spirit and the gifts of the Spirit.

I knew I had a lot to learn, but I couldn't understand what this guy was all upset about. Had his wife burned a hole in his favorite shirt this morning? Being so caught up in what God was doing in and with me, I had hardly noticed him up till now. Later, I found out that his class had gone from around fifty down to ten while my class had grown from three to around forty. Within two more weeks he quit, and his students filtered into the three remaining adult classes.

My class then moved into the sanctuary and soon we grew to seventy-five plus. The Spirit of God moved upon us, and miracles were happening weekly. I would open the class with worship songs and move right into the Word of God. At the close I would have an altar call and pray for the sick and other needs.

It seemed that every week miracles happened: short legs were lengthened, hearing restored, pains relieved, salvations, baptism in the Holy Spirit, financial miracles and so on, all to the glory of God.

Now for that miracle I promised you in the previous chapter.

I hope you're prayed up, because ready or not here it comes. Remember now, I'm only a route salesman for Mothers Cookies, and as a Christian, still wet behind the ears.

It was in the afternoon. I had finished serving one store and was on my way to another. I got a strong impression in my heart to go to Lakewood General Hospital to pray for a woman there. I didn't know anyone in that hospital, but I was certain God had given me that impression. It became so strong that I began to seek the Lord about it. A bit confessed, I didn't know exactly what to do. Then in a humble, quizzical way I asked,

"Lord, if this is really you, please reveal her name to me." Immediately the name Marie Brittenham came to me, not an audible voice but it was supernatural knowledge that the Holy Spirit gave me. I didn't know this woman nor what her need was, so I drove my truck back to the warehouse and took my car to the hospital. I was dressed in my work clothes, no tie, not even a sports coat.

I approached the visitation office and I noticed the visitor's sign at the reception desk. It said *Visiting Hours 2-3 and 7-8 PM*. I looked at my watch; it was 3:30 PM. My heart sank. I thought, Oh no, I should have driven straight over here in my cookie truck. Confused, I just stood there. I thought, Surely there must be a way to get in, but how? Back then hospitals were strict about visiting hours.

Just then the woman behind the desk said,

"Can I help you, sir?"

Still puzzled I said,

"I see your visiting hours are from two to three o'clock ..."

She interrupted with,

"Who is it that you would like to see?"

"Marie Brittenham, Ma'am."

Now, as I stand before God I assure you that nothing more than this was said. The woman proceeded to pick up the phone, dialed the nurse's station down the hall, and then I heard her say,

"Marie Brittenham's minister is here to see her."

Minister? Whoa! I just about raptured! I wasn't a minister, and I wasn't dressed like a minister. There wasn't any reason for her to say that, except that God had somehow put that in her mind. She hung up the phone and pointed down the hall.

"Go down the hall and turn left. Marie is in the second room on the left, in the first bed."

Wow! Was I flying high! Down the hall I went. Marie's door was open and I went in. She was talking on the phone, so I waited. She turned and asked me what I wanted.

"Marie, Jesus has sent me here to pray for you."

Stunned, she hung up the phone and called me over to her. She grabbed me by the arm and pulled me close to her. With eyes as big as pancakes, she said,

"Oh, thank God! I've been praying that he would send someone!"

I introduced myself and asked,

"Why are you here, Marie?"

She replied,

"I have cancer, but they haven't been able to operate because I came down with pneumonia, but I'm just about over that now."

I looked straight at her and said confidently,

"Well, Marie, let's pray and believe God to heal you of both these things, okay?"

"Oh, yes! Yes, Bob, please pray!"

I put my hand on her forehead and prayed that God would heal her from the "top of her head to the tips of her toes." It wasn't a long prayer, nothing emotional, and, in fact, quite simple.

When I opened my eyes I saw a nurse standing at the foot of her bed with a tray of towels or bandages or something. Undoubtedly she was waiting for me to leave, so I promptly excused myself and left. I was only there for about ten minutes or so.

A few days later I called and found out that Marie was still in the hospital. I thought, How can that be? I was confused. I figured, God sent me there, so then why is she still in the hospital? My fear was that maybe the doctor went ahead with the surgery. Marie was eighty-three years old, and surgery would be tough on her. I decided to go and see how she was doing.

This time, dressed in suit and tie, with Bible in hand, I went during visiting hours. When I got to her room, she did the same thing as before, grabbing my arm excitedly. Praising God, she kept saying,

"I'm healed! I'm healed! The Lord has completely healed me!"

Delighted, but confused, I said,

"Marie, if you've been healed, why are you still here?"

"They can't find the cancer, so they've been X-raying me from head to toe looking for it! Bob, when you prayed for me it felt like you plugged me into the wall outlet! A surge of energy went right through my body, and the pneumonia and cancer completely left. Oh, and my toes were healed, too."

"Your toes?" I said. "What was wrong with your toes? You never said anything to me about that."

"Oh, I must have forgotten to tell you. The flesh around my toes was rotting away. They had surgically removed the rotting flesh, but when the nurse came to change the bandages she almost fainted. She grabbed the bed and said,

"My God! My God! Your toes they're like new!"

All I could think of was the goodness of God. I began to receive a revelation from God in light of Ephesians 3:20, "Now unto Him who is able to do exceeding abundantly above all that we ask or think, according to the power that works in us."

It was revealed to me that God will do more than I ask. It was clear that what will happen depends upon how much of His power I have working in me. This is a reflection of how much I love and obey Him, which will produce a like amount of hunger for the Word and prayer as well.

All this love, submission, obedience, reading the Word, and prayer are one. They are all parts of the whole, and they all must work together to produce the greatest results. If any one piece is lacking, as when part of your car's engine is missing, your efforts will not produce the power you intended.

Over the years I've talked to many Christians who say they love God, are submitted to him and pray often. But when it comes to knowing why they believe what they believe, they are stopped in their tracks. This is one of the major causes some get drawn into cults and others into legalism. Many can only quote a few scriptures, and then it's usually their own paraphrase, without clear knowledge of book, chapter, and verse.

You know dear Christian; I look at it this way. It's my soul that's at stake here, and although I read many Christian books and learn from many preachers and teachers, my Bible comes first. No one will have to answer to God for my spiritual condition but me. Therefore, I will "Study to show myself approved unto God, a workman that will not be ashamed, rightly dividing the Word of truth" (2 Tim. 2:15).

God has revealed to me a number of times that the root of the matter is the Word of God with prayer. As I read the Word of God, I am praying over it. I repent on the spot when I see that my life is not in line with God's Word, and I submit to the Holy Spirit to change me right then and there. When I see a promise of God that I'm not experiencing, I claim it by faith and commit to see it manifest in my life for his glory.

I have learned over and over again that it's through an attitude of prayer and obedience that God's truth takes root in my heart and soul. Most of the time I'm anxious to read and pray, but there are times when I don't feel like it. Sometimes reading the Bible is like eating unsalted, unbuttered popcorn in the desert with no water to wash it down. Sometimes praying is like talking to the wall. I have to discipline myself to do it. Discipline is the way of life; without it we go downhill, off course, and sometimes into big trouble.

The Bible asks in Amos 3:3, "Can two walk together, except they be agreed?" The obvious answer is absolutely not. Therefore, walking with God is agreeing with Him and His Word in thought, word, and deed. I can't do that unless I know what God's Word says.

So, as I read and learn God's Word and His will, I'm set free and empowered to make the right choices. I can walk with Him in agreement and receive the peace, joy, and power that he gives to those that please Him.

God, who is all-knowing and all-powerful, answers to no God, for there is no other God. There is the, one-and-only—Jehovah, who answers to no angel, nor to the devil, nor to any power except— the power of prayer. The power of prayer is the only power in the universe to which God yields.

Many Christians have told me they don't know how to pray, so they don't pray at all. Some have even said, God knows their heart and what they are thinking, therefore, no need to pray. Some want to learn from a book or to repeat a written prayer.

There are many good books on prayer, especially those by E. M. Bounds, but the best way to learn is to pray. How did you learn to swim, by reading a book? No, you jumped into the water and started moving your arms and legs. You didn't jump into the middle of the ocean, either; you started out in shallow water and then moved out into deeper water as you learned. So it is with prayer.

Reader, God is waiting to hear from you. Have you called Him lately? His number hasn't changed, it's "Father, I come in the name of Jesus."

By the way, Mrs. Brittenham lived to be ninety-three before God took her home, and she didn't die of cancer or any other disease. She just went to sleep one night and woke up in the presence of Jesus. Isn't the Lord wonderful? How could anyone ask for anything better than all this?

I love to talk to people about Jesus, especially when they respond by accepting him as their Lord and Savior. But whether I'm planting seed, watering it, or bringing in the harvest, it all gives me real inner satisfaction and joy to be sharing his love and forgiveness with others. I have run into many questions and excuses from people, but I never try to force the gospel on them. Although, as far as experiences go, here is a real classic among many that I would like to share with you.

One day I had the opportunity to witness to a man that was obviously well off. He said that I was wasting my time because there was no hope for him, because the rich can't be saved. "It is easier for a camel to go through the eye of a needle, than for a rich man to enter into the kingdom of God" (Matt.19:24–26).

It was clear that he had never learned about this verse, so I took the time to show him. You see, the *eye of the needle* was a low, narrow gate within a larger gate found in the walls around the city of Jerusalem. A camel could only enter through this small gate if it were on its knees and unloaded—difficult—but not impossible.

The saying was a common Jewish proverb that expressed great difficulty. Jesus ended this proverb with these comforting words "but with God all things are possible." The difficulty is that the rich have a difficult time letting go of their trust in riches.

My coworker, Ed, became a close friend and brother in the Lord. We began praying together and started a noontime prayer time. Five of us would stop whatever we were doing at 12:00 noon and find a place to pray for thirty minutes. Each of us had a copy of the same list of needs. Over the months, God performed numerous miracles as a result of these prayers.

One morning, when I arrived at the depot, I reached out to shake hands with Ed. As soon as our hands touched, he said,

"Bob, when you touched me I felt a surge of power go through me and all the pain in my arm and wrist disappeared."
He began to move and squeeze his arm, saying,

"I'm healed, I'm healed."
I didn't feel anything at the time. If this very thing hadn't happened a few times before, I would have had a hard time accepting it. I have learned, however, when you are filled with God's love and faith, others will draw it right out of you like they did with Jesus, Paul, Peter, and many others.

It's humbling to me, but it's no surprise. Jesus said in John 14:12, "Verily, verily, I say unto you, he that believeth on me, the works that I do shall he do also; and greater works than these shall he do; because I go unto my Father." He also said the "disciple should be like his master" (Matt.10:24–25). Therefore, this should be the goal of all Christians. It isn't pride to imitate Christ, it's a command.

As a young boy I was a dreamer, but never in my wildest dreams would I have thought that when I touched someone they would feel any virtue from God through me. As I have said, this has happened often, even in the absence of any prayer, just like it did here with Ed. This is by the grace of God, and among Christians it is the *anointing* of God through the believer.

This is for you as well as me, no matter what your age or level of education. Although I envy the person with a good education resulting in a high IQ, take it from me, you don't need a high-Q in your IQ to be on-Que with God.

On the heels of this miracle, Ed said he believed that God

had called me to the ministry. We talked about it at some length. Ed was convinced of my call, but I was not. It wasn't that I didn't want to be a minister, but I didn't know if God was calling me or if it was just my own desire. The more we talked about it, the more frustrated Ed became. He said that the evidence of the call of God on my life was overwhelmingly obvious.

All I could say was that I didn't want to be presumptuous. I had to know for sure. The great things God was doing in my life proved to me only that God is faithful to his Word. I believe that every Christian should be experiencing these same things. When I read in the Bible "And these signs shall follow them that believe," the words "them that believe" mean anyone, and that includes me. Therefore, I didn't see it as the evidence of God's call on me to anything other than serving Him.

I became frustrated over the whole thing. No, worried is more accurate. Ed was a man of God who had been walking with God for more years than I was old. I admired him greatly. He lived what he believed and always remained true to his convictions. He was an excellent example for me to follow and was used by God to help shape my life. I had begun to fear that he had heard from God and I was too insensitive.

Over and over he tried to convince me. During this discussion, when I said I wasn't sure, his eyes became a flame of fire, his voice thundered like a huge wave crashing upon the rocks, and he said,

"Bob, it's like this. God has handed you the ball and said 'Go for the goal,' but you put the ball down on the ground and said, 'Let somebody else do it!' Bob, I don't believe that God will give you many chances. If you refuse to obey God, he will be forced to overlook you and call someone else."

"Please, Ed," I pleaded. "Don't say that. I'm not being disobedient, I'm just not sure."

He turned and walked away. I was shaken. All I could think about was the possibility of missing God's call? Being young in the Lord, I was not very confident I always heard God's voice in my heart, in my spirit.

Concerned, I climbed into my cookie truck and drove out. Work was drudgery that day. I couldn't concentrate on anything except the awesome thought of missing God. I wanted to go home and spend the whole day in prayer, but I couldn't do that.

The more I thought about Ed's words, the more I feared. I repented, I cried, I asked for forgiveness. I committed myself wholly to God and begged God, "Please don't give up on me. If I have missed you, God, please give me another chance. Show me your will, whatever it is."

Now, I must make this point perfectly clear. I wasn't asking God for a ministry or a gift, only for guidance. I was asking Him to reveal to me, in any way he wished, exactly what he wanted me to do, if anything. I was committed to not jump into anything unless God gave me absolute assurance that it was his perfect will. If He impressed me to stay put and keep doing what I was doing, fine. If He impressed me to set up a foot washing stand on the street corner, it would be fine too. I just wanted to serve God however he wanted me to.

This prayer to God to show me His will went on until almost noon, and I served my stores in a dull haze. I was about to leave a store, I put the key in the ignition to start the truck motor and I heard a voice behind me. Not a thought, nor an impression, nor a message in my heart, but an actual voice saying,

"Bob, take your New Testament out of your briefcase!"

I was thoroughly surprised. I felt a holy presence in my truck, and I was so convinced that Jesus was standing behind my right shoulder that I turned and looked. No one was there. I slumped over the steering wheel and began to talk to myself about hearing things. With the key still in the ignition, I reached for it and I heard the voice again.

"Bob, take your New Testament out of your briefcase!"
This time I knew for sure it was Jesus and that he was standing behind me to my left. I turned to look; still nothing. I cried out,

"Lord, is that you?"

"Yes, Bob! Take your New Testament out of your briefcase!" Wow. This was Jesus, no question. I opened my briefcase and took out my Amplified New Testament. The Lord spoke again:

"Turn to Second Timothy, Chapter 1!"

I couldn't remember a thing from 2 Timothy. My mind was

a blank. Thumbing through the pages I finally found it and turned to chapter one. The Lord spoke again:

"Verse eleven!"

I read, "For the proclaiming of this Gospel, I was appointed a herald (preacher) and an apostle (special messenger) and a teacher of the Gentiles."

Ecstatic, I leaped out of my seat. I began to dance and praise God right inside my truck. I was so elated. I was filled with His presence and thoroughly satisfied in Jesus. I shouted G*lory!* and I sang songs. Then, in humble gratitude, I knelt and prayed, thanking Him with the joy and excitement of a little child.

Finally, I settled down and began praying about my future. I had a little prayer altar where I kept the Fig Newtons. I separated myself to His service for the rest of my life. I said to God,

"Thou art the Potter, I am the clay, have Thine own way, Lord, have Thine own way."

I knew in my heart that God would give me the strength, the courage, and the means to accomplish His will. I asked Him to guide me concerning my job and my ministry. I was ready to do whatever God wanted, but I knew he was *not* telling me to quit my job.

Joyfully I finished out the day and returned to the depot. Ed was late getting in, and I waited for him. When he arrived, I threw my arms around him, hugged him, and thanked him. He stood there with a blank look on his face until I told him everything in detail.

He was almost as excited as I was. We gave praise and glory to God and then I went home and told Sue and the kids. We had another praise party like many others before and later Sue and I talked. We decided not to change anything but just let God guide us as he willed.

Some people have questioned me about hearing an audible voice from God, and all I can say is that I was there, and I know what I heard. No matter how hard I might try, I can't prove to anyone that it was audible; furthermore, I don't have any desire to. God did it, I didn't, and that settles it.

I have often thought that maybe He had to speak out loud to me because I'm so thick headed. No matter, I know my call and my

purpose, and no one, not even the devil can take it away from me. How do I know this? The Bible says in Romans 11:29 "For the gifts and calling of God are without repentance," meaning they cannot be taken back. As I've told many young men and women seeking ministry, "God will put His stamp of approval on the specific call he has put on your life, not to prove it to others, but because the proof goes with the promise.
Just relax and let God be God, in and through you."

Another thing, the method God used to get my attention and show me the call on my life may be different from the way he shows you what he has in mind for you. We need to recognize that God has a plan and a purpose for every one of us, even from before we were formed in the womb.

In Jeremiah 1:5, God said to Jeremiah, "Before I formed you in the belly I knew you; and before you came forth out of the womb I sanctified you, and called you to be a prophet unto the nations." The Scriptures are quite clear on this and happen to mention only a few cases to get the point across.

The Gospels record that Jesus looked out among the people and, having compassion upon them, said, "The harvest is ripe, but the laborers are few." Today the laborers for the work of God are too few. The world is in a world-of-hurt and desperately needs the touch of God's love and healing power that only you and I can give.

We are the Lord's hands, to help and heal; we are the Lord's feet, to go, and we are the Lord's mouth, to encourage, counsel, and preach the Good News.

While we are on the subject of being called by God from *before* we were even formed in the womb, here is something that I have always grieved over. The many hundreds, perhaps even thousands of prophets, apostles, evangelists, pastors, teachers, workers of miracles, doctors, nurses, school-teachers, city, state, and national leaders, and other good people, who have been robbed of their God-given-call by the demon-inspired work of man through abortion.

Oh, I could write a whole book on this issue, my heart grieves so. I often think of the fact that God put a call on my life before I was even thought of by my parents. After I was born, and all my young life for that matter, the devil was trying to kill me to keep me from fulfilling God's call and purpose. But, praise God for Jesus and Calvary!

A few weeks later while servicing one of my larger stores, a Frito salesman approached me and asked me to keep him in my prayers. We had often talked about spiritual things, as well as the legalism his church put upon him. I had shared with him many of the miracles God had been doing in my life. He wanted me to pray about whether the doctrines of his church were correct.

As before, he again explained a few of their laws and rules for being saved and going to heaven when he died. I told him I thought he was the one to be praying about that, not me, but he pleaded with me about it. He said that he knew God heard and answered my prayers. I was flabbergasted.

I agreed to keep him in my prayers and went on my way. I wanted to tell this guy a thing or two about the Scriptures right then and there, as I had a time or two before, but, I felt that if he didn't hear from God on the matter himself, it would be in vain. I didn't know that God had a plan for this guy, and that I would be the tool God would use.

I walked out the back door of the store, entered my truck, and proceeded to pull the cases of cookies needed to fill the store shelves. All the while I had a slight tugging in my heart to stop and pray, but I kept on working. The tugging became very strong, and I said in my mind, Lord, are you telling me to pray about this now?

I didn't hear a voice but I knew in my heart the answer was yes. I started to pray and immediately the Holy Spirit impressed me to get my King James Bible and turn to the book of Galatians. I was familiar with Galatians, having read it a couple dozen times or more.

The Holy Spirit led me to read through five of the six chapters. The Holy Spirit would, shall we say, highlight a verse or group of verses here and there, and I kept notes of them. He gave me a deeper understanding of those verses than I had before.

With this information in hand, I went back into the store and approached the salesman. I explained what had happened in my truck, and he said,

"I just knew for sure it would be that way."

He couldn't wait to hear what God had said to me. I was thrilled and amazed, and could feel a strong anointing of the Holy Spirit upon me.

In the back room of the store, I shared with him all that the Lord had showed me. He melted and wept and thanked God, and me.

He confessed that he was at a crisis in his life, what with his failure to keep all the laws of his religion. He said that it was like a thousand pounds had been lifted from him and he felt free for the first time in his life. All glory to God who is always ready to meet the needs of those who love him and seek him with the whole heart. As the prophet Jeremiah was seeking God, the Bible says, "Then said the Lord to me, you have seen well, for I am alert and active, watching over My word to perform it" (Jer.1:12).

I was working over fifty hours a week for Mother's Cookies and going to school three nights a week. My Sunday school class was steadily growing, and I wouldn't miss a church service for anything. It seemed that miracles were an everyday occurrence in our family. Our son, Robert, carried Bible tracts to school and witness to anything breathing. All the kids were on fire for Jesus and filled with the Holy Spirit. They prayed over every need we had.

One day when Robert was nine, he had a severe attack of asthma. We gave him the usual puff from the asthma inhaler, but it did nothing. I went into some serious prayer in my office and reviewed with the Lord, or shall I say reminded the Lord, of his promises on healing. Not that He needs to be reminded, but I was desperate, and prayer didn't seem to be working.

Robert got worse and worse and was hardly able to breathe. He would look at me while I was praying over him with eyes that said, "Please do something for me!" All I could do was pray harder and harder. I spoke healing to him. I took authority over the asthma. I bound and cast out the devil. I did everything I could think of. I even reminded the Lord of the verses in Matthew 7:9–11 about giving to our children what they need. Robert needed a miracle and he needed it now!

I apologized to my son for my inability to appropriate his healing for him. His response was,

"It's okay, Dad. It will be all right."

He seemed to be accepting that everything was all right when it was obvious that it was not. Once again, God was trying to teach me yet another lesson in faith. I wanted to take Robert to the hospital right then and there, but the Holy Spirit spoke to my heart to "Be still and know that I am God." Although the miracle didn't happen instantly, it did happen within a short period of time that day.

Robert came from the bathroom, looking a little pale, and said he had gotten sick. I asked him what he meant. He said that he had vomited shortly after I laid hands on him in prayer. From that time until this day, Robert has never had another attack, nor has he used any medication for asthma. I look back now and wonder if Robert knew something I didn't know. At any rate, God is faithful, and I am in need of repentance and forgiveness.

Every Wednesday morning TCC held a prayer clinic, miracle healing service, for all who wanted to attend. We had Catholics, Baptists, Methodists, Lutherans, Episcopalians, you name it we had it.

During the song service, Sue felt impressed to lay her hand on the shoulder of an elderly woman sitting in front of her. She knew in her heart that God was going to heal this woman through this simple act. Sue didn't know her, and that stopped her for the moment, but the impression became stronger and Sue obeyed.

After a few more songs the woman turned to Sue and asked if she was the one who had touched her. Sue explained, and then the woman told her about the pain in her legs that prevented her from standing during the singing. She said that she was healed from the time Sue touched her, and then she stood up to prove it. Both of them praised the Lord and hugged each other.

Some have asked me if I have ever missed God's will. My answer is, "More times than I want to remember." One particular time, though, I remember vividly. I arrived at the depot one morning and found Ed not his usual self. I asked what was wrong. He said that his son-in-law had died the night before from a heart attack and that he was not saved.

I had never met the man, and I can't even remember his name, but Ed asked me to add the whole family to our noontime prayer list. So I prayed for Ed and then got out my prayer list and entered his request. At noon, as usual, I prayed for the situation along with all the other needs listed there. I finished the day and went home.

That evening I included Ed's request in my prayers before going to bed. During the night I had a dream where I saw Ed's son-in-law lying in an open casket in a mortuary. Then I saw myself approach the casket and pray, calling him back to life again. He sat up in the casket and said that he had been waiting for me to come and pray for him.

The dream was extremely vivid, and I woke up singing the hymn, "Victory In Jesus." When I got up I told Sue about it and that I had to get to the depot and tell Ed about it. I had to find out where the mortuary was. I had it in mind that he and I could go and pray for his son-in-law and raise him from the dead.

I got to work and found that Ed had already left on his route. I rushed to a couple of my accounts that had to be serviced early, and then raced to a store that was one of Ed's accounts. Bill Castleman was the receiving clerk, and I told him about everything.

He said he expected Ed any minute, so I waited, but he didn't show up. I raced back to the depot in an effort to catch him there, but he was already gone. I called Bill and asked him to meet me at Ed's house, and I went there directly.

I arrived at Ed's house before Bill did and shared my dream with Ed, expecting that he would be as excited about it as I was. He was not! Sadly, he told me all about his son-in-law's rebellion, drinking, and refusal of the Gospel. As far as I was concerned, this had nothing to do with it. I couldn't understand it. Why was he so unwilling to go to the mortuary with me?

When Bill arrived, we talked for some time, and Bill was just as unwilling to participate as Ed was. I was shattered, and my faith was slowly diminishing. The more we talked, the more I doubted, and I left there defeated. I went home confused and uncertain.

I was very upset and I prayed without ceasing. Begging

God for forgiveness, I repented, crying bitterly, knowing that I had listened to man rather than to God. To this day I'm confident that had I put my foot down and gone alone and prayed, the man would have come back to life.

The lesson I learned here, and pray that I will never forget, is that when God gives you the faith to do something, do it! Don't count on anyone else to join you or even to support you. Just do it, and let the chips fall where they may.

I learned another important lesson in all this. It was unfair of me to ask Ed and Bill to go with me. It was wrong to expect them to have the same level of faith that I had. God hadn't given them the dream, hadn't given them the faith, and hadn't called on them to do anything. He called on me—and me alone.

Because I was so upset about disobeying God, I thought God couldn't trust me anymore. Satan had a good time there for awhile blasting me with thoughts that I was through. Fired! God didn't need me anymore. But God reassured me through prayer and the Word that everything was okay and that his call on my life was "without repentance" and couldn't be denied.

So, with my head held high and a smirk on my face, I told Satan to, *Put that in your pipe and smoke it!* With that all taken care of, I jumped right back into the thick of things and dedicated myself even more to the service of God.

That next week I set out to show the devil that I was back in business and was out to save the world. Everything was fantastic. I was praying for people I would approach in my stores. I witnessed to every one of the store managers and employees as opportunity allowed. Some were saved and some received miracles from God.

I remember one tall black man who had such a tender heart. He wept as I shared Jesus with him. He asked Jesus into his heart and was gloriously saved. On top of that, some of the customers got saved, and a few were healed right in the store.

That weekend was glorious with the outpouring of the Holy Spirit. Sue and the kids and I were on cloud nine. We prayed together over everything, big or small. In fact, nothing was considered small.

Nothing would be done or planned without first taking it to Jesus in prayer, and the Sunday night service was the frosting on the cake. But the following Monday, brought everything to a screeching halt.

Chapter 7

Miracles Galore

I was so caught up in the Word of God and the love of the Lord that I no longer had much time for television. Now, more than ever, my interests were being directed by God as he willed. As time went by, many TV programs began to grieve my spirit.

As I gained a greater degree of spiritual discernment, the blatant immorality and out-right rebellion against God, as well as all the violence, drugs, sex, and even murder, were too much for me and my house. I took the small TV outside, hauled it to the top of a small hill, and shot it full of holes.

This may sound absurd to you, or sound like I was losing my marbles, but what was shown on TV grieved me so much that I had to do it. The driving force behind me was the Christian life-style commands set forth in the Word of God, such as "Abstain from all appearance of evil" (I Thess. 5:22), "Be not deceived: evil communications corrupt good manners" (I Cor.15:33), and "He that walks with wise men shall be wise: but a companion of fools shall be destroyed" (Proverbs 13:20), to name a few.

I didn't have a holier-than-thou attitude, and I could associate with non-Christians, for I worked with them and did business with them. But when it came to letting the filth and corruption of things like some TV programs, books, magazines, music, and so on come into my house, I put my foot down and didn't let any of it be a part of our life in Christ.

The Word of God and His Spirit compelled me to seek with

all my heart, soul, mind, and strength, to walk in the Spirit and not fulfill the lust of the flesh. The closer I got to God, the more aware I was of my unrighteousness.

As I would be victorious in one area, the Holy Spirit would reveal another area that needed to be worked on. This wasn't disheartening, because the love and peace of God was always present, and it was much more rewarding than sin was. This separated Christian life-style was all God's doing. He was preparing me for something down the road I had absolutely no clue of.

It was God first, family second, and work came third. I always had a Bible or New Testament with me and read them every chance I got. I studied my memory verse cards every day, seven days a week, and I no longer had any desire for any music other than Christian music. Now it was nothing but good solid praise and worship music for me.

If I wasn't studying, praying, or learning memory verses, I was singing. Songs of praise were constantly going through my mind, and I wasn't bashful about singing out loud as I drove my cookie truck to service my stores.

When I talk about reading the Word and praying, I don't mean fifteen or thirty minutes a day, I mean several hours a day. You don't have that kind of time? Neither did I, until I fell in love with Jesus and his Word. Then I couldn't find enough time. I had to make time. In fact, I've never really found time to do anything. I've always had to make it.

The Bible says that "Where a man's treasure is, his heart is there also" (Matt.6:21). In other words, if you love it you'll spend time with it and pour your life and resources into it. Well, friend, I had had it with the world. It had robbed me of all the time, energy, peace, happiness, fulfillment, and money it was going to. I had found a new life. As the song writer wrote,

> I found a new life, I found a new life.
> If anybody asks you, what's the matter with you my friend?
> Tell 'em that you've been saved, sanctified, Holy Ghost filled, water baptized, Jesus on my mind,
> I found a new life.

Well, that describes me to a tee. I had found a new life and it was the most exciting thing that had ever happened to me. You see, friend, before I accepted Jesus as my Lord and Savior, I was imprisoned by stronger things than jail bars. My prison was doubt, fear, hate, unforgiveness, low self-esteem, hypocrisy, and little reason for living. As the Bible says in John 10:10, Satan came to steal, kill, and destroy me, but Jesus came and set me free and gave me life in abundance.

With all this time spent on "religious" activity you'd think I never had any time for fun, but it's not so. Sue and I were on a mid-week bowling team (she was the better bowler). The whole family went horseback riding on Saturdays, and our three-quarter acre country plot with its livestock was a dude ranch and haven of rest. This was God-ordained family living, full of love, joy, and peace, and we were having the time of our lives.

Now, referring back to the end of the last chapter, Monday morning arrived. As usual I was up at 4 AM praising the Lord in the shower. I dressed in a flash, and headed for the kitchen, where I ate and drank—it was a feast, as I ate the meat and drank the milk of God's Word (Heb. 5:12–14).

My soul needed at least an hour and a half of study and prayer before I went to work each day. Sue made our usual breakfast of bacon, eggs, pancakes, toast, juice and coffee, and we ate together while talking about the goodness of the Lord.

At 7:15 AM I was on my way to the depot, singing and praising God all the way. Sometimes I listened to Christian teaching or music tapes while driving.

I found Dick McAlister, the depot supervisor, waiting for me when I arrived. He led me to his office and told me I was fired.

I couldn't believe it. It took the wind right out of my sails. I felt like someone had stabbed me in the heart. I was putting everything I had into my job, and I loved it. Why? What happened? Where would I find a route sales job that paid as well as this one?

The greater pain was that now, even while doing my best to

live like a Christian, I had failed my wife and family again. Just the thought of it slew me. Was there no end to this pit of despair? Dick McAlister could see I was a basket case there in his office. He had no sympathy for me, and in fact he was angry and harsh.

I asked him why I was being fired. He unloaded on me about the Christian bumper stickers that he had asked me more than once to remove from my truck. I had contended that none of the other men had to remove their worldly bumper stickers, so why should I have to remove my Christian ones?

He railed on me about having a Bible in my truck. I always had a King James Bible on the dash, the Amplified New Testament in my briefcase, and a study Bible in the back with the Fig Newtons.

He blasted me about preaching to the store managers and the customers. That was a real sore spot with him. I asked if any had complained, and he didn't comment; he just said the discussion was closed. I was *fired* and that settled it.

I had known for some time that he wasn't happy with me. I didn't fit in with him and the boys any more. I had made it uncomfortable for them on more than one occasion by not condoning their behavior and being a living witness for Jesus. Now it was all over, *fired, finished,* and *gone*!

I drove home like a whipped pup. The devil had a field day flooding me with thoughts that even as a Christian I was a failure. The magnitude of the situation consumed me. What will we do? Where will I find a job like this one? How long will it take to find a job?

I was making good money, but we were living on every cent I made. How will we make the house payment? The house! Oh, no! Then I remembered that a few months back I had told Sue that I felt God wanted us to sell it in preparation for the ministry. Her response was,

"Well, if you want to move, go ahead, but I'm staying!"

She loved that house. The wide open spaces, the animals, everything; she loved it all. I didn't blame her, I loved it too, but God had spoken to *my* heart, not hers. God had given *me* the desire, faith, and courage to sell it, not her, and now we were sure to lose it. I began to think, Oh God, have I disobeyed you? Is that why this is happening to us? Should I have gone ahead and put the house up for sale anyway?"

I was confused and sorely troubled that I might have missed God's leading. I prayed for help and for forgiveness, and I asked the Lord to give me strength and courage to carry on and provide for my wife and children.

I was determined to prove myself responsible, faithful, and able, but now my zeal for God had backfired on me. As I pulled in our driveway I cried out to God for help like a man who had been thrown to the lions. After a few minutes I mustered up the courage to walk through the front door. Sue was standing inside with a bewildered look on her face.

"Bob, why are you home? What's wrong? You look pale—are you sick?"

Her questions made it worse. How I wished I was only sick. I broke. All I could think of was that I was failing her again. Because of me we would lose our house. I cried like a baby. I was sick to my stomach, and my eyes and nose were running like a faucet. No matter how hard I tried I couldn't stop crying.

Sue kept asking what was wrong, but all I could do was cry. It came from way down deep and overpowered my ability to say a word.

"Bob, listen to me! Pull yourself together! Have you been in an accident?"

Again, her question just made things worse. All I could do was shake my head no. Running to the window, she examined the car. Returning to the couch, she grabbed me by the head and looked me straight in the eye.

"Did you run over someone?"

Still crying uncontrollably, I could only shake my head again. I couldn't speak a word. Then she laid her hands on me and began taking authority over the situation in the name of Jesus.

She prayed like a trouper. Storming the gates of hell, she shook me loose of that retched thing, and I began to settle down. Finally, out of my mouth it came.

"I've been ... *fired*!"

"What did you say?"

"I've been fired. Please forgive me, Honey, I'm so sorry."

"Fired!" she said. "Is that all? I thought it was something serious! Listen to me: it's going to be alright. The Lord hasn't failed us yet and I know He won't fail us now. Bob, I'm telling you, it's going to be all right."

In a stupor I uttered,

"But ... what about the house? Where will I find a job that pays as much as I've been making?"

"The house? Who cares about the house? God will take care of us. He hasn't failed us yet and He won't fail us now."

Flabbergasted, I could hardly believe what I was hearing. The thing that I was so worried about seemed to mean nothing to her now. What a relief!

Still, here I was, God's man of faith and power, and where had all my faith gone? I had been robbed. Satan got in there by means of an old lie that he had tormented me with for years. He had convinced me more than once that I was a born looser, a failure.

You may be asking how he could get to me after all I had experienced with God. Well, you're not the only one asking that question; so have I. It's obvious that my eyes were on the circumstances and not on Jesus.

Jesus is on our side, and he doesn't accuse, the devil does. The Bible says that Satan is a liar, and there is no truth in him, but when these thoughts come I fall into the belief that they're my thoughts, that I create them, that they're true. I somehow forget that they originate with the devil and come from fear.

Since the devil is a liar, I should take these thoughts, turn them around one hundred and eighty degrees, and make a truth out of them. When the devil says I've failed, that means that I've succeeded, and so on. I need to remember that Jesus is our advocate, not our accuser. But at that time, I didn't have this victory, and I felt I had no faith or power at all.

Sue took me by the hands and led in prayer. Suddenly, she stopped praying, squeezed my hand, and smiled. Then, looking me square in the eye she said,

"You'll have your job back in seven days with the same route, seniority, and pay!"

I looked at her like you would look at someone who had three eyes. I wanted to believe her, but it was too good to be true. But she was so full of faith. I could see in her eyes that she really believed what she was saying. Lifting her hands in the air, she praised God and said again with confident assurance,

"It will be so!"

I just couldn't get a hold of it and said with a quizzical look,

"There's no way, honey."

Without any hesitation, smiling like a proud peacock, she said,

"I know in my heart that it will be so, and you'll see in seven days!"

Sue wasn't making this up. This wasn't just positive thinking or positive confession. God had given her a revelation in her spirit, and that's why she knew this in her heart. All prophesy is for naught if it isn't by the Spirit of God, and the test is whether the prophesy comes to pass.

I told her that Mother's Cookies had never hired back anyone they had fired. That didn't faze her; she just said again,

"God has revealed to me that it will be so."

That afternoon I called the Teamsters Union; they said there was nothing they could do for me. I had been fired for insubordination and it was out of their hands and done with.

Sue insisted that we make the best of it by spending the time in the Word and prayer, but I wanted to be out looking for work. After all, I've got to be responsible and faithful, but she kept insisting, that we spend the whole week in prayer and God's Word, and she wouldn't hear of me going out to look for work. Once I dressed in my suit and tie and headed for the front door, and she stopped me, saying,

"Honey, you need to go back and change your clothes and come back out here so we can get into the Word and prayer."

I had never seen her so convinced of God's will. She had always pretty much relied on me to hear from God, but I was hearing nothing. I was on empty. I wanted to believe the same way she did, but I couldn't muster up the faith. Later I realized that God was teaching me to trust Him through Sue, as she had always trusted him through me. When we realized that, Sue and I agreed never to misuse the trust we had in God through each other.

The following Sunday afternoon, seven days later to the day, our phone rang. When I answered it I heard.

"Bob, this is Dick McAlister."

"Um ... Hi, Dick, how are you?"

I could tell he wasn't happy. He got right to it.

"Bob, I want you in my office Monday morning at 7:30 dressed and ready for work, okay?"

"Y ... Yes, sir! I'll be there!"

He hung up without another word. With a quizzical look on my face I told Sue what he said. I had to sit down. Thinking out loud, I said,

"What in the world? What was that all about? Maybe I have my job back? If not my old route, maybe another one?"

Sue was glowing.

"You *will* have your old route back *and* your seniority, just like the Lord revealed to me."

I began to have hope Sue was right, but she was sure-fire convinced it would be so. I thought about it, and I knew that if I didn't have my same seniority, someone else would have my route. It was a good one, one of the higher volume routes of the branch.

As we pondered all of this, and reveled in the phone call being on the seventh day exactly, Sue and I rejoiced and sang praises. Then we gathered family to pray and thank God.

Thinking about it later, even though this experience was painful and humbling for me, it taught me what the apostle Paul meant in Romans 8:18 when he said, "For I reckon that the sufferings of this present time are not worthy to be compared with the glory which shall be revealed in us." In worldly terms, "No pain, no gain," thank you Lord, for counting me worthy to suffer for your Name's sake.

Monday morning came and I was at the depot early. At 7:30 Dick called me into his office.

"Bob, I want you to be in every one of your stores today! I don't care if you sell a dime's worth of cookies, just be in all your stores. I want you to tell every store manager you're back on the route. Do I make myself clear?"

"Well … yes, Dick, does that mean I have my old route back?"

"That's right, the same route."

"But, I have twenty-eight accounts on my route! How can I call on every one of them in one day?"

His face reddened. He slammed his fist down on the desk and said,

"I don't care how many accounts you have or how you do it, I want you in every one of them today! Do you understand me?"

Startled, I answered,

"Yes … I understand. I'll do as you have said … but why do I need to be in all of them today?"

He leaned back in his chair, and with a hesitant look on his face, said,

"Because all your store managers said that if you weren't back on your route by today, they'd throw our cookies out of their stores!"

His answer stunned me. My mouth dropped. My eyebrows flew up in my forehead and I said,

"What? Why? Why would they say that?"

He sneered at me.

"Never mind, just get going, and go to every store before you come back here."

I left, grinning, in glee, not pride. What a relief. I was thrilled and elated, not to mention bewildered. I greeted a few of the other salesmen, got into my truck and headed out, singing praises to God all the way. I called Sue the first chance I got and told her the news. We rejoiced together and thanked God for His mercy and grace.

Almost every store manager had the same reason for wanting me back. They said that I lived what I believed, and that I was friendly, sincere, honest, and reliable. Honest? Reliable? That's a switch! Many of the managers and some of the employees wanted to talk about what had happened to me, but I had a lot of ground to cover and I told them we'd talk later.

We did talk later, mostly about God's grace and mercy in answered prayer. I didn't get home until very late that first few nights, but it was all worth it, and I felt like a million bucks too.

In light of what I had gone through, I got thinking about a poem I ran across one day and really took to heart. I taped it in the front of my Bible and read it often, vowing to make it a living epistle of my life. It's called "The Light of Faith" by Edgar A. Guest.

> *I'd rather see a sermon than hear one any day,*
> *I'd rather one should walk with me than merely show the way.*
> *The eye's a better pupil and more willing than the ear;*
> *fine counsel is confusing, but example's always clear;*
> *and the best of all the preachers are the men who live their creeds,*
> *for to see the good in action is what everybody needs.*
> *I can soon learn how to do it if you'll let me see it done.*
> *I can watch your hands in action, but your tongue too fast may run.*
> *And the lectures you deliver may be very wise and true;*
> *but I'd rather get my lesson by observing what you do.*
> *For I may misunderstand you and the high advice you give,*
> *but there's no misunderstanding how you act and how you live."*

During those seven days off, God had been dealing with me about serving my boss as I would serve the Lord. He led me to many verses that spelled that command out in no uncertain terms like "Let as many servants as are under the yoke count their own masters worthy of all honor, that the name of God and his doctrine be not blasphemed" (I Timothy 6:1) and "Servants, obey in all things your masters according to the flesh; not with eye service, as men pleasers; but in singleness of heart, fearing God: And whatsoever you do, do it heartily, as to the Lord, and not unto men; knowing that of the Lord you shall receive the reward of the inheritance: for you serve the Lord Christ" (Col. 3:22–25).

I pledged my allegiance to God's Word and His will. I served my boss as if I was serving the Lord, in the way the Scriptures said I should.

The Christian bumper stickers had already been removed, but Dick did allow me to keep one Bible in my briefcase. He asked no more of me than that, but I gave him something more anyway. I gave him the respect and obedience he was due as my boss. Never again did I judge or condemn him or the other salesmen with comments or looks of disapproval. I practiced my faith and shared the gospel, but it was with a new attitude and a purer motive. I learned from experience that "All things work together for good for those that love God and are fitting into His plans" (Rom. 8:28, Living Bible).

I learned through this and other experiences that we have valleys as well as mountain tops to experience. On the mountain top we experience peace and joy from success, and we are filled with praise to God for the victory. On the other hand, the valley is a time of trial, testing, purging, cleansing, humbling, grooming, correcting, refining, and, if I'm listening and open to God, a time of training and preparation. After that comes a time of empowering and anointing.

We must remember, with the baptism in the Holy Spirit also comes the baptism of fire, as recorded in Luke 3:16. It is fire that melts the ore; it is fire that cleanses and purifies. The purging fire of the Holy Spirit is hard on the flesh, working on the old nature. This work is done only in the valley, not on the mountain top. Hard as it may be, I will thank God for the valleys and pray that I submit myself to be the clay in the Potter's hand, that He might shape me into the vessel of His choosing. I must always remember, no valleys, no mountain tops.

As my life was getting back to normal, Ed asked me to preach in his church, where he was the Sunday school superintendent. It was a Four Square Gospel Church at 12316 Rosecrans Avenue in Norwalk, and he had set it up with his pastor, R. J. Jones, to have me preach revival meetings Sunday through Wednesday. This would be five meetings in all. With enthusiasm I agreed.

When I drove up to the church that first Sunday morning, I saw a huge banner over the door that read *Miracle Healing Meetings*. I was taken back a bit and thought, God, if you don't show up we are in real trouble.

This was my first time preaching from the pulpit, and I knew

I was way out of my comfort zone. This would be different from teaching Sunday school, but I had to bite the bullet and go for it. Sunday morning I taught on using our faith for healing and asked the people to return that evening for prayer for the sick.

At the evening meeting I took the pulpit and the Lord impressed me to abandon two-thirds of my notes. They were on three 5x8 cards. The Lord revealed that the first and third cards had to go, and the second one was the one I should use. I pleaded with the Lord about it, but I knew in my heart what He wanted, and I obeyed.

I started preaching and the anointing was very strong. It was a short message on faith, fifteen minutes max, and then came the altar call. The Holy Spirit gave me three words of revelation knowledge about needs that were present. First, someone would be delivered from smoking. Second, someone had pain in their back and it would be healed tonight. Third, someone had something wrong with their stomach, and it too would be healed tonight.

I shared the three needs God had revealed, and three people came to the front for prayer. I took authority over the smoking in the name of Jesus and that took care of that. Next was the pain in the back. The woman had a short leg that was visible to everyone, so I had her sit in a chair, and I held her feet together and prayed for her. The leg grew out the same length as the other one right in front of everyone. This kind of miracle has happened many times in my ministry. The pain immediately disappeared from her back, and she was set free.

The third was the stomach problem. This woman was nervous, and as I prayed for her, I felt a special anointing from God. I began to take authority over the problem, even though I didn't know exactly what the problem was. Forcefully I said,

"Satan, I command you to loose this woman and let her go."

My prayer became more and more intense. I was doing battle with the devil and he had to go. There wasn't any shaking, screaming, or anything like that. I issued a stern, authoritative command that the devil had to go and that this woman was being set free and healed.

The following day at work, Ed told me that this woman was his neighbor. She wasn't a Christian. He had invited her to church many times but she never came and he didn't expect her to come this time. He had heard that she had terminal cancer of the stomach. The doctors had done all they could do and gave her only a few weeks to live.

Within the next two days after the healing meeting, the report came to me that she was completely healed. Glory to God! X-rays showed no sign of the cancer. Hallelujah! On top of that, the miracle healing from God had given her the faith to believe in Him. She gave her life to the Lord, and Ed said that she was sharing her testimony with all her friends and bringing them to church as well. Hallelujah! The Lord is so good.

God wants to touch and heal the hurts and needs of His people, whoever and wherever they are. You don't have to be saved to be eligible for a miracle from God. All through history, especially during the ministry of Jesus, the sick were healed, the tormented were delivered, and the oppressed were set free, saved or not. The Gospel was preached to them to repent of their sins, to love God with their whole heart, and obey His commandments. Reader, God is love, and He loves us so much that He wants to bless us more than we can imagine.

Many Christians and non-Christians have told me that they don't deserve anything from God. Deserve? The Bible says that even if we could live a perfect life, we still wouldn't deserve anything from God except judgment. We're sinners by nature and by blood– the blood of Adam.

Think of my early life: did I *deserve* anything from God? No! A thousand times no! What I received was grace, and it's free. Grace is a gift, and a gift cannot be deserved, earned, or purchased. When you receive the gift, you must accept it humbly, without any sense that you earned it. When you receive the grace of God with humility, you will then wish to serve and please God from your heart, like the woman healed of cancer. Nothing you can do will repay God for his gift of grace and love, for the price was paid in full by Jesus Christ.

A few weeks later I got to preach on Sunday evening at TCC. John and Donna Gifford brought their baby girl, about one year old, to the altar for prayer. She had a clubbed foot. I anointed the child with oil and prayed. As I prayed over her, the foot began to straighten out. The people watching became a little hysterical as the foot became normal within a few minutes. We praised the Lord at the top of our voices, and went on with other needs. At the proper time we closed the service to allow people to go home, but many of them stayed and the miracles went on and on.

The miracles began to be talked about all over town. Strangers would approach me and ask me to pray for them, and many were healed. One day a local Nazarene pastor asked me to preach in his church. I accepted and preached Sunday morning and evening, and then Monday and Tuesday evenings as well. There were many miracles, including salvation.

On Sunday morning, the father of a nine-year-old boy asked for prayer for his son, who was in the hospital with spinal meningitis. He had just returned from the hospital, and the doctors said it was hopeless. I had the father come forward, and I laid hands on him and prayed for his son. Monday night this father came to the evening service and testified that his son had been completely healed and was going to be released from the hospital. All praise and glory to God!

Let me digress a little and then come back to the story. Over the years many people have asked me why I don't say "If it be Thy will, Lord," when praying for the sick. My answer is because God has already spelled out his will in his Word, concerning sickness and healing. We are to pray in faith in Jesus' name for the sick and expect a miracle.

God has said in Malachi 3:6, "I am the Lord, I change not." Therefore, when I consider all the words of Jesus, I can see plainly that God wants us to possess an audacity of faith that has no bounds, and to believe all He has promised in his Word and paid for through Christ at Calvary by the Atonement.

Take a close look at Isaiah 53:4–5. Notice that Jesus "bore our griefs" (Literally, physical sicknesses) and "with his stripes we are healed" (Literally, mended, cured and made healthy or whole). I don't know any Christian who would say that Isaiah 53:4–5 doesn't belong to the entire Body of Christ today.

Now look at Matthew 8:16–17, which is in reference to Isaiah 53:4–5. Jesus cast out devils and healed "all that were sick" so as to fulfill this very prophesy spoken by Isaiah. Jesus healing the sick is proof positive that the promise spoken of in Isaiah was for physical healing as well as spiritual healing.

You see, dear friend, the atoning sacrifice of Christ at Calvary is payment in full for every spiritual, mental, physical, financial, or emotional need we will ever have. This is for us today, for you and me. Rejoice, and spread the news that God wants to bless his children with all spiritual blessings in Christ, (Ephs. 1:3).

Also, the Bible says in Hebrews 13:8 that "Jesus Christ is the same yesterday, and today, and forever." This means that what Jesus was, he still is; and what Jesus said, he still says; and what Jesus did, he is still doing today, with us and for us. Glory to God!

I'm an ordinary, rather simple man of no social status and a man of no influence among the educated or wealthy. It's true that I can read and translate New Testament Greek, but I'm neither a scholar nor even a theologian.

So who am I to claim that the authority, power, and gifts of the Holy Spirit experienced by the New Testament apostles are also for us today? Here's who I am: I'm a man saved by grace and called by God to preach the full Gospel of the Cross of Christ. I'm one who simply took God at his word, and as a result I've seen hundreds of mighty miracles all done by God's Holy Spirit.

You see, friend, nobody told me that miracles weren't for today, so when I started to read and believe God's word, I didn't hesitate to believe that miracles occur right now.

I see that God confirms his Word with signs and miracles following, as it says in Mark 16:20. I don't ignore the Scriptures that say "Do not forget all His benefits, for He forgives all our iniquities and heals all our diseases" (Psalms 103:2–3).

These miracles I'm telling you about cannot be done by man alone, whether doctor or magician. What I have experienced are real honest-to-goodness miracles of God. Therefore, since God is the one doing it, isn't it evident that God wants us to pray, believe, and expect miracles? Of course! Miracles don't cost God anything, for he already paid the price at Calvary.

Now, let's get back to the story. The following Wednesday morning at the TCC staff meeting, Pastor Stout asked how the meetings went at the Nazarene church. After telling him about all the salvations and physical miracles he asked me if they received an offering for me. I told him no but that the pastor gave me a check for $63. Looking amazed, he said,

"Sixty-three dollars? Is that all?"

Surprised at his apparent alarm, I replied,

"Yes!"

I showed him the check and explained that the Nazarene pastor said this was all his deacons would authorize. Then the pastor had told me the deacons were insulted because some of their members were telling others that Bob Ford's prayer was the one that healed the boy with spinal meningitis.

The deacons contended that they had also prayed for the boy, and, perhaps it was their prayers that God answered rather than mine. I proceeded to tell the pastor that it made no difference to me whose prayers were answered; the main thing was that the boy's life was saved, God did the miracle, and He deserves the praise, not man.

Immediately, Pastor Stout called in his secretary and said,

"Ruth, I want you to make out a check to Bob Ford for $240 right now."

Turning to me, he said,

"This should make up for the minimum they should have given you."

It was a great blessing to live and minister with people who only want to trust and obey God.

One day a new assistant pastor named Robert Fitts came to our church. Later God used him in a mighty way to disciple me and to open many doors for me in ministry. He also taught me how to play the guitar, even to play it by ear. This was a mighty blessing in my personal praise and worship.

Also, had it not been for brother Fitts, this book probably would not even have been started. Back in the 1970s, he was constantly encouraging me to keep a ledger of some sort about the things God was doing in my life. Had it not been for his advice, I believe that the stories and events recounted here would have been lost and forgotten.

One Sunday evening at TCC, Brother Fitts was preaching on how Jesus called Peter to step out in faith, to get out of the boat and walk on the water. The Holy Spirit spoke to my heart that it was time for me to get out of the boat, so to speak, and go into full-time ministry.

I was to give my two weeks notice to Mother's Cookies and go into faith ministry, which meant I would draw no salary. Instead, I would trust in God for our financial needs. I responded at the altar call and committed to my faith ministry.

Poor Brother Fitts, he was so taken back by it, thinking of the risk I was taking. He assured me that he wasn't referring to me in his message. In response, I said,

"Well, maybe you weren't, but God was!"

I think Brother Fitts began to feel a little responsible for me, which I didn't mind, and it was comforting. We spent a lot of time together in the Word, in prayer, and in ministry. I learned a lot from him very quickly.

He opened doors of ministry for me, including ones in Mexico and the Philippines. He made it possible for me to do a live radio broadcast. All of this was the perfect timing of the Lord and I went into full-time evangelistic ministry completely by faith. Although there were some lean times, God has never failed us. Our only income, other than $150 a month for cleaning the church, was prayed in on a daily basis.

Let me assure you that I didn't quit my job simply because I wanted to. It wasn't some flippant thing that I did out of my own desire or emotion. I took my responsibility as head of the house and provider for my family seriously.

As I studied the Bible I began to understand my responsibility to God, to my wife and family, and to other areas of life. In Genesis 3:16 it says that the man "shall have the rule" over his wife. That doesn't mean to be a dictator; it means that the man's place in the order of authority is over the wife; that it's a leadership role.

He is to be a Godly example of wise, loving, responsible, moral leadership. As in any other chain of command, that means that God will hold the man responsible for the way he fulfills this responsibility.

Like Adam, I and all of us will suffer the consequences of any disobedience to God and his Word. Although Eve was deceived, Adam willfully disobeyed. Man cannot delegate his responsibilities to his wife, no matter how gifted, wise or spiritual she may be. God gave it to the man, in the Old Testament and the New, and that settles it.

I could see that God created the wife, as a helpmate to work with her husband, but He has anointed the man to be the moral leader by example and to be the head of the house. God expects him to keep the enemy—Satan and all evil—at bay, out of his life and his home. I'm not implying that we can force morality on anyone. We are all free moral agents and will answer to God for our disobedience solely on an individual basis.

Further study made me almost wish that I was the wife and not the husband, (see Ephesians 5:22–33). The Bible has a lot to say about the marriage relationship between husband and wife. By the way, that means one male and one female, nuff said?

Ephesians 5:22–24 says that the wife is to submit to her husband "as unto the Lord." That means, among other things, to be true to him, to honor him, to support him, and to respect him. She is to look to him for love, protection, provision, companionship, righteous leadership and direction. Therefore, God expects the husband to acquire and provide these virtues for her, and I'd better not be found lacking. Old fashioned? It's in the Bible, and that's that.

This doesn't means that the wife is to submit to or condone anything that is contrary to God's Word. She is expected to know God's will, to know the difference between right and wrong, between good and evil. She is to help her husband lead the family in righteousness.

Another thing, she isn't a door mat, for she was made from Adam's side, not his foot. She is not to be treated as a servant; God said that Eve was Adam's helpmate, not his slave. She is the half that makes man whole. I know guys, this smacks at our pride. Genesis 2:24 tells us that "the *two* shall become *one* flesh" (emphasis mine). Herein is found a truth worth meditating on, that God made man and woman to—complement each other, and not to compete with each other.

We have considered three verses from Ephesians 5:22–33 that pertain to the wife. Let's look at the nine remaining that pertain to the husband.

They say in no uncertain terms that the husband is to love his wife "as Christ loved the church and gave himself for it." We need to remember that Jesus, our example, came to give and not to take; to serve and not to be served. Men, we are to look at Jesus' life as a check-and-balance to see how we're doing.

As I learned, I saw that my responsibility to God and my wife and family were awesome, and greater than I had ever imagined. All too often I had taken my wife for granted. I had expected from her, instead of giving to her.

I could see that God expected me to love my wife "as Christ loved the church," (Ephs. 5:25) and also to love and *do* for her, "as I love and *do* for myself," (Ephs. 5:28–29). These are tall orders, and I can see that no man can accomplish this without the power of the Holy Spirit within.

I pity the man, or woman, who is simply "religious" and not saved and submitted to the Lordship of Jesus Christ. I pity also him who claims to be saved but doesn't know God's Word. All these people are living a reckless life; like someone groping and stumbling around in the dark without a flashlight. How can one know the wrong path if they don't know the right one to start with?

To do anything apart from God's will would be not only direct rebellion against God but also would be irresponsible and selfish toward my wife and family for which the whole family would suffer. Finally, I'm constantly reminded that God will hold everyone accountable for their actions. As He says in Galatians 6:7, "Be not deceived; God is not mocked: for whatever a man sows, that shall he also reap." Lord, help me to know your righteous ways, and to walk in them, amen!

Now back to the story. When I gave my two-week notice to Dick McAlister, he pleaded with me to stay on, and made a promise that surprised me. He said he'd hold my route open for six months. If I wanted to come back, it was mine for the asking.

Wow! What a difference from just eleven months ago. But I knew God wanted me to burn my bridges behind me, and that's what I did. I'm grateful to God for teaching me how to serve my boss without compromising my Christian principles. The pay-off was in hearing Dick plead with me to stay on and make that promise.

I was happy, no doubt, but I didn't feel proud or as if I had won points. Instead, it humbled me to the core; for as the Scripture says in Genesis 50:20 "what the enemy meant for evil, God can turn around for good." All glory to God, for He had done just that.

Now, let's plunge head-first into this thing called faith, and watch God move in more of His mighty miracles.

---------- *Chapter 8* ----------

The God-Kind Of Faith

Unknown to me, it was time for God to give me a deeper lesson in faith for finances. Youth Crusades of America had come to town, and I went to the meeting. They asked for *faith pledges* of money you don't have at the moment but trust God will provide down the road.

I didn't pledge anything, but I did feel convicted about it. As I left the meeting, the Holy Spirit impressed my heart to return to the meeting and make a pledge. I pulled over to the curb and pleaded with God about it, and I felt strongly impressed to pledge $500. At first I didn't feel I could do that without consulting Sue, but God's dealing got stronger and stronger.

I started the car and went back to the meeting; they were almost all packed up to go. I explained why I had returned and they rejoiced. I filled out the card and off I went. I fully intended to tell Sue when I got home, but I couldn't seem to find the right time to do it. Within the week we received a letter thanking us for our pledge. The letter was a complete surprise to me, and guess who opened it? Shocked, Sue said,

"$500 pledge! What's this all about?"

I explained sheepishly, and she was sure I had lost my marbles now.

The letter said that we could make twelve equal payments rather than one lump sum, if desired. That was $41.67 that we didn't have. We talked it over and finally decided that what was done was done. We would both trust God for the money and honor the pledge.

As a demonstration of our faith, we took from our grocery money and made the first payment right away. My monthly school tuition was due, and boy, did we need a miracle.

As God would have it, nothing came in. The whole month went by without money for my tuition. We were just about living on bread and water, and we spent no money on anything but our bills. No meals out, no entertainment, not even a soda pop or cup of coffee.

Income for the month was only a few small offerings from services I had preached. Therefore, we decided that if the money didn't come in by my next class, I would have to drop out of all my classes. No money came in. Now I'm questioning this whole thing in my mind and intently seeking God about it all. I must admit, I was more than a little confused and concerned.

I went early to my Greek language class to tell my professor I would be dropping out of school. First, though, I sat through the whole class. For some reason I didn't feel right about leaving. After class was over I waited along with others to talk to him in private. There were only about four of us remaining when the miracle happened.

A stranger stepped into the classroom and asked if there was a Bob Ford in the class. I didn't recognize him, but I did respond. When I responded, he asked again if I was Bob Ford, and I said that I was.

He pulled out his wallet and removed two checks. As he was endorsing them over to me he said that these checks came in his mail that day. He said that while removing them from his mailbox the Holy Spirit impressed him to give them to a "Bob Ford at Melodyland School of Theology." He didn't know me, but he followed the leading of the Spirit in his heart.

I was astonished, to say the least. He went on to say that the two checks came from a company that had gone bankrupt. They had owed him money for over a year, and if the checks weren't any good, it was between God and me alone. The checks totaled $664.34. Wow. What a miracle. I deposited the checks and they cleared. Glory to God! You know, friend, what Jesus said to Martha, he still says today "If you can believe, you will see the glory of

God."

The first thing we did was write a tithe check out for $66.44. Next, we paid off the balance of the pledge, $458.33. We paid my tuition, and then we went waltzing down to the grocery store with almost $50 to spend, which in those days bought a heaping cart full of groceries. Isn't the Lord fantastic, amazing, and marvelous?

We couldn't wait for Sunday morning. We wanted to put that tithe check in the offering so bad we could hardly contain ourselves. Pastor Stout and his wife were on vacation in Hawaii, and Rev. Hobart Van was preaching. At the end of his message, Hobart asked to receive a love offering for Don and Ann Stout because they were running a little short of money, but now Sue and I only had eleven dollars left, and the gas gauge was sitting on empty.

After I put the tithe check in the general offering, the Holy Spirit spoke to my heart again.

I was to put the eleven dollars in the love offering. I hesitated, thinking, All of it, Lord? We need at least a dollar for gas. The tank is on empty! With that car, when the gas gauge said empty, it meant empty. By now the offering bag was in my hand. I took out the ten dollar bill and put it in, keeping the one dollar for gas.

Now the bag was gone, and I didn't feel good about it at all. The Holy Spirit spoke again—with conviction. I couldn't take it. I got up, ran to the usher, and gave the last dollar we had. What a relief; nothing feels better than obeying God.

When it comes to giving, Sue and I figure it this way. God, being the Creator of everything, actually owns everything anyway. We're only stewards of what He loans us. The tithe, or ten per cent, is a part of it, and, if God, for whatever reason, wants more, or even all of it, who are we to say He can't have it?

Believe me, when God asks for it, give it to him, even when others think you're being foolish, for when you do, you're in line for a blessing that will knock your socks off. Just be sure that it is God and not your own doing. If it's truly God, then the miracle will follow. Jim Elliot said, "He is no fool who gives what he cannot keep to gain what he cannot lose."

From the outset, Sue and I had an understanding with God. We promised to tell no one but God of our needs. No long faces, and no sign that we even had any needs. There would be no telling others that we need prayer for food or money or gas or anything for that matter. If we needed something, then Sue and the kids and I would all pray together alone and trust that God would hear and answer.

We figured that if we were going to trust God and go into the ministry on faith, we would do just that and trust only in him. By this time we had learned that He was big enough to do it without us trying to help him out.

Although this is how we felt led to move with God, I'm not saying that people should never share their needs. That's what the Body of Christ is all about; caring and sharing, but don't say you believe God for something, but at the same time tell everybody about it.

Here is an experience I had right along this line that should make my point clear. Once while walking through a shopping mall a friend of mine told me he was trusting God for a new pair of western boots. They were made from some special exotic leather and were very expensive. He just happened to take me into the western store that had the boots, and he showed them to me. I commented that they were very nice, as well as very expensive, and let it go at that so as to get on with other shopping.

To make a long story short, he didn't want to leave the store, and I became uneasy about it. I tried to leave, and then he told me that God wanted me to buy him the boots. I said,

"You can't be serious!"

I knew in my heart that God had not impressed me in the least to do that.

He insisted and said,

"You need to buy me these boots."

"Why?" I asked.

"Because I believe God wants me to have them."

Then I told him, in no uncertain terms, that he'd best put his faith in God alone and not in me. He was not happy with my answer and told me that I needed to sow some financial seed and buy him the boots. I told him that he would do best to let it go, and I left without him.

Earlier when I said the gas tank was empty, I meant it—empty. But I drove that old Chevy for three days without running out of gas. I never said a word to anyone about it, and each day I went to the church, called on the sick at three different hospitals, and ran errands for Pastor Stout and the staff. No gas went into the tank, but the car kept going anyway.

Then, on the third day, late in the afternoon, a brother came up to me and said that God had impressed him to give me his gasoline credit card. Here we go again. God is so faithful.

That's not all. Within two weeks, $917 came in through various means. A brother asked me what percentage of increase that was to the original $11 we gave to Pastor Stout's vacation offering. I told him I was too busy with the next miracle to figure it out. Just think, I could have missed the whole miracle for one measly dollar.

Let me tell you friend, when you get to the bottom of your purse, you're at the top of His. He owns the cattle on a thousand hills. All the silver and all the gold is His. Nothing's impossible with God. The impossibility is all with us when we measure God by the restrictions of our unbelief. The Bible says in Mark 9:23, "All things are possible to him that believes."

All, not some things, not most, not a few, not a little, but a*ll* things! Praise His Holy name! When your heart truly belongs to God, your heart and his heart will be one. As His Word says, "He will give you the desires of your heart" (Psalms 37:4), all because they are His desires in the first place.

One day I told this miracle of the gas to a group, and one of the brothers, Ted Kyle, questioned me with a doubtful eye. I reiterated to him that I had only obeyed the Lord. A few days later he came up to me with a strong rebuke, saying that I had fabricated the whole story and he was angry with me.

His premise was, he had tried it, even though he had money in his pocket to buy gas. It didn't work for him, and he and his family were stranded miles out in the boondocks, out of gas, of course, and he had to walk to town to get some. I was astonished, and I informed him that he had tempted God, whereas I had obeyed Him.

Many people talk about faith today, thinking that faith allows them to step out and do whatever they want and then God is obligated to come through. Not so, of course. God pays for what he orders, but he has nothing to do with man's foolishness. Presumption is not faith, it's foolishness. Faith is following God.

Jesus said that he did only the things he *saw* the Father doing, the things he *knew* in his heart. He didn't mean the things he saw with his eyes. That's not walking by faith, that's walking by sight, and if ever a man walked by faith, Jesus did.

I say that I'm following God, and I believe that I am, but I've made as many mistakes as anyone in this area. That's how we learn. At times I've been sure that God, by His Spirit, was leading me to do this or that. When I bombed out, I didn't give up. I've had cancer cases that didn't get healed; in fact, they died.

So what am I to do, quit? Wait a minute here. Who's doing the healing, me or God? I can't heal anybody—only God can. I'm only a vessel, just like anyone else. My job is to keep this vessel clean, full of Him, empty of myself, and I must practice His presence. Now let me be clear here; for there is a lot of teaching going around about this that is contrary to what I mean.

When I say practice His presence, I mean to act, think, and talk as if He is physically with me at all times. This kind of attitude will keep me in check, so to say, and cause me to be more sensitive to the leading of the Holy Spirit, and I must keep my eyes upon Jesus and his atoning sacrifice at Calvary as well. Then, and only then, I'm empowered and led to go on believing and praying for the sick and the lost, and leave the results up to God.

The Bible says in Hebrews 11:1 that faith is the substance and the evidence of things hoped for. Much has been said about this, but let's keep it simple. I like to put it this way: this kind of faith simply means to know. When Hebrews chapter eleven talks about faith giants, what stands out the most? They all *knew* what God wanted them to do. They knew, either because God had spoken to them audibly, or because he had given them a revelation in their heart, in their spirit.

That kind of knowing isn't in your head. It's not logic or reason. In fact, knowing in your spirit might be contrary to everything your mind tells you. Go back over all these miracles I've been telling you about and you'll see what I mean. The revelation knowledge that God gave Sue about getting my job back in seven days just appeared. It wasn't logical, it didn't seem possible, and it hadn't been asked for. It simply needed to be believed and acted upon.

When God reveals something to you that he is going to do, he gives you a gift of faith, a knowing in your heart. Revelation knowledge from God means that the thing is as good as done. No need to be prayed for, only accepted or acted upon and received.

Often God has given me faith for something that has nothing to do with any specific scripture. I don't mean to say that it's contrary to his Word. It's always perfectly in line with it. When God speaks to my heart to do something not related to any scripture, it's considered a personal Word from God, given when He desires a certain action.

This is as much the Word of God as the Scriptures are. Because that Word is from God's own mouth, so to speak, whether it is audible or heart knowledge. At that very moment, God gives a gift of faith for the specific occasion so as to motivate me into action. My mind may be saying, Don't even try it, it's not logical, not reasonable, but my heart, my spirit, is impressing me to do it and it will be so. Like the $11, or the miracle with Mrs. Brittinham, and others.

Rev. Don Piper, a Baptist preacher, wrote a book called *90 Minutes In Heaven* by Cecil Murphy. He tells his story of dying in an automobile accident on January 18, 1989. After being clinically dead for an hour and a half, another Baptist preacher, the late Rev. Dick Onerecker, came upon the scene of the accident, and God spoke to his heart to pray for the dead man in the red car.

It took a while for Onerecker to get up the courage to obey God, but when he did, God raised Don Piper from the dead. Quoting from the book,

"God spoke to me and said, 'You need to pray for the

man in the red car.' Dick was an outstanding Baptist preacher. Praying for a dead man certainly ran counter to his theology. I can't do that, he thought. How can I go over there and pray? The man is dead."

Here is a perfect example of what I've been talking about. When God spoke to Dick Onerecker to pray for Don Piper, it was the Word of God to Dick, and he had the obligation to obey, just as he has to obey the written Word of God. Dick obeyed the Word of God in his heart, Don Piper came back from the dead.

Why didn't God raise him from the dead by Himself? Because God has instructed in his Word that we are his instruments to heal the sick, raise the dead, cast out demons, and preach the Gospel of the full atonement of Christ. Wow, aren't we privileged.

I have had asthma all my life. I've prayed for others with asthma, and they've been healed. Why not me? Only God knows the answer to that but I continue to believe for my healing anyway.

One day I was in town when I had a sudden, severe asthma attack. I needed medication and drove a short distance to the pharmacy. The store was closed, but I went to the door and looked to see if anyone was still there. I was wheezing and hardly able to breathe; the slow, exhausting walk from the car took all the energy I had.

Just then I heard an awful sound. I turned and saw that a German shepherd had jumped over the fence and was coming straight for me. I stood frozen in my tracks. It looked like he had a Mohawk haircut; the hairs on his backbone from head to tail were standing straight up. His lips were rolled back and a seething growl was escaping through his teeth.

Void of all strength, I couldn't run or try to defend myself. I needed a miracle, and I needed it now. Hardly able to breathe, I stood there wheezing, saying out loud, "Jesus. Jesus. Jesus." I looked that dog straight in the eye as he approached me and over and over I spoke out, "Jesus! Jesus!" I only said *Jesus*, nothing else, but in my spirit I was taking authority over the intent of that dog simply by speaking out the name of Jesus.

The dog continued to charge me. Was I frightened? For a moment, yes, but then faith took over. The dog thrust his mouth against my left leg. I didn't even flinch. As stiff as a post I was looking down at him now, still saying the name of Jesus. This dog put his front paws around my leg so as to press his mouth against it in order to bite me.

He went all around my body, crashing against my legs over and over with his mouth, but he couldn't bite me. It was as if his mouth was taped shut. He finally backed off, still growling and with the hairs on his back still straight up.

Let me tell you, this was a hair-raising experience for me. But just as God had shut the lion's mouth for Daniel, so did He shut this dog's mouth for me. The aftermath was, the asthma attack was gone as soon as the dog was out of sight.

Looking back, if God had healed me earlier, I would have missed out on this miracle. I love Him. I will always love Him. He is my best friend. He is my God, my Lord, my Savior, and my soon-coming King. I remembered a couple verses of Scripture where God said to the apostle Paul "His grace was sufficient for him." He said that "God's strength was made perfect" in Paul's weakness, as it was made perfect in mine. Glory to God!

Soon after, God gave me a vision of doing battle with Satan and the Holy Spirit led me on an in-depth study of the authority that believers have in Jesus. This study went on for many months, and I read every book I could find on the subject. Summarizing my findings, I'll give you the revelation God gave me, and the key for victory over the devil.

There is power in the name of Jesus, but only when we are in him and under his authority, as the example of the centurion in Matthew 8:5–13 who exercised the authority of the leader he was submitted to. But, we must believe with our whole heart that we have the authority of Jesus. There is no room for doubt. When we are in line with this, Satan knows our name, and adds us to his list of those possessing this authority.

Don't be alarmed that Satan knows your name; in fact, this is a good thing. For example, when some unbelievers, vagabond

Jews in the New Testament who were exorcists, tried to cast an evil spirit out of a man, the evil spirit said that he didn't know these unbelievers. At the same time, the evil spirit said that he did know Jesus and the apostle Paul.

As Acts 19:13 says, "The evil spirit answered and said, Jesus I know, and Paul I know; but who are you?" This proves that a believer's name is known in hell, as well as in heaven. Thank God that our names are written and known in heaven, but only known in hell.

Going deeper now, let's look at a few Greek words in Luke 10:19. The King James Version says "Behold, I give unto you *power* to tread on serpents and scorpions, and over all the *power* of the enemy: and nothing shall by any means hurt you," emphasis mine. These two words (power) are two different Greek words, and have different meanings.

We see here that Jesus has given us power over Satan, *Behold, I give unto you power*. This first word power is *exousia*, literally, delegated authority, denoting freedom of action and the right to act in Jesus' place. Jesus said that he gave us this freedom and this right as a delegated authority over *all* the power of Satan.

The second time power is used in this verse it is *dunamis*, literally, supernatural power. So, to press the point, what Jesus has said here, literally, is that he gave us the freedom and right to act, in his place, as his delegated authority over *all* of Satan's supernatural power. No wonder Satan works so hard to keep this truth from the Body of Christ.

Now let's think about this a little further.

A police officer has no power over you unless he is under the authority of the police department. When he says, I arrest you in the name of the law; there is no question as to whether he has the authority to do so.

The same applies to the teaching in Luke 10:19. Jesus has given us the authority to arrest the works of Satan, nullifying his power and stopping his actions, even reversing their effects. All we have to do is be, and act, under the authority of Jesus, which means to submit to him and obey him. I guarantee that when you operate in this truth, you will see miracles you never thought possible, just as I have.

When we operate in the glorious name of Jesus, we are acting in faith and obedience to God's Word. When Satan knows that your name is written in heaven, and that you are under the authority of Jesus, and operating by faith in his authority, the devil knows he is defeated.

The only question is this: Do you know that you have the authority of Jesus to work the works of God? Like I stated above, the utterance of the mighty name of Jesus alone, in faith, will produce the desired end without some long, flowery, highfalutin, meaningless prayer. You know what I mean, the kind of prayers some pray to make the on-lookers think they're spiritual.

One Wednesday morning, Pastor Stout had started the prayer clinic service at TCC when I walked into the sanctuary a bit late. I had just reached the back row of chairs when the Holy Spirit spoke in my heart. Out of the corner of my eye I saw a wheelchair on the front row; I could only see the back of the person sitting in it. The Holy Spirit impressed on me that this person would walk today.

Man, was I excited. I sat there waiting for Pastor to do something. I expected God to use him; after all, he was conducting the meeting. His prayers were often followed by miracles.

After a while Pastor Stout fixed his eyes upon me and called me to the front. He said he felt impressed that I had something to share. That was an understatement. I always had something to share, so I walked forward, Bible in hand.

I opened my Bible and asked everyone to turn with me to the particular text. Then, I looked to my right and saw the man in the wheelchair. My faith swelled within me. I knew this man would walk. I just knew it.

I closed my Bible, laid it on the podium and walked over to him. Taking him by the hand I said,

"In the name of Jesus, rise up and walk."

His wife stood up and put her hands on his shoulders, holding him in place, and shouted,

"But he can't walk!"

I looked at them with compassion and faith.

"Oh, but God says he can."

Then I proceeded to pull him up out of the wheelchair. That's when the test of my faith came. His right leg was no bigger around than a small baseball bat, and as I started to pull him to his feet I could see this. For a second or two it felt as if someone had removed something from my chest: my faith. I felt a breath-taking emptiness. My mind said, Let him be, let him sit there in that wheelchair and say a nice little prayer for him and tell him to believe God for his healing, and then go on with other things.

But I was determined to believe God and not my mind. My heart said to pull harder, to pull him up and out of that chair. Dear reader, if I've learned anything about miracles it's this, don't try to make things easier for God or you'll miss the miracle altogether. For further study on this essential key, look at 1 Kings 18:20–39, where Elijah poured tons of water on the sacrifice, and then asked God to light it on fire.

So I pulled harder and said to him with authority,

"I command you to walk and be healed in the name of Jesus."

Bless God, he did just that. He walked unassisted across the front of the church. His wife was crying for joy and the crowd went wild, so to speak. I'm the kind of guy that doesn't care for, or promote, fleshly theatrics or drama, but genuine excitement like this is from God, and for God's glory, and it deserves a celebration.

People were crying for joy, raising their hands in the air, thanking Jesus, and praising God. The man went home healed, and within two weeks his leg returned to normal size. He not only walked, but he and his entire family walked into the arms of the Savior and experienced the joy of salvation. Here we see again—the miracle first—and born again second, just like it happened to me. God is pouring out his love, are you getting your portion?

Almost 2,000 years ago, Peter and John went to pray and had nothing to give the lame man except the blessing of God (Acts 3:6–7). Let me tell you, that's more than enough. God is never short on what it takes. He's the God that's more than enough.

When the apostle Peter reached out and lifted that man to his feet, then and only then is when his ankles and legs became strong. Peter said that it was all done through faith in the name of Jesus.

Jesus wants us to operate in this same kind of faith. He said so in Mark 16:17-18, "And these signs shall follow them that believe; In my name shall they cast out devils; they shall speak with new tongues; they shall take up serpents; and if they drink any deadly thing, it shall not hurt them; they shall lay hands on the sick, and they shall recover." This verse states that these signs shall follow them that believe. It doesn't say these signs will only follow the preachers or apostles. It says believers. That means you. Do you believe?

Don't question it, just believe it. It's God's Word, not yours or mine. Some Christians have said to me that these verses shouldn't be in the Bible. Shouldn't be in the Bible? "Careful now," I tell them, "this is God's Word," and God says in 2 Timothy 3:16 that every word of it is inspired. That means that every word of it is "God breathed." It goes on to say that every Word of God is profitable to us, and that God's Word will completely furnish us for every good work.

Some people are so busy whittling the Bible down to their size that it's no wonder they lack the power of the Spirit. They say the power of God is not for today. Some say, "But that's not the way our church believes." Others say, "My father never believed it that way," and so on and so forth.

Why do they say these things? Because it's easier to deny the power is available, than to admit they are lacking in it. It's no wonder why they never see any miracles. They have removed the power of God. Oh, Lord, help them to see the light.

I had many discussions and shared many miracles with my father, witnessing to him every chance I got, and this wasn't easy. He had a hard time accepting anything from me, even though things had been settled between us. One day though, in the midst of one of these discussions, he said,

"Son, the devil can do miracles, too, you know. You need to be careful about all this."

It was obvious that his boyhood church doctrines were getting in his way. I looked him right in the eye and said,

"Dad, many, many people are being saved, baptized in the

Holy Spirit, healed, and then attending church and Bible studies, worshiping and praising God, and serving God as never before. You don't really think this is the devil's work, do you? What possible glory could the devil get out of all this? And remember, Dad, Jesus said in Mark 3:24 that 'a house divided against itself can't stand.' Therefore, if the devil was doing this, he would be destroying himself. No, Dad, on the contrary, this is the work of the Holy Spirit, and God is getting all the glory."

Shortly after this discussion my father went to a revival meeting and was gloriously saved and filled with the Holy Spirit. He started attending church regularly and witnessing for the Lord in public places. His attitude about Blacks and Hispanics did a complete flip-flop and the love of Christ showed through him in a mighty way.

At church he would raise his hands in worship and sing out the praises of Jesus. I might add, Dad had a very good singing voice. Finally, after all these years, my Dad and I have something in common, and, thank God, we're good friends now too.

Shortly after becoming a Christian, I came across an anonymous poem that spoke to me so strongly I taped it in the front of my Bible. It's called How Readest Thou?

> Tis one thing friend, to read the Bible through,
> another thing to read, to learn to do;
> Tis one thing too, to read it with delight,
> and quite another thing to read it right.
> Some read it with design to learn to read,
> but to the subject pay but little heed;
> Some read it as their duty once a week,
> but no instruction from the Bible seek.
> Some read to bring themselves into repute,
> by showing others how they can dispute;
> While others read because their neighbors do,
> to see how long twill take to read it through.
> One reads with fathers "specs" upon his head,
> and sees the things only as his father did;

Another reads through Luther, Wesley, and Scott,
and thinks it means just what *they* thought.
Some read to prove a pre-adopted creed,
thus understanding little that they read;
And every passage in the Book they bend,
to make it suit that all important end.
Some people read as I have often thought,
to teach the Book instead of being taught.

Many miracles happened at the TCC prayer clinics and I am only mentioning a few of them. I've tried to describe a few here, but my words don't do justice to the extent of the miracles we saw.

One man, a diabetic, came forward for prayer. After prayer he asked me if he should continue to take his insulin. I told him that it wasn't up to me, it was up to God. I advised him to continue taking his medication until he either heard specifically from God not to or had a reaction from the medication. A few days later he said that every time he took the medication he had a reaction, so he reduced the dosage. Within a week he was off his insulin. He showed no sign of diabetes from then on.

Once when I had a two-hour layover in the Denver Airport I wanted to use the time to lead someone to Jesus. I could easily have approached anyone there with the gospel but I sensed that God would have me wait on Him and pray. The longer I waited, the more anxious I got.

I was hungry and wanted to get something to eat, but I didn't want to miss God's direction. I sat down and pressed into God for about thirty minutes in prayer. With no real leading yet, I stepped up to a food stand and bought a hot dog and soda pop. As I turned around to find a table and chair I saw a young man buy a book published by the Moonie's (a cult). The Holy Spirit spoke to my heart and impressed me that this was the one to go after. I threw the food in the trash barrel, grabbed my briefcase and headed his way.

He had quite a lead on me and I had to walk fast to overtake him. I began to wonder what I would say and asked the Lord for help. I approached him from behind and started walking beside him, while catching my breath. He looked my way and I glanced at the new book under his arm and said,

"Do you understand the teachings in that book?"

Somewhat puzzled he said,

"Well ... no I don't, do you?"

We stopped walking and he handed me the book, expecting me to explain it to him. I introduced myself and learned that his name was Mark, and said,

"If you have a few minutes, could we sit down to talk?"

"I'd love to. My plane won't be in for over an hour."

"That's great, Mark. Now, about this book, may I ask you a question?"

"Sure, fire away."

"Are you seeking spiritual truth?"

"Yes, I am. In fact, as soon as I bought this book I asked God to please send someone to explain it to me."

"Well, Mark, God has heard and answered your prayer. The moment I saw you buy that book He spoke to my heart to approach you about it."

"Really! Thank God! I've come to the end of my rope. Everything in my life is all mixed up. I can't seem to find any answers to what life is all about and no one seems to have any answers for me."

"Can I ask you another personal question?"

"Sure, go right ahead."

"If you were to die today, are you sure you'd go to heaven?"

"No, I'm not sure at all. I'm tormented by my past sins and I can't find any peace of mind at all. But how can anyone know for sure if they'll get to heaven?"

(Mark is a perfect example of a person who is already *convicted* and only needs to be *converted*. There will be more about this in the next chapter).

"Well, Mark, let's back up for a minute and talk about this book you bought. You see, it will teach you about a man's philosophy, his theory, his views on religion, but this is only his opinion. On the other hand, this Bible I have here will teach you the truth about spiritual things and give you the answers you are looking for. Answers to your questions about life and how to know for sure you'll go to heaven. Which one would you rather talk about?"

"Bob, if you can explain the Bible to me, please do. I've tried to read it, but it doesn't make sense to me."

"I understand, Mark, but first, do you believe that Jesus is the Son of God?"

"Yes, I do."

"Do you believe that he died for your sins?"

"Yes, I believe that also."

"Then let's take a look at what Jesus had to say about some things."

I took Mark through about a dozen scriptures and then asked if he would like to pray to receive Jesus as his personal savior and Lord. He was eager and we bowed our heads in prayer.

I led him through what's called the sinner's prayer, where he confessed and repented of his sins, invited Jesus into his heart, and asked the Holy Spirit in to change and control his life. He was gloriously saved. I told him that if he ever had any doubts about his salvation to read John 5:24 and 1st John 1:9.

Then I taught him about prayer, praise, and how to read the Bible. I talked about the importance of church fellowship as well. Before we parted I got his name and address so I could send him some literature; then I asked him what he wanted to do with the Moonie book. He said he didn't want it, so I disposed of it for him

Brother Fitts had organized a witnessing get-away in Venice, California, and invited me to come along. I was assigned a few teenagers and a section of houses to canvass. We took off with our Bibles and hand-out Bible tracts and began knocking on doors. We were able to give some literature to a few people, but most people didn't want to talk to us about God or Jesus, or for that matter, anything to do with religion.

Street after street it was all the same, and the kids were getting discouraged. They begged me to leave the assigned area and go about six blocks over to the beach where there would surely be "riper fruit." I knew what all was there–the babes showing off their bikinis and the hunks showing off their muscles. It was Muscle Beach, where Arnold Schwarzenegger worked out. I had to tell them over and over that we were not going to the beach and we would finish our assignment no matter what.

On the last street, three or four houses from the end, we rang the door bell and heard a woman ask from the side yard what we wanted. We said we were handing out Christian literature and would like to talk with her about it. She shouted out,

"I'll be right there; don't go away. I'll be right there. It will only take me a few minutes but don't go away."

We all looked at each other hoping we didn't have a loony on our hands. When she came to the front door she asked again exactly what we wanted. We said again what we were doing and asked if we could talk with her.

She threw open the door and asked us excitedly to please come in. We were caught a little off guard, but we went in and were treated like prized guests. She brought us lemonade, iced tea, and cookies. She said that she had been praying that God would send someone to answer her questions about Christianity. When the kids heard that they jumped up from the couch like popped-corn in a hot pan and shouted—*Hallelujah!*

We spent a good deal of time there answering her questions and then led her in the sinner's prayer to receive Jesus. She was gloriously saved and couldn't thank us enough for stopping by. We left literature with her, and I got her name and address so as to follow up on her later.

Well, these kids were so excited they couldn't wait to get back to the home base and tell everyone all about it. You see, this was the first person that any of these kids had ever led to the Lord, and now it wouldn't be the last, for sure.

My courses at Melodyland School of Theology were coming to a close, and Betsy, our 1960 Chevrolet, had almost 200,000 miles on her. She was a faithful little buggy. Treating her like as if she were human, I used to pat her on the dashboard and say, "Bless you, Betsy, bless you."

Three months earlier I had installed her second rebuilt

generator; they came with a 90-day guarantee. The previous one had lasted just over three months, and the current one was going on four months old.

As I was entering the freeway, the generator light came on. This meant that it was no longer charging the battery. There was an old familiar noise coming from under the hood, too. Just like the other one, this generator was beginning to squeal and disintegrate. These were inexpensive generators, and you get what you pay for. In an act of faith (and desperation) I put my hand over the red light indicator and said,

"In the name of Jesus I command you to be repaired. I command you to operate properly and to charge the battery."

As I removed my hand the red light went out and the noise ceased. Ecstatic, I shouted,

"Praise the Lord!"

Here's the rest of the story. The generator stayed in that car and worked perfectly for another 53,000 miles, when we traded the car in on a new one. Yes, my friend, as God's Word says, "All things are possible to him that believeth." And you can take that to the bank, too. What a fantastic, marvelous God we serve! As I said before, He is more than enough. Praise His wonderful name!

Everything was happening so fast we didn't have time to comprehend it all. It was like riding in bumper cars at the fair, getting hit from all sides. We were always bumping into a miracle or some new revelation that was changing our lives and taking us deeper into the knowledge and love of God.

There was never a dull moment. Although we had already seen more miracles and blessings than most of the people we knew, we had no idea of the glorious things that were about to happen.

Chapter 9

Moving On

With the prompting of the Holy Spirit in our hearts, Sue and I knew it was time to put our little ranch up for sale and down-size in anticipation for the next move in ministry. It wasn't easy, but we knew that obeying God was best. We listed our home for $49,500 and signed a contract for six months.

This also meant we had to sell our livestock. We called a mobile slaughter house and that took care of the pigs. They were mighty good eating. The turkeys had already been eaten as had the chickens. The ducks were adopted out, and that left only the horses.

We ran an ad in the newspaper with a brief description of each horse and the price we were asking. I didn't know it at the time, but Sue didn't want to sell her horse.

It was a white and grey quarter Horse mare, and she was a good one. Only about five or six years old, she still had plenty of life left in her. When people came to look at the horses, Sue would tell a little white lie and say that her horse was already spoken for. The person who had spoken for her horse was, herself.

All the other horses sold quickly, and I couldn't understand why this horse hadn't been bought until one day when I was home and some people came to look at her. That's when Sue coughed-up the facts, and told me how she felt. It was sad for her to see her favorite horse go, but we knew in our hearts that God was requiring this sacrifice to the future ministry He had planned for us.

My horse was a Palomino gelding with a long blond mane.

His blond tail was so long it touched the ground. He was a trained parade horse who knew all the fancy steps; prancing forward or sideways with high deliberate steps. When we went down the street, he'd put on a show that brought all the neighbors out to see.

He'd cock his head in and up and stand tall, prancing down the street sideways and in-line with perfect steps and the pride of the herd written all over him. You could hear his distinct clippity-clop blocks away, and he surely thought every street was a parade platform.

Our families, friends, and neighbors couldn't understand why we had to sell all this for the ministry. We couldn't explain it all to them, but we had to obey the leading of the Holy Spirit. We knew that would be best, even though we didn't have any details of what this ministry would be. We knew we were being asked by God to follow him in faith and that the details would be revealed later.

Shortly after listing our house, Brother Fitts asked me if I'd be interested in going to Mexico to preach and hold healing meetings in a Mission about forty miles across the border. I didn't speak a word of Spanish and couldn't see how it would work, but he said that an interpreter would be available to assist me.

After talking it over with Sue, I decided to go for it. Brother Fitts took care of the details and made all the necessary contacts. We set a date with the Mission leaders and arranged my transportation.

Off I went to Mexico for nine days. I had been there once before, when I was a teenager. I went to Tijuana to have tuck-and-roll upholstery installed in my car. My brother, Dick, and another friend went along, and we stayed on this side of the border for safety reasons. We had heard about all the bad stuff that happens down there. Boy, do I thank God for that decision now.

Brother Carlos, my driver and interpreter, drove me from my house to the Mission in his van. On arrival he instructed the women to prepare a meal for me, since I hadn't eaten all day. He was to return soon, but soon in Mexico could be many hours.

I was shown to my room and found that it had only a mattress on the floor and one little table. There was no closet, just a couple of hooks on the wall. There was no door, just a curtain. The floor was bare concrete; the walls plain plaster. For light, there was a bare bulb hanging from an exposed wire with a pull-chain. There were no pictures on the wall, no mirror, no shelves. Carlos left me there with no one who could speak English. I was *way* out of my comfort zone.

As I looked around to see exactly what I had gotten myself into, I saw that the kitchen door leading to the outside was off its hinges and there were live chickens in the kitchen. Not only were they on the kitchen floor, they were on the counter-tops, even while the food was being prepared. This was almost too much for me; I'm a clean freak when it comes to food.

My anxiety was relieved a bit when I saw that everyone there was radiant with joy and trying their best to accommodate me and communicate with me. I felt such tremendous love and acceptance from them that I was almost able to ignore what my eyes were seeing. The women would chase the chickens off the counter-top and out the door, and then they'd come right back in again.

There was running water. It looked cloudy, almost scary. Then I realized that, thank God, water for drinking and cooking was delivered in five-gallon bottles every day. I had been told, in no uncertain terms, "Don't drink the tap water unless you want to be very sick." The refrigerator was old, maybe from the 1930s. The stove was an old fashioned gas range with a propane bottle next to it on the floor.

The toilet facility was a detached 6'x6' room outside with, I was glad to see, a flush toilet. However, I was told not to put any paper down it or it would plug up. Also, the sewage was piped directly outside and ran in an open trench, which explained the terrible stench I had smelled from the time I had arrived.

The next day when I used the toilet I had forgotten about not putting paper down it, and I plugged it up. The men had to remove it and clean out the mess, put in a new wax ring, and reinstall the toilet. I was so embarrassed I wanted to disappear.

As I looked around at all this, my mind went back to when I was a child. My mother had to make our living room end tables out of orange crates stood on end. Then she covered them with large doilies that she made out of empty feed sacks from our rabbits and chickens (a couple of hundred, combined). She even made our shirts and my sister's dresses out of empty feed sacks. As a young boy, I thought we were poor, but in comparison to what I was seeing in Mexico, we were well off.

The ladies had finished fixing the meal and motioned for me to sit down and eat. I obliged them, but no one else was eating with me. I didn't understand why not, but I couldn't ask them about it, so I prayed over the meal and began to eat.

The refried beans were the best I had ever tasted, made from scratch, of course, and the handmade tortillas were excellent. The jalapeños? Wow! Talk about hot, my mouth was on fire! I wanted water but didn't know how to say it, so I motioned frantically. One of the men got me a glass of milk, and it put the fire right out. I learned that milk works better for fire in the mouth than anything else. Thank you, Jesus.

I didn't recognize the other food on my plate, but I ate it in respect and with deep gratitude for all the effort and love they showed me. One of the items, in a sauce of sorts, had a strange honey-comb look to it. Later I learned that it was tripe, or goat stomach.

It was a large plate of food, and more than enough, but out of respect I ate every bit of it. As I was finishing the last bite, one of the ladies pointed to the plate and said, "Mas? Mas?" Not knowing what she was saying, I thought maybe *mas* meant *good*. Wanting to show my gratitude, I said, "Mas."

Immediately the ladies grabbed my plate and went to the kitchen to return with another full plate of food. I took one look at it and realized that *mas* must mean *more*. The harder I tried to communicate, the more trouble I got into. I wanted my interpreter, but he wasn't around. I felt helpless and so inadequate. All I wanted to do was to thank them and bless them. With that being out of my reach, I became more and more frustrated.

I went to my bedroom and took out my Bible. Sitting on my mattress, I started to read. One of the men came in and tried to tell me something, but I couldn't understand what he was trying to get across to me. Finally, he took me by the arm and escorted me into the front room, which was the sanctuary. He gave me a table and chair to use for study and brought me a glass of water.

My Bible lay open, and he pointed to it with a puzzled look on his face. He began reverently to touch the pages. Talking in Spanish, he pointed out my hand-written notes on the bottom and sides of the pages, as well as the colored pencil highlights I had put in the text. Later I learned that this man didn't know it was alright to write in your Bible.

Carlos returned, and I finally got to talk to all the brothers and sisters at the Mission. I explained my confusion and gave them my deepest thanks for their love and generosity. They not only treated me like a king but reverenced me to such a point that I felt uncomfortable and humbled at the same time.

I learned that this is the way they treat any man of God, and believe that the Bible instructs it, emphatically. I began to realize that these simple, loving, poor and uneducated people had a lot to teach me, and the rest of us for that matter, about humility, sacrifice, and serving others.

Two meetings were scheduled for Sunday, and the weekly evening meetings were held at 6:00 PM. On Saturday evening 6:00 PM came and went, and only a few people were there. I asked if we should get started and was told that we would be starting soon.

After fifteen or twenty minutes I asked again and was told the same thing again, without any sense of urgency. This was difficult for me; I was raised to be prompt. My dad taught us that it was disrespectful to keep someone waiting for you. He would rather be thirty minutes early than one minute late.

At about quarter to seven we started singing hymns, all in Spanish, and I inquired again about officially starting the meeting. Carlos told me that many people lived a great distance away and had to walk, some carrying babies or walking with small children.

I was flabbergasted and asked how far they had to walk. He said that some had to come from a number of miles away. This cut me to the quick. In the States nobody would even think of walking that far to go to church. What an education I was getting, and I think that Brother Fitts knew all along that this experience would be good for me. Of course, he was right, and I still thank God for it today.

When I was introduced to the congregation I was told to take all the time I needed with my message. After preaching for about an hour and a half I started to close the meeting, asking people to come forward for prayer, salvation, healing or anything they needed.

Carlos told me to go ahead and pray for the people but not to close the meeting yet. He said that these people came to hear me preach for as long as I wanted and that they would stay all night, if needed. I couldn't even comprehend it.

Never before had I ever heard of people so hungry for the Word of God. Oh sure, I had read of revivals long ago like Azusa Street and such, but nothing like this in our day. This touched me deeply, and a new and different anointing fell upon me to teach and not to preach. I felt led to let them ask questions about the Bible and I'd do my best to answer them.

During the altar call a number of them were saved. A few were baptized with the Holy Spirit, and many were healed of all sorts of things. One lady had so much pain in her body she could hardly stand even with help from others; she had tears of pain running down her face and she moaned in agony. The Holy Spirit moved on me in such a way that I told Carlos to repeat my prayer for her word for word. It was short and simple, "Satan I command you to let her go. Amen."

As soon as he repeated the prayer, she jerked as she straightened up and shouted out in Spanish,

"Thank you Jesus!"

All her pain was instantly gone. As her friends talked with her, touched her and rejoiced with her, they too were inspired to believe God for healing.

As I continued the meeting I felt led to teach word studies concerning key words in critical Bible verses such as Luke 10:19; John 14:12, Matthew 28:19–20, and others. This was a slow process, because every word had to be interpreted. I learned that some of our English words don't translate well or not at all, and I had to search for different words. Around 11:00 PM we finally closed the meeting with abundant, joyful singing, and I went to my mattress and slept like a baby.

The meetings grew until people were outside looking in

through the windows and the open front door. Because chairs took up too much room now, only the elderly and the women with small children could sit, and everyone else had to stand. They stood for hours on end and kept asking for more. Thank God there were no building capacity codes.

On a number of occasions I found myself losing my voice because of all the preaching and praying. This was a real challenge to me, and many times I had to take a short break and call on God to heal my voice in order to continue. He always came through, and not one meeting was cut short.

Ever since God so graciously saved me I've wanted to be in the category of people who make things happen. I've learned there are three kinds of people in this world: the ones that make things happen, the ones that watch what happens, and the ones that wonder what happened. It's not a matter of education or finance, but choice.

After becoming a Christian I committed to serve and not to be served, to give and not to take. In the daily action of that, God makes many things happen in and through me, all for His glory. I cannot imagine being saved, sanctified, satisfied, and *sitting*. When God saved me, His grace and love motivated me to get off my butt and into the battle.

I asked Carlos if it would be possible to go door-to-door to witness and pray for the sick during the day. He was delighted, so we took one of the elders from the Mission, and set off. I said,

"Let's knock on the door and ask if there is anyone sick or in need of prayer inside to find someone to preach the gospel to."

This is one of the most powerful methods of evangelism, one that Jesus himself not only used, but commanded us to use in Matthew 10:7–8, saying, "And as you go, preach, saying the kingdom of heaven is at hand. Heal the sick, cleanse the lepers, raise the dead, cast out devils: freely ye have received, freely give." A similar message appears in Acts 4:29–30.

If there weren't any sick inside, we would present the gospel anyway and then invite them to the meetings. Almost every home was the same, little furniture, maybe one picture on the wall, and no carpet or rugs on the floor.

Let me sum it up this way; if they had any possessions, you might say, they were all either in their pockets or hidden somewhere else. But there was one thing that most of them did have, and that was the peace and love that passes understanding. I wondered if they even knew they were living in poverty.

I can't even begin to tell you how many successful encounters we had as we ministered in these homes, but one stands out that I must mention. An elderly man had an infected toe. It was huge, terribly discolored and inflamed from the infection. Just seeing the size of it made my own foot ache.

As I prayed through the interpreter the swelling went down, the pain went away, and the natural color returned. The old man was so taken that he lost his composure and broke out in deep sobs of thanksgiving and joy. He and the entire family accepted Jesus as their Lord and Savior right there and then, all glory to God.

While on the subject of witnessing, please let me share my heart with you. In Luke 9:59–62, where Jesus is discussing the cost of discipleship, he condemned weak commitment as much as he did out right refusal of commitment. He said through these Scriptures, as well as a few others, that when a person makes the decision to become a disciple, he or she is committing to being actively involved in the work of a disciple, and the first work is to win souls. Jesus said that this work was, in fact, putting our hand to the plow, (verse 62).

Many people ask me about how to witness, and I've taught many seminars on the subject: Evangelism Explosion, One-verse Evangelism, Four Spiritual Laws, Lifestyle Evangelism and more. However, I have always found one thing to be true. Witnessing to the lost does not flow out of a head filled with methods and techniques—*how*—but flows out of a repentant, thankful, committed heart that has put its hand to the—*plow*.

After training hundreds of Christians in—how—to witness, I have often been grieved at how few actually use their training they received and shared their testimony and the Gospel with anyone at all.

Then again, I have seen those who were saved and were so

grateful to be saved from the punishment of their disobedience to God and His Law that they would preach the Gospel to anyone who would stand still long enough. For the most part, they didn't know a thing about—how to do it.

Now brace yourself, because what's coming up is paramount to being a faithful disciple of Jesus.

You know, contrary to God and His Word, we invite people to get saved; but God *commands* it! "But now He commands all men everywhere to repent" (Acts 17:30). Instead of driving people to the nets of salvation by using *God's Law*, many try to attract them by preaching the benefits of salvation: love, joy, peace, prosperity, a better job, a raise in salary, a promotion, happier marriage, etc.

We surely wouldn't want to tell people that they could, and surely will, suffer persecution, trials, tribulation, suffering, and attacks from Satan, would we? That might scare them off and we sure don't want that!

But that's why eighty percent of those who make a decision for Christ, later turn their back on him, walk away and have nothing more to do with the church or Christians. You see, they believe they were told a lie. Their decision for Christ was based on benefits, not on true sorrow for breaking God's Law and on genuine repentance of their sins.

Now you might be thinking, "Hey Bob, hold on a minute. As Christians we are not under the Law any longer." Yes. You're right, as Christians we aren't, but until a person becomes a true born-again Christian, that person is under the Law and will be judged by the Law.

You see, until they truly see exactly what they're guilty of, and truly repent and commit to Jesus as their personal Lord (Master, Ruler) as well as their Savior, they are under the Law. And, the Scriptures say this is to be applied to all mankind and not only the Jews.

Romans 3:19 says, "Now we know that whatever the Law says, it says to them who are under the Law: that every mouth may be stopped, and all the world may become guilty before God." Then again in 1st Timothy 1:8–9 we read, "But we know that the law is good if one uses it lawfully, knowing this: that the law is not made for a righteous person, but for the lawless and insubordinate, for the ungodly and for sinners."

When it comes to the knowledge of sin, we must understand that it is "missing the mark of perfect righteousness" with God. Romans 4:15 says, "For where no Law is, there is no transgression."

Therefore, as is obvious in this last verse, eliminate the Law from the unsaved, and he will not see his transgression nor will he be convicted of his atrocities against God, nor his need for true repentance. For example, if we didn't have any speed limit laws, no one would be guilty of speeding.

Likewise, by means of the Law of God, the sinfulness of sin is completely exposed. Charles Finney said, "If you have an unconverted sinner, convict him. If you have a convicted sinner, convert him." Remember Mark back in the Denver airport? He was already under conviction and only needed to be converted. Reader, this works. It's likened to the law of a successful salesman; create the need for your product, and you will surely close the sale.

If we were to take a quick tour through the Gospels, we would see that Jesus used the Law to convict sinners. He dealt with sinners in a way that showed his recognition of the Law's validity and, although he forgives sin, he also rejects those who as his professed followers practice lawlessness, as set forth in Matthew 7:23.

Jesus was a Jew talking to Jews, and Paul was a Jew talking to Gentiles. Look at what the apostle Paul said about the Law of God (concerning all mankind) in Romans 7:7, "What shall we say then? Is the Law sin? God forbid. Nay, I had not known sin, but by the Law: for I had not known lust, except the Law had said, Thou shalt not covet."

This is why he was so enthusiastic about the Gospel. He not only knew he was guilty of disobeying God's Law, but he also knew exactly what he was guilty of. He also knew that none of us can work our way out of it. In receiving the free gift of salvation, he was elated that he was now no longer under the Law as set forth in the Ten Commandments and was saved by grace through faith in Christ.

Being free from the deeds of the Law didn't mean that Paul was now free to sin. He was now under a new law, "For the law of the Spirit of life in Christ Jesus has made me free from the law of sin and death" (Rom. 8:2). All of this is why I'm so excited and enthusiastic about my own salvation and compelled to share it with others, as these authors did.

S. Chadwick said,
> *Truth without enthusiasm, morality without emotion, ritual without soul, are things Christ unsparingly condemned. Destitute of fire, they are nothing more than a godless philosophy, an ethical system, and a superstition.*

Paul S. Rees said,
> *Revival and evangelism, although closely linked, are not to be confounded. Revival is an experience in the Church; evangelism is an expression of the Church.*

Witnessing is easy. I tell people to remember one thing: *Don't try to be the Bible answer man. Just stick with sharing your testimony.*

When I say your testimony, I don't mean all the details of your past as I did in the beginning of this book. Tell about being redeemed from the judgment of God. Tell about the peace and joy you have in knowing that you, as a Christian, are free from the Law. This alone will usually get them asking questions. Don't forget to tell them how good it feels that God has forgiven you and that you know you're heaven bound.

Focus on what you have been saved from: Hell. Don't dwell on the many blessings you've experienced since you accepted Jesus as your personal Savior and Lord. That will only give them a false hope, for trials and tribulations will come. Don't tell them that their life will get better or easier, for it may not.

The only promises you want to make are that they, as a Christian, are forgiven and reconciled to God and that they will spend eternity in heaven instead of hell, only because they are truly sorry for their sins, have truly repented of them, and have accepted Jesus Christ as their Lord (Master and Ruler) as well as their Savior.

Sometimes a person will tell me that they're saved by grace and don't have to do any good works, because Jesus did it all for them. I say, "You're exactly right. Jesus did live the life and pay the price for our salvation and therefore, we are saved by grace."

Then I direct them to Titus 2:11–12 which says, "For the *grace* of God that brings salvation has appeared to all men, teaching us that, denying ungodliness and worldly lusts, we should live soberly, righteously, and godly, in this present world," emphasis mine.

Therefore, if one is truly saved by grace, then that same grace is all the while working in them to produce the righteousness of God in their thoughts, words, and deeds. That's why the apostle James said, "For as the body without the spirit is dead, so faith without works is dead also" (James 2:26).

Often after meeting someone or striking up a conversation about the weather, sports, or whatever, I start witnessing to a person by saying, "Say, are you a Christian?" If the answer is yes, I let the conversation take me where it will so as to discover whether they're really saved.

If they answer no, I say something like "May I ask why not?" Then they usually start telling me a whole list of reasons why they aren't. All the while I pay strict attention, and let them know that I am genuinely interested in them. Then, after they've exhausted all their excuses, I gently begin to tell of all the peace and joy I have in the fact that I know for sure that I'm saved from an eternal hell and going to heaven, and that I have a personal relationship with God through Jesus. This will often spark their curiosity and get them asking questions.

I have often had people tell me that they don't wear their religion on their sleeve. Without being sarcastic, I tell them that I don't either, but I do wear the love of God all over me and all through me.

If a person is truly born again, he or she, as Jesus said, is like a candle that lets its light shine so all can see, not one that is hidden under a bushel.

Has God lit your candle as he has mine? Well then, for Pete's sake, let's get out there and let our lights shine for Jesus. Let's all let our lights so shine that we quench the darkness that is so prevalent in this world. And remember, it's the Holy Spirit that does the work, we just speak the words.

Don't let the devil tell you that your contribution is too little, or insignificant, or that you are wasting your time. Every little bit helps, and, with God, nothing done in the name of Jesus is little. You may not be the one that received the five talents or even the two, but you have at least been given one, as recorded in Matthew 25:14–30. So, as Jesus said, "use it or lose it."

Reader, Jesus is talking about our souls here (verse 30). In my next book, the sequel to *Wrongfully Accused,* you will read of my little thirty-minute contribution to the work of God in Monterey, Mexico. Unknown to me at the time, God used that contribution to ultimately touch and change thousands of lives all over the world. Praise His Holy Name!

In closing on this subject of witnessing to the lost and sharing our testimony, let me share with you something that God showed me over and over in His Word.

All through the Bible, Old Testament and New, the message from God is the same. God did not give us *suggestions*, but c*ommandments;* and He did not ask for *partnership* with us, but *ownership* of us, for He is Master, Lord and King.

While I was on that first mission to Mexico, after every meeting the elders took up an offering, and after the nine days of meetings, the total offerings amounted to around $13 in US. They presented it to me with great joy and honor, but I begged them to keep it, for I could see that they needed it much more than I did.

After a lengthy discussion, they convinced me to accept it. They said that the people needed to give so that God could bless them and give back to them, and that they were all planting seed into God's treasury and not mine. Once again, I was so humbled that I broke into tears and thanked the Lord for counting me worthy to learn all these lessons.

I returned home with the $13 and found that no money had

come in while I was gone, and that we were out of food as well. We couldn't even pay the monthly mortgage, but we never slipped in paying our minimum tithe to the church.

We had some income from leather-work that I had been doing (I learned the craft as a teenager). I made Christian belts, purses, bowling bags, Bible covers and other items. All these items had Christian insignias such as the fish (IXOYE), a Greek acronym for "Jesus Christ God's Son Savior," or a carved cross.

Some of them even had Scriptures stamped into them in block letters. The belts all said Praise the Lord or Jesus Is Lord stamped on them in bold letters. All these items were placed in a few Christian book stores on a consignment basis.

Every week I would go to these stores and collect the money from the sales, usually about $100 a month. Sue and the kids helped by putting dye and finish on the items and by installing buckles on the belts and clasps on the purses.

With what money we had we paid the utilities and put gas in the car. I gathered the family together and we listed everything we needed and laid our hands on the list and prayed.

We did this every day for several days and still nothing came in, but we all held tight to our commitment to tell only God of our needs and not to broadcast them to anyone else. Once again, our premise was that God will meet our needs, and then we'll know for sure it is God and not man.

The devil began again to attack me and cause chaos in my mind. We had about a half jar of peanut butter, some spaghetti but no sauce, a can or two of vegetables, a little milk, some juice, and a few other staples, but nothing that would make a meal.

I began to think that I better do something quick, but I didn't know what to do. I wasn't hearing anything from the Lord, and I wondered if I had missed his leading. Do I share our needs? Do I get a job? Is there something we can sell? All this confusion and questioning was due to the fact that I took my responsibility to provide for my family very seriously, and when things didn't look good I felt responsible. Hello, Lord. Are you there?

That afternoon all seven of us went into serious prayer, not that we weren't serious before, but now we're pounding the Throne like never before.

That evening, as Sue was about to try to make something out of what we had, the doorbell rang. She opened the door and a woman we didn't know stood there with two bags of groceries in her arms. She walked right in like she owned the place and looked for the kitchen. We said, "What's this?" She said that the Lord had told her we needed some food, so here she was.

She put the bags down on the kitchen table and left before we could thank her. We were dazed, but ecstatic. The devil had had his day with my mind, but now he was going to get his due. Scripture says in Proverbs 6:30–31 that "When a thief steals, he must pay back seven fold," and although the devil stole some of our time, energy, and peace, now he had to pay it back many times over.

I want to take a moment to talk about *persistent* prayer, the prayer that brought about the miracle in the story above. Reader, if you can get a firm hold on this, believe me, you will break the devils back.

Let's look closely at Daniel 10:1–14, you'll see that Daniel had prayed and fasted for twenty-one days, before the answer came to him by means of an angel. The first thing the angel said was that he had been sent from God with the answer on the first day Daniel began praying.

Then the angel said that he had to call upon Michael the archangel to *withhold,* or *hold back,* the demonic spirits that prevented him from delivering the message to Daniel, and that this took twenty-one days. The testimony of the angel proves that if Daniel had not persevered in prayer and fasting for the full duration of the conflict, the battle in the heavens would have been lost, and he would never have received the answer.

These spirit forces that are active today in heavenly places also appear in Ephesians 6:12. Considering all these verses, look at what happened in the heavens when Jesus was baptized. In Matthew 3:16 it says that "the heavens were opened unto him," indicating that the heavens were closed and had to be opened by an act of God, who acted forcefully so that He could send the Holy Spirit in the form of a dove upon Jesus.

This all confirms that there are evil spiritual forces in the heavens that are intent on interfering with, or holding back, the blessings of God and the answers to prayers that are intended for us.

Jesus talked about persistent prayer in Luke 11:5–10, where a man went to his friend's house during the night and asked for some bread. The friend said that he could not accommodate him because it was late and his family was in bed.

In those days, among commoners, the beds were spread out on the floor, blocking the front entry. You couldn't open the door without disturbing someone. But the man kept on knocking until the homeowner realized that nobody was going to get any sleep until he opened the door and gave the man some bread.

Jesus ended this story (verse 9) with "ask, seek and knock," in Greek, these three words are in the continuous tense, meaning we are to keep on asking, keep on seeking, and to keep on knocking.

Now I know that all of this goes cross-grain with some that I have encountered, for they believe it demonstrates a lack of faith to pray for something more than once. Well, it may surprise some of you that I believe that too, but only when it's appropriate to the situation.

When the Holy Spirit impresses upon my spirit that more than one prayer and maybe some fasting are needed, it would be foolish and disobedient of me not to obey. There is a place for the one-time prayer, and appropriate to keep praising God for the answer until it comes, but to say that this is the only way is to ignore the teaching on persistent prayer and to put the Holy Spirit in a box.

Back to the story, we started going through the bags of food to see what we could put together for dinner, separating produce from canned goods, bread and so on.

Then the door-bell rang again. We almost didn't hear it, what with all the excitement over the food. I went to the door and opened it, and a middle-aged couple was standing there with two bags of groceries apiece—four bags of groceries! They brought them in and added them to the two we had. Amazed and delighted, we were all looking at each other.

Within a few minutes, two groups of people had arrived with

loads of food. It's hard to believe, but before the night was over, five or six different groups, all strangers, had come to our door with groceries, and none of them stayed to visit or explain. We didn't recognize any of them. Some said nothing at all, others simply said that the Lord instructed them to do this.

By the time it was over our refrigerator was completely full, and the pantry couldn't hold any more. We had food piled on every countertop, on the kitchen table, and out in the living room stacked high on the coffee table and the end tables, and even in the bedrooms. Beloved, God is faithful, and he is way too good for any of my words to even try to explain his goodness and grace.

Okay, now the house had more food in it than ever before at any one time, but we still didn't have the money to pay the mortgage. We got together and decided that not one cent of whatever income we would get would be spent on anything except our tithe, utilities, gas, food and then the mortgage, in that order.

When the mortgage fell two months behind, the bank sent us a notice of foreclosure. This was a surprise. We read over our mortgage contract and found that after only thirty days in arrears they could do this.

We did have a few couples look at the house, but no offers came in, so we discussed our options with our real estate agent. She said that dropping the price wouldn't do any good, because the price was already below market. We just needed the right person to come and see it.

I had a few preaching engagements, plus the $150 for cleaning the church, so we could pay for one month arrears. We worked with the bank's mortgage manager, who was a Christian, and he was sympathetic and willing to give us extra time. He was good friends with the owner of a Christian book store in Lake Arrowhead that didn't carry my leather goods.

The mortgage manager arranged for the store owner to give me a call. I took samples of purses and belts to show him and he ordered a large amount of all items. He asked how long it would take me to get them to him. Not realizing his intention, I asked if he could take orders for me, and kindly, but firmly, he said,

"Absolutely not! I want you to deliver the complete order and I'll pay you the full wholesale price up front as soon as it arrives."

I was almost speechless. I thanked him from the bottom of my heart and rushed home to tell the family and get to work. We had plenty of materials in stock, and two weeks later we delivered the goods. This was enough to pay the mortgage for another month, but it didn't put us any further ahead because of the time that had passed.

Then a couple from back east made an appointment to see our house. They liked it and made a full price offer, but with the stipulation that they could wait until the moving/storage strike back home was over to close the deal. The strike had been going on for a couple of months, and all indications were that it would be over soon.

We signed the offer and began looking for a smaller, older house to rent that was close to our church. Nothing we looked at was right, and the strike kept on going too. We were four months behind and the bank was getting antsy. We told them we had a pending sale, but that didn't seem to matter to them.

Then the mortgage manager said that he was being transferred and someone else would be taking over our account. The new manager called and told us he needed all payments made up within thirty days or he would foreclose on the loan.

Our real estate agent was torn up and couldn't understand why we were so calm about it all. We told her about Jesus and the miracles God had done for us, but she just couldn't believe along with us.

As the days went by she would come to see us, thinking that we surely would be troubled, instead, we prayed for her, to help her find peace about what was happening to us. She asked what we would do if the bank took our house. We said we were willing to live out in the street if that was the Lord's will. She cried and shook her head, and we consoled her once again.

On the thirtieth day, a Friday around noon, she came to the house and said that the moving/storage strike had just ended. The only problem was that the buyers could not get the money to us so that we could get it to the bank by 5:00 PM closing time.

Apparently everything they tried to do would not work in time because of the three-hour time difference. Our agent was a basket case, and we felt very sorry for her, but all our prayers, counseling, and witnessing were of no consolation. She was still baffled by our peaceful attitude.

At 4:30 PM she came and told us that the buyers were working with their financial agent to send the money directly to our bank. At 4:50 the phone rang, and … You guessed it again. The bank manager said he had the funds in hand and would not foreclose on our home. This was back in the mid 1970s, long before the high-speed transfers we take for granted today.

By the way, in case you're thinking these miracles were common place, that we began to take them for granted, let me tell you, every one of them is like a breath of fresh air, like a new wave of God's love and grace. Every miracle brought us closer to Him and deepened our commitment to Him.

We had sixty days to be out of the house and into another one, so back to the drawing board we went. We asked Pastor Stout to please make an announcement in church that we needed a house to rent. He agreed, but while making the announcement he slipped up and said that we needed a house to buy.

A couple visiting the church for the first time approached us and said that their home was for sale. We tried to explain that we only wanted to rent, but the Holy Spirit spoke to our hearts to go and take a look at it. Thinking that maybe we could talk them into renting it to us, we followed them home.

The Holy Spirit spoke to our hearts again, saying that this was our new home, and we were to buy it, not rent it. We went through the house and the yard, and we were certain that we wanted it. The owners were Asian, and Christian, praise the Lord. We made an offer and it was accepted, so we started packing in preparation for the move.

Not long after, Bill Castleman approached me and invited our family to join him and his family on a three-week vacation in Idaho. I said that the timing was not good because we would be moving during that time and thanked him anyway.

Then, after the movers moved everything in, we discovered that our new house was infested with cockroaches. They were everywhere, even some dead ones in the face of the built-in oven. How did we miss all this? God must have closed our eyes to it, for surely we would never have bought that house if we had known this.

We called an exterminator and he said that he would have to put a tent over the entire house and fumigate it for about a week. We took the clothes and other things we needed and left everything in their boxes, letting the "bomb squad" have at it.

Just in the nick of time I called Bill and asked if his offer to join them in Idaho was still open. He said that it was and that they were leaving in the morning to make the two-day trip.

We packed our things and off to Idaho we went, following Bill. He was going to stay at his in-laws' farm (Roland and Marry Meyer) in American Falls. We were invited to stay with them too, and we were looking forward to it, but on Saturday evening we got separated from Bill, took a wrong turn and had to backtrack a long way. We didn't show up until about 1 AM on Sunday morning, too pooped to pop.

Tired, worn out, and hungry, but happy to finally be there, we drove up the long drive to the huge farmhouse on several hundred acres of farmland. There to greet us were Bill, his wife Linda, and her mother Mary.

We had just started talking when Linda's sister came out and joined us, introduced herself, and said that I was scheduled to teach the adult Sunday school class at 9 AM. Thinking she was joking I laughed and said,

"No, I don't think so. We're here on vacation."

She went on to tell us she had recently returned from California and that she had attended one of my meetings. Small world, huh? I wondered, "Is God up to something we don't know about yet?"

She said that after Bill said we were coming with him she asked her Assemblies of God pastor, Pete Peterson, if I could teach the class and, guess what? He agreed, but, because we were on the road she couldn't tell me about it. I tried to get out of it, but she persisted, and I gave in.

I got about two hours of sleep. When I woke up, I dressed quietly and told Sue I'd be right back as soon as the class was over and that I'd get some rest then. She said something like "Oh, good, Honey," and went back to sleep. I slipped out the door and went to the church alone.

Pastor Pete sat in on the class, as I expected; after all, he didn't know me from Adam. When the class was over he told me that I'd be preaching that morning as well. I said I was exhausted from the trip, I'd only had a few hours of sleep, and I didn't want to do it. He wouldn't take no for an answer. He led me out to the sanctuary, introduced me to his wife and a few others, and told everyone that I was preaching this morning.

I preached that morning, that evening, and Monday, Tuesday, and Wednesday evenings as well, all in his church. On Sunday evening he told his congregation that they would be having 6:00 PM meetings Monday through Wednesday. He encouraged everyone to be there if at all possible and to invite their friends and neighbors as well.

The church was packed every night with both members and nonmembers. Sister Peterson was on the phone to every Assemblies of God church within a seventy-five-mile radius, and all but two of them scheduled me to preach. During this three-week vacation I had only three days off, and on the other days it was one or two meetings, lunches with pastors, and so on.

About a week or so into this "vacation" the Lord gave me a vision. I saw myself gathering a group of people together and physically building a church. Out of that group I saw other groups raised up that were affiliated with the first group. I saw joyful singing and dancing in praise to God as people became saved and filled with His Spirit.

I knew in my spirit that it was to happen here in Idaho, specifically in Pocatello. Ironically, Pocatello was one of the two cities that never did invite me to preach. In the vision I even had the name of this church: it was the Idaho Christian Center. I decided to tell no one except Sue about this vision. I'd just wait and see what God brought about. For the moment, I put it out of my mind.

When we went to Idaho, I didn't plan to teach a Sunday school class, or preach for that matter, much less pioneer a church. On top of all that, never in my wildest dreams would I have imagined that I would serve God in apostolic ministry, which you'll hear about later.

In Idaho for these three weeks I began to understand the workings of God in the recent past as He was preparing us for what was to come. Knowing that God plans and works out things better than I do, I decided to keep my fingers out of the pie and just let Him do it.

This book isn't big enough to tell you of all the miracles, salvations, rededications and other things that happened in all of those churches, but I want to mention a few.

Aside from the obvious spiritual and physical miracles, the pastors were telling me that they were seeing new life in their members that they hadn't seen for years. Their excitement was contagious and was producing new converts. I was told on numerous occasions that attendance was up not just from new people but because members came to church more often.

What I learned was that Idaho is mainly a farming state, and most farmers (as well as non-farmers for that matter) found it convenient to miss church when they didn't feel like going, especially if the weather was bad. Now all of that was beginning to change.

One of the churches I was called to preach in was the Assembly of God in Albion, Idaho, a small town about forty miles west of American Falls. The pastor's last name was Wonder and he liked to be called Brother Wonder. I thought it was kind of neat; here we are in the miracle working business and one of God's servants is named Wonder. It works for me.

It was on a Sunday morning, and as usual I sought God for the message He wanted me to preach to these people. Unless God tells me to, I never use some sermon I've preached elsewhere, no matter how good it was or how much response it produced from the people.

I had been seeking God all week for this church but I wasn't satisfied in my spirit that I had anything from God yet. All I had was John 3:16. So I asked Bill Castleman to drive me to the church and to pray like mad all the way there until I had a word from God. Bill was most willing to accommodate me and prayed softly out loud every mile we drove.

Mile after mile was the same. All I had was John 3:16, and I couldn't see anything that stood out for me to emphasize. I know this is one of the most powerful verses in the Bible, but I didn't have any unction from God concerning it that morning.

I cried out to God, "Please Lord, give me something for those people, anything," but no matter what I looked at in the Bible, I came up blank. I kept coming back to John 3:16. I became troubled, seeking harder and harder to hear from God, and now we were just a few blocks from the church.

John 3:16 is a familiar verse that says "For God so loved the world that he gave his only begotten son, that whosoever believes in him should not perish but have everlasting life."

I told Bill my plan. I would have him open up the service with his testimony and look my way every once in a while for a signal that I was ready. Then he was to turn it over to me.

All the while Bill was speaking, I was searching the Scriptures and praying. He spoke for ten minutes, then fifteen, then twenty. Sometime after thirty minutes, he ran out of things to say and turned it over to me. I still had nothing.

I approached the pulpit and began to confess that I only had one verse for them. I told them I had been seeking God for the entire week and all that came to me was John 3:16. I asked them to turn to the passage with me, and that's when it all happened.

As soon as I read the verse out loud, the Spirit of God hit me like a ton of bricks. The anointing was so strong I could hardly stand.

God pointed out the word *believeth*, whose biblical definition is, *trust in, rely upon,* and *cling to*. I expounded on the necessity of believing in Jesus, and that true Biblical believing is obedience to God and His Word.

Then the Holy Spirit spoke to my heart to turn to Luke 6:46. I read, "And why do you call me, Lord, Lord, and do not the things which I say?" The sermon then took a whole new turn and went in the direction of making Jesus *Lord* meaning Ruler and Master, and not just Savior.

Verse after verse came to me as God gave me direction, and the anointing got stronger and stronger. At the end of my sermon I asked for anyone present who had never made Jesus the Lord of their life, the Lord of their thoughts, words, and deeds, to come forward.

The entire congregation, with the exception of two young men sitting in the back, came forward, including the pastor, his wife, his elders, and his deacons. The two young men in the back who didn't come forward had entered the sanctuary soon after the service started, while Bill was speaking.

I looked at the people at the altar and figured that I must not have made myself clear. I asked everyone to please take their seats again. The second time I put forth the invitation in clearer terms, and the exact same thing happened again. I was befuddled, to put it mildly, and once again asked everyone to please go back to their seats again.

This time I spent a good deal of time explaining exactly what I meant, and for the third time I opened up the altar for those who had *never* made Jesus the *Lord* of their life. All but the two young men once again came to the altar and knelt for prayer.

I couldn't take it any longer. I said,

"Brother Wonder, surely you've done this already, haven't you?"

Humbly weeping and shaking his head, his response was a very emotional,

"No!"

Moved with compassion, I stepped down from the platform and instructed Bill to minister to the two young men in the back while I proceeded to pray with all those at the altar.

It was a glorious time of genuine weeping in repentance, receiving God's forgiveness and complete dedication of mind, body, and soul to Jesus, the master of the universe and the Savior of our souls.

At the close, Bill came forward and announced that the two young men had given their lives to Jesus and had accepted him as their Lord and Savior. This was the first and only time I've witnessed a move of God that so motivated and propelled an entire congregation in unison, and in such brokenness to dedicate heart-to-heart with God and to His Lordship. All glory to the One who sits on the Throne and Rules and Reigns from the Heavens.

Every church where I ministered received a love offering for me during each service. Every now and then someone would put some extra money in my hand. Never had I seen so much money appear in so short a time, there was almost—$4,000 there.

Most of the time I had Bill drive me to the meetings simply because he knew his way around and I didn't, so I always gave him half of the offering for his time and expenses. In every church where he assisted me I always had him share his testimony and help in prayer at the altar as well. I had taken him under my wing to train him in ministry as Paul trained Timothy.

I preached in the Assembly of God in Blackfoot, led by Rev. Richard Bradshaw. Blackfoot is a small town of about 4,000 about twenty miles north of American Falls and Pocatello.

I arrived a little early for the Thursday evening service, and Rev. Bradshaw and I talked about the order of the service. It was an off night—they usually met on Wednesday—and he didn't know how many would show up. I was there that night because I had no other opening that week.

It was a small group, but once again the anointing was very strong. After a few miracles happened at the altar, Rev. Bradshaw said he needed to see me and discuss something with me in private. I wondered what was up, he reassured me I had no need for concern, and I agreed to meet with him at a local restaurant, where he told me of a dream he had a few months before.

In this dream he saw a young man come to town with a new anointing for miracles that stirred the hearts of the people into a genuine, deep relationship with God. He also saw that this young man would pioneer an interdenominational Spirit filled church that would develop other churches as well. The frosting on the cake was that he was to help this young man in any way that he could to do the work that God was sending him out to do.

I just sat there in amazement as he expounded on his dream. It was as if he was present when God gave me the vision and gave it to him at the same time. I hung on every word as he spoke. Then he said,

"I need to know if you are the young man in my dream."

What could I say? I was so taken by it all that I couldn't even speak. He leaned forward, and stared into my eyes, and asked the question again. He seemed concerned because I hadn't responded. I apologized and tried to explain that I was so astonished my head was spinning. I settled down and told him of the vision God had given me; he pledged right there and then to help me in every way he could.

I felt he needed to know some things about me first, and that I needed to pray the whole thing through. I told him I wasn't even an ordained minister yet, nor was I a pastor of any church. I told him I'd be returning to California to submit to my Pastor and to have him and the elders pray on it. He agreed this was the right thing to do and that he would be praying for me as well.

Then he asked me to return the following week for another meeting—he was sure it would be a packed house this time. I agreed, and at the full-house meeting the following week the blessings of God flowed once again like a mighty rushing river.

The vacation came to a close, and Roland and Mary Meyer said that if we ever wanted to return to Idaho we were more than welcome to stay with them. They urged us to move to Idaho to teach, preach, and perhaps even start a church. They pledged their complete support, as did others in their family, if God led us in that direction.

With all that had happened during these three weeks, not to mention the vision and its confirmation, I couldn't wait to get home. I was so anxious to share with Pastor Stout and the elders that I could hardly sleep. Unknown to me though, I had a surprise waiting at home for me that caught me way off guard.

Chapter 10

The Mission, The Message, and The Means

It was a long trip home. I was like a kid waiting for a Christmas morning that doesn't come fast enough, full to the brim with the blessings and presence of God. In my mind I went over the vision God had given me, wondering how in the world I could do anything like that.

Nevertheless, I had a confidence beyond understanding that somehow I could do it, with God's help and leading, of course. I was sure of what God had shown me. He had confirmed it, and now my thoughts were focused on *how* and *when* to begin.

We arrived home with a pocket full of money, found that all the bugs were dead, and jumped right into a major house cleaning. We cleaned—every inch of that house. We washed and scrubbed floors, walls and ceilings; we shampooed all the carpets. I took the built-in oven apart and cleaned it, and we went over every inch of the kitchen.

We stayed in a motel while we cleaned and painted, set up beds, and so on. Then we began to unpack our belongings and move in. With the seven of us and a few other helpers we made quick work of it and settled back into our daily routine.

The first chance I had, I shared the vision I had in Idaho with Pastor Stout and the staff. I told them how God used me with all the churches and about the confirmation from the Blackfoot Assembly Pastor and his pledge of support for me. I shared that God wanted me and my family to move to Idaho and pioneer a church there.

To my surprise, the only person that showed any enthusiasm about it at all was Brother Fitts. I was disappointed, to say the least. The more we talked about it in that meeting, the more I could see that I was getting nowhere. In parting, Pastor Stout said that he would share it with the elders at the next meeting.

Thanks to Brother Fitts, who had trained me to submit to the leadership and not be afraid of trusting God through them, I had a settled peace about it all. I submitted, as I had been taught to do, and with a proper attitude too.

Sue and I decided to leave it with God to deal with. We believed He would show Pastor and the elders, and then surely they would support us. When we thought back on how God handled my job at Mother's Cookies, and many other things for that matter, we were confident that God didn't need any help from us on this one, either.

We went on as usual, carrying our assigned duties: teaching the Bible studies, cleaning the church, attending the usual meetings, all with joy and peace from on high. This went on for three months without a word from Pastor Stout about Idaho.

Then one night after the staff meeting, Pastor Stout asked me to remain for a few minutes. Privately he asked me if I had given any more thought to Idaho. I told him it was constantly on my mind and in my prayers. He asked what Sue and the kids thought about it, and I said they were all in favor of going.

Then he asked, "What do you believe God is saying to you about it?" I spared no words in expounding on my certainty that God wanted me to pioneer a church in Pocatello, Idaho, and that I was waiting on God to reveal the same to him and the elders.

Then he told me that he and the twelve elders had met again the night before about it and had come to a decision. He said their decision was unanimous. I was hanging on every word. He said that they knew I was to go, and they had decided to subsidize our Idaho ministry to the tune of $1,000 a month for a year to get it up and going.

Wow. I was ecstatic, and filled with such joy and gratitude that I lost control and hugged him as never before. I practically danced out of the church.

I got home and told Sue, and we talked about all the marvelous things that God had done and would be doing in the lives of two simple, undeserving people like us. We had no idea how all this would come about, and the more we thought about it, the less of a plan we had.

Brother Fitts and I met often, and even with all of his experience and wisdom, we still didn't come up with an image of what was going to happen. I began to realize that God would reveal His plan to me only as I took one step at a time in faith.

This was pretty scary for me. Even though I've seen God do great and mighty things in our lives, this was unchartered waters— the kind you can drown in.

Sue and I were sure of our mission, but we didn't know what to do first, what would make things happen. I mean, exactly how do you go about *planting* or *pioneering* a church? Talking it over with Pastor Stout and Pastor Fitts didn't help much either, they didn't know the first thing about Idaho or what we might be up against.

Pastor and the board of elders had committed to supporting us financially, but they didn't want to get involved in the mechanics of it. That led us to more prayer, and seeking God as to where to start.

After days of intense prayer, God led me to call the Meyers in Idaho and tell them the good news. They were elated and renewed their offer of lodging and help. I thanked them and told them we were praying to get the Lord's perfect will and timing and that I would be back in touch.

We had only been in our new house for four months, and it seemed as if one part of our life was tripping over another. We began asking God if we missed something or if we were moving too fast.

God began to move on my heart to test the waters, by taking a trip to Idaho to see how committed the people really were. I called the Meyers and told them of my plans, and they said they would pass the word around. They did some advertising and rented a chapel. When I arrived I held a week of meetings there.

About twenty people came to the first meeting. Roland and Marry and two others I knew were there. I welcomed everyone and introduced myself.

Immediately the Holy Spirit spoke to my heart. It was a word of knowledge. Someone had pain in their right shoulder, and God was going to heal it tonight. I shared the word, but no one responded. I shared again, still no response. I said it a third time and a woman in the front row elbowed her husband's side and said,

"What's the matter with you? You know he's talking about you. Why don't you say something?"

He looked frightened, looking back and forth from her to me. I went to him and said,

"Don't be alarmed, Sir. Do you have pain in your right shoulder?

A little reluctantly, he answered yes. I said,

"Sir, you don't have to do anything. I'm going to pray, and God is going to heal you."

I placed my hand on his shoulder and said, quite calmly,

"I the name of Jesus Christ of Nazareth, I command your shoulder to be healed and made whole, amen."

Then I asked him to move his arm in a position he hadn't been able to without pain. Slowly he began to raise it in the air. As he did his expression changed from fright, to delight. Soon he was waving it all around and saying there was no pain. He and his wife came to every meeting that week, all without any more pain.

Miracles were evident at every meeting, and I felt impressed to ask if anyone would be interested in hosting a home Bible study. Five people signed up, four couples and a single college girl in her mid-twenties.

We met and I told them I would commit to being in Idaho every other week to lead the study groups. Their job was to invite friends and neighbors and to have no less than five people attend the study group. If they couldn't get five couples or five nonrelated friends to commit, they were to call and let me know. Some of the groups met in the morning and some in the evening, depending on work schedules, and I showed up and taught and prayed for any needs.

Everything went as planned until I got to the college girl's home. The first thing I saw was that there weren't any cars out front or in the driveway. I began to think I was at the wrong address, but

I checked and I was at the right place. I parked in the driveway, and as I was getting out of my car the girl opened the front door.

Standing with her on the steps I asked if any others were here and she said that no one was able to make it. Then she said that she had prepared lunch and some dessert and that the two of us could study together, alone. Although I didn't feel that her intentions were pure, I also didn't want to accuse her of anything. I simply said,

"You're asking me to violate my principles and my convictions by being alone here with you, and I will not do that. If you can get a group together, call me and we can make arrangements, okay?"

Instead of letting it go at that, she tried again to persuade me to come in. I had to be firm and tell her how disappointed I was with her. Then I left, and I never saw her again.

Let me share with you another part of my personal life. My parents raised me to be modest and trusting, and, honestly, I'm a little too trusting. I need all the help I can get from God. When I married Sue I repeated my vows that I would not only remain with her, but be true to her all the rest of my life. This was more than just words to me, and I meant it with all my heart. By the grace of God I have never broken my vow, and I have never had a sexual relation with anyone other than my wife.

At this writing, in 2009, I am 69 years old. I have faced the same temptations that everyone else has, but God put it in my heart never to violate this precious trust between a man and his wife. I have often had the honor to instruct many teenagers and young adults alike to "keep yourself from immoral sex sins," for the Bible says they will eat you up like a cancer. This issue is addressed clearly in Proverbs 7 and in Galatians 5:19–21 and in 1 Corinthians 6:15–20, to mention a few.

Some people have called me old-fashioned and said I am not keeping up with the times. Call me what you like, I have peace with God and man, and I've never had to apologize to my wife and children for a moment of lust. For those who have fallen, there is forgiveness, and I preach this grace of God strongly and sincerely. But you must repent, never go back to that lifestyle, and separate yourself from *all* things that tempt you to. That includes getting rid of pornographic books, films, videos, CD's, magazines, Web sites, and perhaps even some of your friends. Don't stop there, but invite the Holy Spirit into your heart to empower you and keep you clean.

Concerning the planting of churches and doing the work of the ministry, I read the following passage in a book called *Power Through Prayer* by E. M. Bounds. He said,

> *The glory and efficiency of the Gospel are staked on the men who proclaim it. When God declares that 'the eyes of the Lord run to and fro throughout the whole earth, to show Himself strong in the behalf of them whose heart is perfect toward Him,' (2 Chronicles 16:9), He declares the necessity of men and his dependence on them as a channel through which to exert His power upon the world.*
>
> *This vital, urgent truth is one that this age of machinery is apt to forget. The forgetting of it is as baneful on the work of God as would be the striking of the sun from his sphere. Darkness, confusion, and death would ensue.*
>
> *What the Church needs today is not more machinery or better, not new organizations or more and novel methods, but men whom the Holy Ghost can use – men of prayer, men mighty in prayer. The Holy Ghost does not flow through methods, but through men. He does not come on machinery, but on men. He does not anoint plans, but men–men of prayer.*

With this vital truth, and the confirmation of the Word of God and the call of God on my life, I forged ahead to preach, teach, and win souls. I was confident that God would pioneer this church through me even in the absence of things that seem necessary for success. You see, I didn't know that I couldn't do it, so I just went out and did it.

Philippians 4:13 says, "I can do all things through Christ." It says *can*, not hope, not maybe. You see, success and victory comes in *cans* not can'ts. To be honest, I was only doing what I felt led to do as the Holy Spirit guided me.

Did it take faith? You bet it did. I wasn't going by any past experience; I was only following the Holy Spirit. I didn't fully realize at the time that this was all God wanted me to do, or expected me to do: just follow His lead.

I'll confess, I often felt that if I just had a manual on this thing of pioneering a church, I could at least know where I was going. But all I could do was follow what leading I had, moment by moment and day by day. That was a wonderful lesson that God taught me. Even now, after twenty-five years of church planting, the only manual I have, or need, is the Bible and the leading of the Holy Spirit by prayer, prayer, and more prayer.

Speaking of prayer, seminaries can't teach you how to pray; books can't teach you how to pray. The secret of prayer is to pray in secret. One of the most blessed things I learned in my early stages of ministry was that, although it is an awesome thing when God calls on a man and lays hold of a man, the even greater wonder is when a man calls on God and lays hold of Him.

One of these Bible studies was held at George and Cindy See's home. A young couple named Paul and Jeannie Neibaur attended and was obviously feeding on every word. Paul came from a Mormon family but became a Christian probably through Jeannie.

I was praying for people as usual, and Jeannie said that she was born with a short leg. She told how her mother always had to make one pant leg shorter than the other for her. So I asked her to lie down on the floor as straight as possible. Everyone could see that one leg was, quite a bit shorter than the other.

I instructed everyone to keep their eyes open during my prayer. I also said that no one was to touch Jeannie. This was an attempt to demonstrate that God will do the miracle all by Himself and that no tricks were used. As I prayed, her leg grew out slowly and steadily.

People began to gasp and raise their hands to their faces in awe. Jeannie became my personal church secretary and faithfully served in that capacity for many years. She even helped spell and grammar-check this book many years ago when I first started writing it. Her husband, Paul, a gifted peace maker, became a deacon, then an elder, and to this day both of them are good personal friends.

The very first week I was there I felt led to go to the local radio station, KWIK, and check on doing a short Sunday morning teaching broadcast. I hoped they would give me a discount.

They offered an 8 AM thirty-minute spot no charge. Wow. Did I hear that right? Yep. They said if I wanted it I could have it. Of course I wanted it. I jumped at it, but they didn't think that anybody would listen to teaching for thirty minutes straight and suggested I also play some Christian music. It sounded good to me, so we shook hands on the deal and set up the schedule.

They had a ton of Christian music at my disposal. I would take my place in the studio about 7:45 AM and wait for their On the Air signal and then do a live broadcast at 8:00. I made a recording for the following Sunday's program, along with the music in between, to be played the week I was back home in California.

No one but us insiders knew that the second program was recorded. The station said that they received calls on those Sundays from people wanting to talk to me, and they had to tell them I wasn't available to take calls.

As soon as my feet hit the ground in Pocatello I met with some strong resistance. I had never experienced such attacks. The obstacles and resistance to this new ministry of planting a church in Pocatello grieved my heart, but God kept prompting me to think back on the precise details He used to reveal His call on my life.

The Scripture the Lord gave me from the Amplified Bible mentioned a "special messenger." What did that mean for me?" I knew what it did *not* mean: someone special or superior. Over time, God revealed to me that this mission would include a special message.

The mission and the message were basically two parts of the whole, but more complex than I realized. To pioneer a church that would impact the entire city for Christ, was a given. I learned later it was only a by-product of the mission and the message. The main focus of this revelation was something God didn't show me until He knew I was ready.

The mission and the message were divided into two levels; the pastors of the evangelical churches, and the members. God had sent me to influence the pastors and the members in breaking down denominational walls of division. This was more than I bargained for, and way past my level of confidence, but no matter how things looked to me, I knew that God would not send me to do this work without a special anointing to accomplish it.

Pastors and believers in Idaho never asked each other "Are you a Christian?" If you weren't a Mormon they would ask if you wore the same label as them; "Are you a Baptist? Are you a Lutheran? Are you Assembly of God? Are you a Nazarene?"

If you answered no, you were held at arm's length. You were outside the circle. If this isn't a house divided, I don't know what is. Jesus said a house divided can't stand, and I could see that this house was in shambles. God help us! It's as Jesus said, "Ye blind guides, which strain at a gnat, and swallow a camel," (Matt. 23:24).

The apostle Paul rebuked the church at Corinth for the same spirit of division and labeling (1 Cor. 1:11–13 and 3:3–7). I would say to people, "So you're a Baptist, did the Baptist die for you? So you're a Lutheran, did Martin Luther die for you? No, Christ died for you, and that makes you a Christian. You belong to the whole body of Christ, no matter what label you or they cherish."

Romans 12:5 says, "So we, being many, are one body in Christ, and every one member's one of another." And again in 1 Cor.12:12–14, "For as the body is one and has many members, but all the members of that one body, being many, are one body, so also is Christ. For by one Spirit we were all baptized into one body—whether Jews or Greeks, whether slaves or free—and have all been made to drink into one Spirit. For in fact the body is not one member but many."

When believers march in submission and obedience to the

drumbeat of the blood-stained banner of Christ, they belong to God, and whatever belongs to God, belongs to the whole body of Christ.

For the record, we all have our likes and dislikes, our preferences. One style of worship fits me and may not fit another, that's fine, but let's not be exclusive, but inclusive. Even as Christians we can't all be right, and we can't all be wrong, but if we try, we can all get along.

Let's work together as much as possible and fulfill the command of Jesus, "A new commandment I give to you, that you love one another; as I have loved you, that you also love one another. By this all will know that you are my disciples, if you have love for one another," (John 13:34–35).

I realize that many pseudo-Christians occupy the pews of many or our churches, and Scripture says to rebuke them and be separate from them. That's because they practice ungodliness and refuse to repent and live for Christ, not because they don't agree with me in all doctrine.

"But now I have written to you not to keep company with anyone named a brother, who is sexually immoral, or covetous, or an idolater, or a reviler, or a drunkard, or an extortioner—not even to eat with such a person," (1 Cor. 5:11).

Also, "Do you not know that the unrighteous will not inherit the kingdom of God? Do not be deceived. Neither fornicators, nor idolaters, nor adulterers, nor homosexuals, nor sodomites, nor thieves, nor covetous, nor drunkards, nor revilers, nor extortioners will inherit the kingdom of God," (1 Cor.6:9–10).

You may be thinking, "Hold on a minute, Bob. If we don't have sinners in our church meetings, how can we get them saved?" That's just it. We have it all backward. The meeting of the saints is for prayers, teaching, praise and worship, not preaching, and not evangelism.

Preaching is for the lost, teaching is for the saints. Jesus said, "As you go, preach." Preaching is to be done in the market place, in the highways and byways, on the job, in the store, at your neighbor's house, and wherever the lost are.

In Matthew 28:19–20, Jesus said to first make disciples, second to baptize them, and third to teach them (the baptized disciples) to observe all things I have taught you. When we try to teach the deeper things of God to the unconverted sinner, we are going at it backwards; for without the Spirit they can't understand or receive the knowledge of God.

Yes, the apostles preached in the Synagogues and Temple courts, but that's where the lost were. The Synagogue and Temple meetings were not gatherings of Christians either, but Jews, and they needed to hear the Gospel, not the teaching the born again believer needs to hear.

Evangelism is to take place outside. The meeting of the saints, the believers meeting, is to be inside. Once the lost is converted, then and only then should they be invited into the believers meeting to take part of the teaching, and the sacraments, and to offer prayers, praise, and worship to God. But we have turned our church meetings into evangelistic meetings, and as was evident to the apostle Peter, we have "spots in our love feasts."

Jesus never told a Pharisee to stop being a Pharisee. He never told a Sadducee to stop being a Sadducee, but he did tell them to stop being hypocrites.

He told them to repent, to love God with their whole heart, mind, soul, and strength. He told them to stop making things so difficult for the people, by heaping upon them the traditions of men, and forsaking the commandments of God. They had shut-up the kingdom of God to others, and themselves. Sadly, this is the predominant world view of the Church today. We need a house-cleaning, a temple-cleansing. Will you join in and be part of it?

Okay, I'm off my soap-box.

Realizing God had chosen me to be the catalyst for unity among the churches, and not having a clue how or where to start; I left it with God, and went about my business. In time He showed me that the mission (unity) would be accomplished as I followed the guidelines of the church in the New Testament. Our fellowship was to be patterned after the Biblical pattern, and that would speak louder than any words simply spoken about unity.

Yes, we would have a building, but it would be used for

believer's meetings, not for evangelism. Granted, the lost filtered in, as is common in our day, and you can't stand at the door and refuse to let them in. They heard the unadulterated Word of God, experienced dynamic praise and worship, and saw miracles to boot. Many were saved and filled with the Holy Spirit, because they saw that our "religion" was real, and with power.

    The message was the easy part. I was to teach in-depth, the full Atonement of Christ, which includes the baptism with the Holy Spirit with visible miraculous signs following. This teaching would bring Christians into a deeper, fuller, more committed relationship with God.

    Also, it would produce the fruit of the Spirit in their lives and develop a boldness of faith for miracles that would be commonplace in their lives. This would be like a light in the dark, drawing bugs.

    I knew that as our new fellowship grew, we were to be humble and not prideful. We were to be gentle, loving, and gracious. Learning our Bible so as to know why we believed what we believed, we would be fully prepared to share our faith and knowledge with others in the power and love of the Lord.

    As the radio broadcast became more popular, I got a few threatening letters and phone calls. I was disappointed, but I could deal with it. It's always comforting to know that the devil is upset with what you're doing for Jesus. But what grieved me most was the discord and competitive spirit among the local pastors.

    There were two ministerial associations in town; one was liberal and the other conservative. I chose the conservative, but only about four or five ministers out of thirteen evangelical churches attended. There was very little love between them. For the most part, it was ineffective and unproductive, and I stuck out like a sore thumb.

    The irony was that before I arrived, some of the ministers were enemies, but now they put their differences aside, joined forces, and attacked me. It was much like the Scriptures say in James 3:14–16, "But if ye have bitter envying and strife in your hearts, glory not, and lie not against the truth. This wisdom descendeth not from above, but is earthly, sensual, devilish. For where envying and strife is, there is confusion and every evil work." It was obvious to me why so few ministers attended.

At first, I just kept my mouth shut. I was the new kid on the block and didn't want to make any quick moves. After a while, though, I was impressed that someone had to get this thing going in the right direction or this city was never going to see the full blessing of God.

The animosity between the Christians and the Mormons was bad enough, because hatred destroys, but to have such strong feelings of division when we're supposed to be on the same team was sad. As I analyzed all this, I could see this mountain had to be removed.

This was the most difficult part of the mission that God had for me. It took tons of prayer, tolerance, love, and work even to get the wheel moving in the right direction. I constantly cried out to God for prayer warriors. Our entire church was in constant prayer over this. At times I thought it was hopeless. It took almost ten years to see that mountain move.

In California, as a licensed minister, I attended the ministerial meetings with about twenty-five pastors from the churches in the area. Some were not of the full gospel persuasion. We had only three objectives: draw closer to God, draw the saints closer to God and pray for laborers to bring in God's harvest. Doctrine was not on the agenda; loving God and winning souls in the spirit of unity was.

I want to be clear: I'm committed to unity, but I do not believe in unity at *any* cost. When it comes to the nonessentials for salvation, I'm tolerant, looking for an opening to share the full gospel. But when it comes to the essentials of salvation by grace through faith, that's another thing, and I'll go toe-to-toe with anyone on that.

If someone wants to argue doctrine with me just to have an argument, I have no time for it. That's what the devil wants us to do so that he can cause discord and division among the brethren and keep us from building up the Body of Christ.

I have had many discussions with pastors and others over differences in doctrine, but all are in the spirit of research and learning, rather than attack and division. Even Brother Fitts and I, as close as we are, don't agree on every little thing. Be assured of this one thing though: we are committed to unity. If one of us gets off track, the other can bring him back on line because of our mutual respect and love for each other.

One of the things that I loved about Pastors Stout and Fitts was that they always sought for unity and love among the brethren. They always said they were not interested in stealing anyone's sheep but only in helping people grow in the Lord.

A well known prophet of God, Rev. Dick Mills, said, "You must be winsome, if you are going to win some." A verse in Proverbs says, "A brother offended is harder to be won than a strong city."

In Pocatello in 1975, it was difficult for the pastors even to pray together. At one meeting, one of the ministers mentioned bringing in Rev. Billy Graham for some evangelistic meetings. One of the ministers said that if *he*, pointing at another minister, was going to be a part of it, then he wanted nothing to do with it, and he stormed out of the room. That ended that.

As the years rolled by in Pocatello, some of the ministers who refused to get with the program of unity were being replaced by new ministers. Eventually we had ten or twelve ministers meeting monthly for prayer. We prayed to draw closer to God, to draw the believers closer to God, and to win (and disciple) souls for Christ.

These monthly prayer meetings then rotated from church to church, which was a great step forward. As the old guard was replaced, most of the new pastors also desired unity, and their contribution was refreshing, helpful and fruitful. In the early 1980s, we began to have special services at one or another of the churches. Victory in Jesus is so sweet.

I went to Idaho to pioneer a church, but I made clear from the outset that I had no intention of drawing people away from other churches, known as stealing sheep. I wanted visitors, especially the Assembly of God people, to hear this from my own mouth, but I want to say more about stealing sheep.

I believe a local church can be compared to a restaurant. If the food is good, people will go there to eat and tell their friends about it. If the food isn't good they'll not only tell their friends about it, but look for another restaurant.

So it is with a church: if you are well fed with solid teaching, worship, and miracles, you'll stay. If not, you'll look for another church. When the sheep are moving of their own accord, it isn't stealing. Besides, the sheep don't belong to anyone but God: they're the sheep of His pasture.

Because I was totally committed to winning people to Christ, and wanted others to catch this evangelistic vision with me, I didn't need to steel any sheep, but when it came to soul-winning in Idaho, I was in for an education. In California it was easy, but here in Pocatello—let's just say it was easier said than done.

This was Mormon country, and trying to get people to witness to their friends and neighbors was like telling them to jump off a cliff without a parachute. Wherever I was, in a store, at the mall, doing business with someone or whatever, I was telling people about Jesus, our church, and the vision God had given me concerning unity among the believers.

Once in a while someone would go out with me to share the Gospel, and I would encourage them to "do the work of the ministry for the edifying of the Body of Christ," as it says in Ephesians 4:12.

It's the saints, or believers who are commanded to "do the work of the ministry," not the apostles, prophets, evangelists, pastors or teachers.

I had never seen so many Mormons in one area. Pocatello has a higher percentage of Mormons than Salt Lake City has. At least half the people I would approach were Mormons. This was all new to me, but I knew that God was "for us and not against us," as Romans 8:31 says. I never forgot to thank God for the training about Mormonism that He led me into back in California, living next to the Peelers. Yes. God does all things well, and His timing is perfect.

When I moved to Idaho to pioneer a church, I realized that God was providing the means: workers, open doors, wisdom, anointing, and finances. I took one step at a time as He guided me. It was risky, but I didn't care. I was absolutely sure of my calling. I took courage in the fact that God would not leave me out there to be made a fool of and not accomplish what He wanted done through me.

When I looked back on how God audibly called me to the

ministry and the exact verse He spoke to me, had it not been for such a dynamic experience, I might have bagged it all, tucked tail, and gone home. Why? Because it was tough work: emotionally, spiritually, and physically.

I traveled back and forth every other week for three months before I moved to Idaho. Sue and the kids remained in California, as our house was now for sale. I stayed with Roland and Mary Meyer, and they treated me like a king.

The Episcopal pastor in Pocatello, one of the few who accepted me early on, supported our ministry by renting the ISU Campus Chapel to us for $35 a month. What a blessing he was. At the time they had no campus minister, so it stood empty and unused.

It only held about 80 people, but it was a good start. At the beginning we had no Sunday school, no song leader other than me, no hymnals or song books, and no musical instruments. We did have a nursery, praise God.

After about six weeks Sue and the kids made a trip to Idaho to visit. It was good to be back with the family; I really missed them, but God had called us all to a short-term sacrifice that would pay benefits down the road. They stayed for a week, and then returned to California to maintain our house.

Sue hated to drive and this was a long two-day trip each way, about fifteen hours. She drove halfway and then spent the night in a motel with five children ages five to thirteen. The beautiful thing was that our children were disciplined and well-behaved. Often, after being in a restaurant for an hour or more, people would stop and comment on how quiet and well-behaved they were.

The church became a non-profit 501(c)3 corporation in 1975, the same year I returned to California and became an ordained minister of the Gospel of Jesus Christ.

I named the church Idaho Christian Center (ICC) as I had received in the vision. We grew in size and spiritual strength as did the Bible studies. We had a Wednesday morning group in Jim and Denise Estel's home and Bible book Store in Blackfoot. We had two evening groups in Pocatello and one in American Falls.

We had a few people coming from Ashton (about seventy-five miles north of Pocatello) Idaho Falls (fifty miles north) Blackfoot (twenty-five miles north) and American Falls (twenty miles west) to our Sunday morning and evening services in Pocatello.

At one of our morning worship services, while I was greeting the people as they arrived, a woman named Unice Neu whispered in my ear, pointing at her son David,

"He sings."

I thought to myself, "Oh no, another mother who thinks her kid can sing."

I took a liking to this young man and his wife Claudia, who had a gentle, sweet spirit about her. One evening they invited me over for dessert and coffee and I jumped at the offer. During our visit, Claudia mentioned that Dave could sing and offered to play a tape of one of his performances. I said I would love to hear it.

Before Dave had sung four or five lines, my breath left me, and I was in awe. He could do more than just sing; his voice was one of the most beautiful I had ever heard. It can lift you right up to the throne of glory. Waves of the Spirit's anointing rolled over me again and again.

Another thing, Dave could sing a cappella better than most professionals can sing with a million dollars worth of accompaniment. Without hesitation, I asked him to sing in church, and he accepted my offer.

On Sunday morning I announced to the fellowship that Dave Neu was going to sing for us, even though we didn't have any accompaniment. The majority of the people didn't know Dave or his singing ability, but when he started singing, everyone was awe struck as I had been.

As time went on, Dave sang in many local churches, held Christian concerts, and even made professional recordings that sold in various Christian bookstores. Dave became one of my deacons and later on an elder. He was an eloquent preacher and teacher of the Word, and highly admired by the fellowship and the community. To this day this precious couple remains very close, personal friends.

When Dave and Claudia lived in Pocatello they would come over to the house and stay until about one or two in the morning. We talked about the Bible and the Christian life and would cook up some thick juicy steaks with all the trimmings and have a feast.

Sue and I really miss those days. We drew from them such wisdom, strength and true companionship; Claudia was just the perfect friend for Sue, and Dave is a genius, as far as I'm concerned, someone I needed and enjoyed having at my side. We could always count on their support. They are good people. I repeat, just good, honest, faithful, down-to-earth, good people.

By this time I was teaching Bible studies in Rockland (population a few hundred), American Falls (two thousand), Blackfoot (four thousand), Inkom (five hundred), and Pocatello (forty-five thousand) along with a number of counseling appointments during the week.

The radio broadcast was all live, an hour long from 8:00 to 9:00 AM and, still free, glory to God. With only an hour between the radio broadcast and the morning service at 10:00, it was a wild rush home to get Sue and the kids. We had an evening service at 6:00 PM, and I was beginning to suffer physically.

I learned that in Idaho, people are rather territorial. All you see between cities is potato and wheat fields for twenty or thirty miles. The people are brought up to go to church in their own city or they're seen as traitors. This brought pressure on many families and friends to remain loyal to the church in their own town.

In winter when the roads were covered with snow and ice, our attendance went down. The fifty-mile, one-hour drive from Idaho Falls could take two hours in severe conditions. Very few would brave it, especially those with small children, and I didn't blame them.

Once when the weather was severe I could only drive about five miles an hour in blowing snow. It wasn't falling; it was gusting horizontally across the road. I had to lower my window to see the center line on the road. The wind chill factor was thirty degrees below zero and my heater was blowing cold air on my feet. The following morning, my tires were frozen to the concrete in the carport. I had to break them loose with a sledgehammer before I could move the car.

People would come to me and apologize for not being able to attend Sunday services because of the pressure from family and friends. I consoled them, prayed for them, and told them to take it to the Lord and trust Him to work it out.

Some said their church was dead, the worship service was lifeless, the preaching was dry, and there were never any miracles. I could see that these people were in as much bondage as the Mormons were; it was just a different kind of bondage.

This is one reason why church growth was a lot slower than it would have been in California. An even more important reason was that most Christians here were too intimidated by Mormonism to go out and share their faith, or even invite others to church. I could see that I had my work cut out for me. The work that the Lord called me to do in Idaho was a special work, and only later would I fully understand it.

After about six months, many of these people couldn't take it any longer and made the drive to Pocatello to join the outpouring of the Holy Spirit.

A number of them confessed to me that they had been sitting in church for a number of years, some all their lives, singing lifeless songs, listening to dead sermons, and never seeing any miracles.

Then there were a few who told me that they had attended church for years, and were very religious, but never saved until they came to ICC. They would tell us that our worship service was heavily anointed, that it was like singing with the angels. They were learning things from the Bible that they never would have imagined possible and were beginning to know *why* they believed *what* they believed. Soon they were memorizing Scripture verses right and left, which changed their lives dramatically.

The house back in California finally sold and now my family was preparing to join me in Pocatello. Along with everything else I was doing, I started looking for a house to rent.

We needed at least three bedrooms, and I wanted something warm and cozy. I was in for a shock. After looking through real estate ads for about three weeks and coming up with nothing to even look at, I sought advice.

Every three to five years in Pocatello, it came about that there were more people than housing. The only way to get a rental was to pay a fee to an agency that put you on their client list. I paid the fee and was listed as number twenty-five, way down at the bottom of the list. In the meantime, I kept on looking.

Finally our name came up on the list and the agent had two places to show me. They were dumps, horrible, and I couldn't see how any landlord could even think of renting them. The agent said that if I refused them someone else would rent them and I'd have to wait for something else to become available. I passed on it and went into prayer again. Now I only had a week before Sue and the kids would arrive.

The agent called to tell me about an old, run down house with only two bedrooms. It was the only thing available, so I took it, praying that something better would come up, and we moved in.

The boys had to sleep in the living room, and as the winter closed in on us, the house got colder and colder. We soon learned that the house had no insulation in the walls and the front and back doors leaked air all around them, especially at the threshold. The kitchen window would not close all the way and left a small open area at the bottom.

Numerous calls to the landlord did no good at all, and he said that the condition of the house was why the rent was so low. It wasn't low at all; in fact, it was quite high, and the only reason he could get that much for it was the poor housing market at the time.

Concerning the kitchen window, we just had to plug the hole, and, on top of it all, the house smelled old and musty. There was a bad odor coming up from the unfinished basement, which had a dirt floor. Later we learned that the people before us had pet monkeys and kept them down there.

Looking at this, my mind went back to Mexico, where the chickens were on the kitchen countertops, and the open sewage in the streets. We weren't far from that right here on Buell Street in Pocatello.

Brother Fitts was getting requests from other ministers and friends to make a trip to Manila, in the Philippines. He told them about me, and they wanted me to come along with him. It would be a seventeen-day trip with a twenty-seven hour flight one way with layovers.

Two things excited me about it that made me say yes. One was that we were invited to preach and teach in Catholic churches, as well as homes, on the baptism with the Holy Spirit and the gifts of the Spirit, and to pray for the sick.

The other was that we would be able to investigate the so called-faith healers who claimed to perform surgery without leaving any mark of the incision. Faith healing surgery turned out to be fake, nothing but sleight-of-hand. I took still and video pictures from behind them that showed the trickery, methods and props that they used to deceive people.

We preached two or three times a day, thanks to the women who set up everything with the priests and home study groups. Some home groups were as large as twenty-five people, and they treated us like kings and fed us some of the best meals I've ever eaten.

One time we all went to an upper-class Chinese restaurant in downtown Manila. I like Chinese food, but this was different. You know, I can't believe that people eat some of that stuff. The waiters brought deep fried chicken feet that still had the toenails on them, fish-eye soup, and I won't even mention some of the other things. But, glory to God; we saw a ton of miracles, salvations, baptisms, and deliverance from superstitions and demonic oppression. It sure was good, though, to get back home and off of that cramped Airplane.

Get ready now; here we go with the next big miracle.

With the housing market like it was, and being so disappointed with the house on Buell Street, we continued to cry out to God. He had to have something else for us. One day He led me to look for a lot where we could build a house. There were plenty of lots for sale, and I would stop and look at one and then sit in my car and pray about it. This went on for a week or so.

Then while driving up on Freemont hill I came to Oasis Street, and I saw a number of lots for sale. At one the Holy Spirit spoke to my heart and said this lot was mine. It gently sloped up in the back, and there was a large open field behind it that went a thousand feet or so to the top of the hill. I jotted down the lot number, street, and the agent's name, and off I went to his office.

I asked for the agent I wanted to see and found I was already talking with him. I told him about the lot and said I wanted to put a down payment on it. He looked it up and said it was already sold and they hadn't put a Sold sign on it yet.

I proceeded to tell him that God had told me that it was mine and I wanted to give him some money to hold it for me. He just laughed and said that a prominent and wealthy person had bought the lot and he was absolutely sure that the sale would go through.

I very kindly told him that I knew the sale wouldn't go through and that I also knew the lot was mine. He became angry and almost left me standing there alone in the front office. I tried to put him at ease. I took my card out of my wallet and handed it to him. He took a deep breath and said he couldn't take any money on the lot, because it was against the law.

I said I understood, and in the event the sale happened to fall through, would he please call me first. He reiterated that he knew it wouldn't fall through, but he took my card.

I drove away in perfect peace knowing in my spirit that the lot was mine and felt no need to call the fellowship or anyone else together to pray about it. Sue and I thanked God each day saying "Thank you Lord for this lot you have given us." It was a case, not of asking God in prayer for something, but of praising Him for what He has already said is yours.

A week or so later, my phone rang. You guessed it again. Boy, reader, you're getting pretty good at this. The agent sheepishly said that somehow the sale had fallen through and if I was still interested I could come down and place a deposit on the lot. I told him I'd be right there. With a meek and gentle spirit, for God has no place for pride or arrogance, I pulled out my checkbook, wrote a check for $10.00, and handed it to him.

He took one look at it and said,

"Ten dollars? you've got to be kidding. You can't hold this property for ten dollars!"

I told him I didn't get paid until next week and this was all I had for now. He became quite heated, but finally accepted my check. He made it clear that this would hold the property only until next week, when I would pay the remainder of the down payment. I kept my word, and the property was now officially ours. Isn't God wonderful?

Now let's admit it, that's a pretty good story, but here we go again with the rest of the story.

Sue and I looked through the phone book for a contractor. We didn't want a Mormon; we hoped there was a Christian. We felt impressed to call a contractor by the name of Erhardt Andersen.

He invited us to his home and, eager to witness to him, I asked if he was a Christian. He said that he was. He and his wife, Inga, attended the Lutheran church in town. After some discussion we settled on a plan that had four bedrooms, two baths, a living/family room, a two-car garage, and a basement 2,500 sq. ft. in all.

I told him I had done some construction and could help out. I also had a plumber in the fellowship who would donate his labor, and the heating and air conditioning would be donated by our good friends Charlie and Linda, who owned Lotshaw Heating & Air in California. We drew up a contract with Erhardt for $27,500 and shook on the deal.

We went to the bank and made application for a construction loan. We only asked for $30,000, but after reviewing our building plans the bank decided to put $58,000 in a construction account to cover their appraisal price.

We started building immediately, and things progressed rapidly. Erhardt was a well-respected contractor in town, and although he didn't move at a fast pace, he could do the work of two men. The work he did was perfection perfect, just like an old-time Danish craftsman. He had one part-time helper along with me and my family, and I did all the electrical work and helped form and pour the concrete basement walls.

While we were building the main floor joists and installing the floor sheathing, another payment for the lot came due. We didn't have the money in our checking account to make the payment, so I went to the bank where we had the construction loan and asked the manager if he would let me use some of the construction loan money to make the lot payment.

He came unglued. He jumped up out of his chair shouting, "You mean to tell me that the lot isn't paid off? You can't build on a lot that isn't paid for!"

I stood there speechless. He asked me what the balance was on the lot, and I handed him the contract. He and another bank employee made a phone call and did some figuring. Then they wrote out a check to the real estate company for the entire balance. They gave me the check and some other papers and told me to go right over, pay it off, and get the paperwork done at the title company.

Reader, I can hear you saying, "You mean that the bank never checked to see if you owned the lot outright?" That's right, and I never gave it a thought either. Good thing God's in charge, isn't it? You know, He's so good it just tickles me pink!

We finished the house in seventy-two days. It was an absolute joy to move in, not only because of all the space it had, but it was clean and airtight. By the way, we built the house for $29,357. Thank you, Jesus, for everything!

Easter Sunday came, and it was time for church. The building was packed out. One of our members was an advertising salesman employed at the radio station (KSEI) in Idaho Falls, and he arranged to do a live service over the radio that would incorporate both KWIK and KSEI. He, and a few helpers, set up the equipment and tested it, and when they gave me the signal, I was on the air.

The Lord had led me to preach on the crucifixion of Christ in graphic detail. This wasn't the usual resurrection sermon on a happy Easter-egg-hunt day. One thing I knew for sure, if God wasn't in this one hundred percent, the service would be a total flop. This drove me deep into prayer, seeking His perfect will.

During the months of preparation, the Lord had spoken clearly to me about this service. He gave me a number of graphic mental pictures that I was sure, with the help of the Holy Spirit, could be indelibly painted in the minds and hearts of the fellowship.

I started preaching, first laying a foundation, and when I got into the heavy stuff I began to weep. I had cried a number of times during the preparation of the sermon, and I thought it was done with. As I continued, I cried even more. I wasn't the only one weeping; many in the fellowship were too.

It got to the point that I could hardly speak. I just mumbled a few words here and there. I felt agony in my heart, in my spirit, as I envisioned the crucifixion of Jesus. The Holy Spirit took me, and the people, deep into the event so vicariously that almost everyone was crying in repentant sympathy and adoration to God.

We were all being broken and changed by His sacrifice and love. When I got to the end, I said that the beating with the cat-o'-nine tails that ripped his back to shreds didn't kill Jesus, and the railroad spikes driven through his hands and feet didn't kill him either.

No, Jesus died of a broken heart, broken over you and me. It's a fact that the sac around his heart filled with fluid to the point that his heart was crushed. The pain that he suffered in his body, as severe as it was, was nothing in comparison to the pain he suffered in his crushed and broken heart over you and me.

The altar call was right there in the pews, everyone broken, crying, repenting, and pledging their allegiance to the creator of all things, Jesus.

During the next week many people of other churches, as well as some pastors, told me it was one of the best sermons they'd ever heard. I even got calls from some Mormons who said they were strongly moved by my message. They said they weren't supposed to listen to our broadcast, but they were thankful that they did.

A few others told me they had even missed their own church service because they just couldn't leave the radio broadcast.
This is what God can and will do if we just cooperate with Him, follow His will, and let Him have these earthen vessels to use for His glory. All praise to His glorious name.

I was stoked for the following Sunday, and the little chapel was packed to overflowing. We started a Junior Church for ages five and up during the service in a building down the street, so as to have more seating for the adults. As time went on, the Holy Spirit got sweeter and sweeter, and miracles were as regular as clockwork.

But one Sunday, right before the sermon, the devil dropped a bomb on us that changed everything.

---------- *Chapter 11* ----------

Attacks, Obstacles, Challenges, Robbery and Blessings, Too

The service opened as usual with a heavy anointing of praise and worship. As the worship was coming to a close, an usher called me to the chapel entrance door. When I got to the door I saw a man outside in priestly clothing motioning for me to come outside.

I didn't recognize him as any of the local pastors, but I approached him with my usual big smile. I introduced myself and put out my hand to greet him. He looked down at my hand in disgust and said,

"I want you out of my Chapel when your service is over, and you can't use it anymore! Do I make myself clear?"
I tried to regain my composure as I said,
"Do I know you?"
He said no and told me he was the new campus minister. The chapel was his, and we couldn't use it any more. He turned and left without saying goodbye.

This encounter knocked me for a loop. The thing that I couldn't understand was how a man of God could treat me and our fellowship like that. How could a minister throw other Christians out in the street with no warning? Where would we go? Where can we find a place in one week?

I did my best to hide my emotions, because I didn't want to put a damper on the service, but I knew I had to inform the fellowship that we needed a new place to worship and we needed it fast! It was very cold outside. We needed a proper building. I put my sermon aside and told the fellowship what had happened. We discussed some possibilities, said some prayers, and sang a few more songs of praise before we left the chapel for good.

During the following week people checked out anything that even looked like it might work: large homes, the senior center, store fronts. The only thing available that looked like it might be suitable was the Irvine Junior High School auditorium. It was large, with theater type seating, a large platform, a podium, and a built-in sound system. The auditorium sat empty most of the time, used only on special occasions, and never on Sunday.

The building was old, but it was well kept up and the rent was within our means. There was plenty of parking on the street, and across the street. We told the school principal about our service times, Sunday morning and evening only wanting to make sure we had heat. He gave me the janitor's name and phone number and said he'd know we'd be there on Sunday. We got the word out to the fellowship in every way we could think of trying not to miss anyone.

Sunday morning I arrived at our new facility early to pray, as I always did. I unlocked the door and got hit in the face with a blast of air that felt like it came from the North Pole. I went to the wall thermostat and it read a frigid *thirty-eight* degrees! I tapped on the thermostat to see if it was stuck, but it didn't move. Had the janitor forgotten to turn on the heat? I got out my little phone directory and gave him a call, and he said he had turned the heat on at 6 AM.

He explained that it takes a while to heat that large room with its twenty-five-foot ceiling. I asked him if he could turn the furnace up higher, and he said it was already up all the way. The furnace was an old boiler system with heat radiators all along the walls of the auditorium. I walked around touching the radiators to see if they were working. They were so hot you couldn't keep your hand on them. It was going on 9:30, and the thermostat had inched up to thirty-nine degrees, no higher. Church would begin in thirty minutes.

The people began to pour in, and got the shock of their lives. Nobody took their coats off. One woman was wearing a mini-skirt (in that frosty weather!?). When she sat down on the cold seat, she jumped up again and just stood for a while.

I explained the situation to everyone and we all agreed to not let the devil have the victory, and to go ahead with the service. We opened with a prayer and sang a while, but it was so cold in there I could hardly turn the pages of my Bible. I began to shiver, along with everyone else, so we closed the service early and determined to make sure it didn't happen again. A committee was formed to look into the heating and because we couldn't use the classrooms we continued looking for another building.

The following Sunday it was a different story. I opened the door and another blast of frigid air hit me. "What's this?" I thought, "How can this be?" I looked at the thermostat, and this time it read forty-five degrees. I called the janitor, and he said he had turned the heat on 3:00 AM. The up-shot was that the principal would not allow the heat to be turned on the day before just for us. His reasoning, it took so much coal that it was cost-prohibitive.

A number of people who came said they were sorry but they just couldn't take it again. They turned around and went home. I learned real soon that this church planting thing is not all fun and games. Sometimes it's the hardest thing you'll ever do.

My wife and children were beginning to suffer under all that was happening, but what else can we expect when we're at war with the devil over souls? He attacked God in the heavens, he attacked Jesus in the wilderness, and he's attacking the church, you and me, right here and now.

As recorded in Romans 8:37, "We are more than conquerors through Jesus" and in 2 Corinthians 10:4–5, "The weapons of our warfare are not of flesh and blood but are mighty through God to the pulling down, overthrow, and destruction of strongholds." Sometimes Satan wins a battle here or there, but don't ever forget this; he will never, never win the war. Praise God!

We found a store front right on the main drag in town on Yellowstone Avenue, the newer part of town, and the rent was reasonable. But we did need to do some remodeling for classrooms and an office for me. This only took a few weeks, thanks to all the help from the fellowship and one of our members who was a contractor.

Surprisingly, we did a fantastic job of it. While still in the school auditorium we settled with the principal to pay whatever it cost to allow the heat to be started well enough in advance for comfort, and it did pay off while preparing our new place, thank God.

A week before moving into our new facility, I met Jim Spencer, a former Mormon elder, who had become a Christian while reading the book of Romans. It completely freed him of all the bondage of legalism and false religion, but it thrust him into an attack from Satan that threatened his marriage and his future.

After talking with him and hearing his testimony. I asked him to share all that he had told me with our fellowship at a Sunday night service. He accepted, and it was a moving experience. We became close friends, and he grew so mightily in the Lord and His grace that he pioneered a church in Idaho Falls called Shiloh Foursquare Church. Later he became a district superintendent with the Foursquare Gospel Church, Inc.

He went on to develop a ministry to Mormons called "Through The Maze," which is still going strong all over the nation and perhaps the world.

He has written a number of books, and his first, *Beyond Mormonism*, is riveting. I read it from cover to cover in one sitting and knew right then that Jim was called of God to a work that very few are called to do. His website is **www.beyondmormonism.com.**

I strongly suggest that even if you have no interest in Mormonism for the moment, look into it, not just for your own sake, but for someone God may put in your path someday. Remember, in 2 Timothy 4:2, God commands us to be prepared with the doctrine of the Gospel of Jesus Christ in season and out of season.

We moved into the store front on Yellowstone and grew so much that we bought a sixty-six passenger used school bus. We transported people from Idaho Falls, Blackfoot, and Fort Hall to Pocatello for the morning services. Brother Jim Estel not only drove the bus but also did all the upkeep on it.

Denise Estel set up a book ministry within the sanctuary for people who wanted Christian books or who couldn't make it to her bookstore in Blackfoot. These are fine, dedicated and committed people who love Jesus with all their hearts. Jim has a precious spirit not often seen in men and will often weep at the mention of the love and grace of God.

He became a deacon and then an elder, and later I appointed him superintendent of our Christian school (K–12). Yes. You heard it right. We started an Accelerated Christian Education school called River of Life Christian School.

Sue taught the kindergarten class. Neither of us had any formal training in education, but the ACE foundation in Texas trained us in running an ACE school. On our return to Pocatello we took the plunge, as we seem to be doing all the time.

The school had forty-two students, and by the time Sue had finished the first year of kindergarten, her students knew all their phonics and could spell and read near the first grade level. A few made it to the second grade level.

The tuition was kept low, and the church fellowship subsidized the school and a few families who couldn't afford full tuition. Teachers were paid a salary, but teaching was more a volunteer service than a job.

None of the teaching staff, including my family, ever got free or discounted tuition. I received no salary from the school, and Sue was the lowest paid teacher on staff at $100 a month.

The local public school superintendent, along with his assistant, came unannounced into our school one day demanding to see me. In front of all the students and teachers, he told me in no uncertain terms that we could no longer continue with our "illegal" school.

I ushered him into my office, reprimanded him for his unprofessional actions, and sat down to talk with him. ACE training had taught me that he couldn't shut us down, but I showed respect for him as a person and as a public school official. Remember, I learned to maintain an attitude of respect when I was at Mother's Cookies, and I thanked God once again for the lesson.

I knew this attack was spiritual, that Satan was behind it all. When the devil comes against me with this kind of attack, I realize immediately that he wants me to get angry and start mouthing off.

That will only quench the Holy Spirit, and launch me into a battle with the flesh.

It isn't easy to stay in control, and I haven't always had the victory, but when I do, it pays big dividends. I'll admit, my old nature would've loved to call these guys a few choice names, but then I would be guilty before God, and have lowered myself to that of a common heathen.

Once as I read about Michael the Archangel and Satan having a dispute over the body of Moses in Jude verse 9, the Holy Spirit showed me that Michael didn't make any railing accusation against Satan but simply said, "The Lord rebukes you." If it's good enough for an archangel, it's good enough for me.

Satan may be our enemy, but nowhere in the Bible are we given the right to defame or slander him or his God-ordained position. The same goes for our conduct among others. Scripture says "Let no corrupt communication proceed out of your mouth," (Ephs. 4:29). Such conduct will only discredit us, grieve the Spirit of God, and quench the flow of His love and power in our life.

I hear Christians call Satan derogatory names, but that, my friend, is contrary to the Scriptures and Christian conduct. You only need to call him to the attention of the "name that is higher than any other name under heaven," Jesus! Another thing, remind Satan of the three words uttered by Jesus on the cross, words Satan has never gotten over: *"It is finished!"*

If you're under the authority of Jesus, you can say, or even whisper, "Satan, I rebuke you in the name of Jesus!" After that, you can walk away with a smile on your face, and the victory in your hand.

The public school system pressed down on us with relentless force. Soon it was costing me and the entire staff a lot of time and effort to counter their attacks, and we were becoming weary, but shortly God came to our aid.

A couple came to my office with their two boys about seven and nine. The seven year-old, Billy, was missing about half of the side of his face from his cheek-bone down to his neck. He could hardly speak clearly enough to be understood. I'm a big softy, as you may have noticed, and when the compassion washed over me the tears began to flow. When his mother said his name I called him to me, inviting him to sit on my lap. I wanted to show him that I accepted him as I would any other child.

Billy was shocked, unsure of me, and he looked over at his mother. When she said it was all right, he still hesitated. I could see that he wasn't accustomed to such acceptance from strangers.

He finally came to me, and I lifted him up and put him on my left knee. He was still hesitant, and I said a few gentle words to him and went on talking with his parents. They told me that the public school couldn't help him because of his physical deformity and inability to communicate. The other kids made fun of him and called him "freak" and "monster."

This ripped my heart, and the longer we talked, the closer I hugged Billy, letting him know that he was with a friend. He just stared at the floor until he saw a tear fall from my eye. When he saw that my eyes were full of tears, he put his right arm around me and hugged me real tight, saying something I couldn't understand.

I asked his mother what he was saying, and her words broke me to the core.

"He's telling you that it's all right, God will make everything work out okay, and don't cry."

I couldn't take it any longer. I broke down in tears, wrapped my arms around him and hugged him and told him that I loved him very much. We just hugged each other and sort of rocked back and forth in my chair. He cried and kept telling me that he loved me. That settled it; the boys were enrolled immediately.

From the first day the boys were well accepted by all the students and teachers. They did exceptionally well academically and socially, and we learned how to communicate with Billy. He was a joy and an inspiration to all of us.

Next, a Mormon couple came to us with their two daughters, seven and ten. The seven year old was academically challenged and had been told by the public school system that she was retarded and couldn't succeed. The sad thing is that her parents believed it too.

They told us right out that she was retarded and couldn't learn like the other kids. We observed the child and saw that she didn't have any of the usual signs of retardation. Academically challenged, yes, but retarded? We didn't believe so. To us it seemed that the family had been brainwashed. The child was still in kindergarten at seven and would stay there another year if she remained in school at all.

The parents pleaded with us to give her a chance. After considerable discussion and sharing about our Spirit-filled Christian school, including a robust kindergarten program, they enrolled both of their girls.

It was a tough row to hoe. We had to pray constantly over this younger girl, take authority over the devil and plant in her mind and that of her parents that she was not retarded. This task took Sue and the rest of us two grueling years of constant prayer, counseling, teaching, and reconfirming the Scriptures and the promises of God to the family.

Finally the truth broke through, the girl went on to excel and become a fine young lady, later marrying and having a family of her own.

All during this time the public school superintendent was watching us like a hawk, challenging us on everything he could come up with, but God prevailed and we won the victory. Finally we were no longer being harassed.

One day the superintendent and his assistant came to my office again, this time by appointment. They asked me, actually pleaded with me, to take some other children they couldn't help. They said that most of these kids were real troublemakers and needed a disciplined environment.

The school board had already arranged for financial help through the State to pay the tuition. But there was a catch: I, the school, and these students would have to submit to their authority. Hum, kind'a sounds like the same offer Satan gave to Jesus in the wilderness, doesn't it? I respectfully declined and told them exactly why. They left, disappointed, and I never heard from them again. After that we never had any more trouble with the public school system.

The move to Idaho was challenging and filled with trials,

but it also had its good times. Our youngest, Michelle, maintained her love for horses. We bought a five year-old mare and named her Mandy, and Michelle and Mandy won many ribbons and trophies for show, running barrels, and dressage. We bred Mandy and she had a beautiful foal.

Robert was our skateboard fanatic, he was a natural. Eric took to motorcycles and could tear up the hillside trails like they were nothing.

We bought snowmobiles and a trailer, and we'd take off to Yellowstone National Park and ride into Old Faithful and the big lodge. We'd make a whole day of it, riding all through the park and taking pictures of buffalo, moose, elk, deer, and everything else we saw. We'd stay for two or three days at our favorite motel and dine at some mighty fine restaurants.

Every year the boys and I would go hunting for elk, deer, pheasant and sage hen. Boy, there's some real funny stories to be told about those trips. The boys tell the stories best. These were real bonding times, still etched in my memory. There were the family camping trips to Scout Mountain, Copper Basin, Corn Creek, Wild Horse and other adventures. Then there was fishing the Big Lost River, let me tell you, fishing in Idaho is as good as it gets.

In between, the boys and I would practice trap shooting. We had our own clay-pigeon launcher and got to where we could hit twenty-four out of twenty-five a good deal of the time. Then when the weather was good enough, we'd take the four-wheel drive pickup into the hills behind our house and tear up the countryside.

An important event for us was the annual church family camp-out at Copper Basin. For seven days we had a great time and stored precious memories of time spent with the most wonderful saints of God ever.

A Mormon man named Ray would come to my office to argue doctrine with me. He told me he had the truth and the only viable priesthood was through his church. With everything else that was going on at the time, I saw this as another attack from the enemy, and I wasn't up for it, but I had a check in my spirit keeping me from telling him not to return.

I made it clear that if he wanted to discuss doctrine in a civil way I would, but if not, the conversation was over. It was hard on him. At times he stormed out of my office. But for some reason he kept coming back. Every time, usually because of some doctrinal question he had, I showed him Scripture and told him about the saving grace of God through Christ and not works or religion, but he would refuse it.

He had heard about the miracles our people were experiencing. He tried to tell me they couldn't be real because we weren't under the Melchisedec priesthood of the Mormon Church. I showed him in Scripture that the Melchisedec priesthood was only a type of Christ's priesthood and that Jesus is our high priest. All born-again believers are a kingdom of priests unto God. When I asked him if he had seen any miracles in his church like the ones our people talked about, he usually got mad and left.

I shared with Ray over and over again that the reason he couldn't see the real truth in the Word of God was that he had a veil over his spiritual eyes, as it says in 2 Corinthians 3:14–17. He refused to accept Jesus as his personal Lord and Savior and accept salvation as a gift apart from works or a religious system.

I shared this with him in love, but it angered him. I was surprised that he continued to come back. I was never namby-pamby with Ray. I spoke to him in love, but always with the confidence and authority of Christ.

Ray visited often for almost a year, sometimes weekly. I could see that he was troubled and had no peace about his salvation, and he often said he didn't know if he would make it to the heaven I talked about. He tried to convert me, which is unusual for Mormons; they usually send out their missionaries. Then again, the missionaries already knew of me. Either they didn't want even to try it or their church told them to stay away.

He took up a lot of my time, and we didn't seem to get anywhere, but I kept in mind with Ray the wisdom I learned from my brother in the Lord, Jim Spencer:

"The truth without love is too hard, and love without the truth is too soft."

With all of this "new gospel" and "new revelation" that Ray

said the Mormon Church had and I did not have, I often shared with him two powerful scriptures in the Bible: Malachi 3:6, "For I am the Lord, I change not" and James 1:17, "from the Father of lights, with whom is no variableness, neither shadow of turning."

Then I would lovingly drop the Holy Ghost bomb from Galatians 1:8: "But though we, or an angel from heaven, preach any other gospel unto you than that which we have preached unto you, let him be accursed." The word *accursed* here means to be doomed to eternal punishment.

Every time Ray came to me he got the truth in love, sometimes firmly, but always in love and with the authority and anointing of the Holy Spirit.

His reaction often made me think that he surely wouldn't be back, but Ray always returned. Then one day he was more open than I had ever seen him. He said, in so many words, that all along he could see that I had a real peace about my salvation and talked about Jesus and God as if they were my friends, which, of course, they are. He said every time we talked doctrine, the Bible proved his doctrine to be wrong. Wow, this was music to my ears!

At the end of this discussion he asked me if I would pray with him to accept Jesus as his personal Lord and Savior. I said,

"Ray, are you ready to accept the free gift of salvation by grace and grace alone and trash all your good works as payment for salvation and discard religion as a means to go to heaven, now and forever?"

He answered with a big yes and then began to cry. Between sobs he began to tell Jesus, without any coaching from me, how sorry he was for his sins and for not believing in his Word. I didn't need to lead him in the sinner's prayer; he had a better one than I had at the time.

At the end of his prayer I laid hands on him and prayed for him to receive wisdom, insight, and revelation from God's Word, and for them to take permanent root in his heart. Then I took authority over all false doctrine and cast it out of him. We cried together, and for the first time, hugged each other.

For the first time ever, Ray left my office with a smile on his face and a song in his heart. Almost every day after that, for about a month or so, he came by to thank me and tell me of all the good things that were happening in his life. He was even holding Bible studies (no book of Mormon any more) in his home.

Now others were asking him the same questions he had been asking me. This was such a victory for me that it was as if a hundred or more souls had just been saved. Who knows, maybe there will be even more, all because Ray is sharing his testimony with others.

We grew to a point that we had to have two morning services with Sunday school in between. The facility soon became too small, and when the lease became due for renewal, the landlord doubled the rent.

Off we were again, looking for something else that would work for us until we found a permanent place. Adequate buildings in Pocatello were scarce, so we rented the local Grange building and did a lot of remodeling.

At the same time I started a live one-hour broadcast on the local public TV channel. I taught the Bible, advertise our church and school, and told of our vision and our ministry goals. I had local Christian musicians from other churches share their talents, and this alone was a demonstration of unity in the body.

The message of unity within the body of Christ was taking root, and pastors and believers were beginning to act like Christians.

Our River of Life Christian School was in need of funds, and a few of the members came up with the idea of selling hot dogs at various places. They were three for a dollar and we sold a ton of them. At the same time we handed out material about our Christian school along with Bible tracts.

The fellowship held a huge garage sale, but the weather turned bad and everything had to be taken inside and set up on tables. Things went fine until some items were stolen during the night by thieves who broke in through a window.

They took TVs, fishing poles, camping gear, a very expensive camera with multiple zoom lenses, the entire sound system, $350 from the petty cash drawer and more. When I saw what had happened the Lord spoke to my heart so strongly that His voice was almost audible. He said He was going to show me the house where some of these things were hidden.

When the police arrived, I spoke to the detective in charge and told him what the Lord had told me. He looked at me like he was looking at a wacko, and passed it off. We gave him a description of everything we could see was missing.

For the next couple of days I spent most of my time driving up one street and down the other, giving the Lord the opportunity to point out the house where the goods were stashed. I didn't get any leading, and I was getting worn out, so I went back to my office to pray.

I locked the door behind me, began to pray, and the phone rang. I thought, Don't answer it, just keep on praying, but I realized it might be Sue, and I picked up the receiver. It was a young Christian friend, Larry Gish, who had attended a few services in the past but had moved out of town.

This guy was a real talker, and I just wanted to end the small talk and get on with praying. After a few minutes or so he asked me to join him for lunch at a restaurant. I told him that I was not available, but he persisted and said he was only in town for the day and just wanted to fill me in on what the Lord was doing in his life.

My head said no, but my heart (ever so lightly) said go, and I found myself arranging to meet with him. After about an hour, during which he talked and I half listened, he said,

"Well Pastor, enough about me, how are things going for you and ICC?"

Planning to make it short, I told him a few of the positive things and then casually mentioned the burglary and that I needed to get going. He jerked his head back and said,

"What? Someone broke into the church?"

Reluctantly I began to tell him all about it. When I said that the sound system had been stolen he leaned forward and asked me to describe the pieces. Noticing his strict concentration, I went into detail:—a 7" reel-to-reel Radio Shack tape recorder, two five-foot black speakers, four small cassette recorders, a couple TVs, and so on. Without hesitation, he said,

"I know where they are!"

My mouth dropped, and I just about fell out of my chair. I asked him how he knew where they were. He proceeded to tell me that the night before, when he arrived in town; he had visited some relatives at their house and saw every one of the pieces. He said that they were in the basement of their house, and that they claimed to have bought them at a garage sale.

Right then and there I asked Larry to accompany me down to the police station. He said that he couldn't do that and that the police and his relatives must not find out who ratted on them. He asked me to promise not to reveal his name, and, reluctantly, I did make the promise.

So I asked him for the name and address of the person who had our items. He wrote down the address and said that he couldn't divulge the name to me. Then he said he had to get back on the road and wished me Godspeed.

I drove straight to the police station, asked for the detective that was in charge of the case, and told him that I had the address where our items would be found. He asked me how I got the information and I told him of my meeting with a friend. He asked who this friend was and I told him that I was not at liberty to say.

After a lengthy discussion he stated that there was absolutely no way he could get a search warrant without the witness who saw the items with his own eyes. He asked me over and over to tell him who it was, and I almost broke my word, but I couldn't do it. I pleaded with the detective. "There's just got to be a way! The stuff is there, I know it is!"

He looked at me with visible disappointment and asked me for the piece of paper with the address on it. I handed it to him and he said he'd see what he could do. After about fifteen minutes he came back into the room in a rush, grabbed his coat, and told me we were going to the court house to get the search warrant.

Surprised, I asked,

What happened?

He said the address belonged to a repeat felon who had a warrant out for his arrest and that just maybe the felon would be there. He hoped that while searching the house we would find the stolen items.

I waited in the car with the other officer while the detective got the search warrant. As we drove, he told me in no uncertain terms that when we got to the house he didn't want me to say a word. I was instructed to stay back behind the other officers and that if any rough stuff happened I was to run and get back into the police car.

I began to realize that this was getting serious and my heart was pumping overtime. There were two police cars and four officers, and we all pulled up to the house at the same time. One officer immediately went around to the back of the house and another stayed off to the side at the front.

The detective and the other officer and I went to the front door and rang the bell. The second officer told me to stay close behind him. He had his hand on the gun in its holster.

As soon as the door opened, the detective flashed the search warrant in the woman's face and pushed his way in, telling the woman who he was looking for. The second officer and I were right behind him. Standing in the living room, the detective asked where the wanted man was and the lady repeated that he wasn't there.

The detective and the officer quickly looked into the rooms on that floor and then took me by the arm to the basement stairs and told me to follow them down. The detective took the lead, then the officer and then me, and we all moved slowly and cautiously down the stairs and into the basement.

Just as Larry Gish had said, all the sound equipment and one of the TVs were right out there in the open. The detective asked me to look closely at all of it and to make no mistake in identifying anything. Things began to relax, and I started to confirm each piece as the detective made a list. Then a discussion broke out on the issue of placing all of it into evidence at the police station.

Just then the detective shouted to the officer, who jumped in front of me to protect me, and a scuffle began on the other side of the bed on the floor. My heart was beating so fast it sounded like a machine gun.

The officer pushed me down to the floor, dove over the bed, and held the wanted man while the other officer handcuffed him. They pulled him up on the bed and read him his rights. As a result of this arrest, two others involved in the robbery were arrested the same day. All of them were under twenty years old.

The story gets even more intense. I was thanking the Lord in prayer, and He impressed my heart that I would find the expensive camera. Learning from the last episode, I didn't go out looking this time.

In one of my many discussions with the detective I happened to mention that I would find the camera. This time it was different. I had his undivided attention, and he asked me for every detail. He asked me how I knew when the Lord spoke to me, what it sounded like, and so on. It was a good time of witnessing that I didn't even have to go out and look for.

I told him that I didn't have any details about how I would find the camera yet, but I assured him that the Lord would reveal to me what I needed to know when the right time came.

Two or three times the next day he called me to see if the Lord had said anything to me yet. Every time he called I told him I'd call him as soon as I knew anything. He said he couldn't believe the peace and confidence I had over the whole thing, and during every conversation I got to tell him a little more about Jesus.

The next day still nothing happened, but at 2:00 AM the phone rang next to our bed. When I answered it, the person on the other end said he had our camera and he wanted to return it to me.

Reader, are you keeping track of all these miracles? I'm telling you, God's alive, and He is just as much the same miracle-working God today as He was in Biblical times.

At first I thought I was dreaming, so I got out of bed and took the phone into the living room, making sure I was fully awake. As we talked the young man told me he heard that the Lord had given me the address of the other items, and he just wanted to return the camera and not get in trouble. He felt that if he didn't call me and make arrangements, the Lord would give me his name and address and he would be arrested. This phone call lasted for over an hour, so I'll stick with the highlights.

He was only eighteen. This was the first time he had ever done anything like this, he said, and he was very sorry. He said he had just started mixing with the wrong crowd and knew that he had to cut off all relationships with them. I witnessed to him about sin, judgment, and Jesus, and he said he wanted to repent and accept Jesus into his heart as his Lord and Savior.

Testing him, I said that if he wasn't serious about changing his life and becoming a Christian he could just leave the camera somewhere for me to pick up. He insisted that he really wanted to change and repent. This young man, too, was already *convicted* and only needed to be *converted.*

Later that day we met and made the exchange. I got the camera, he got Jesus. I'm glad he got the best of the trade. I never gave his name to the detective. He asked me more than once, but I only gave the young man's name to Jesus.

During the trial the defense attorney attacked me in every way he could, trying to make me look like the criminal. In one of his attacks he asked why a minister wouldn't just forgive rather than take out vengeance on these poor kids who were undoubtedly raised in a dysfunctional family.

He drilled me on hearing from God about the address where the stolen items were, which the detective had told him about. His whole attitude was arrogant and facetious, and he was doing his best to make me out to be a fool. He wanted to know if I often heard "voices," making a mockery out of the whole thing. When I repeatedly said "no comment" to his line of questioning, the judge said forcefully,

"Rev. Ford, you will answer the question!"
I replied,

"Your honor, with all due respect, I'm not the one who's on trial here!"

The judge was not happy with my response. He reprimanded me and stated that I must answer the question. Then, after a short pause, I said,

"I stand on my Fifth Amendment rights!"
Finally the prosecuting attorney spoke up and got things off into another direction.

After three days of trial proceedings, the jury went to deliberate, and within fifteen minutes they returned with a verdict.

Even though two of these boys were repeat felons, they all received only six months probation. There was no restitution, no community service, not even an "I'm sorry." I learned that the judge had valued all the stolen property at less than $100 and gave no credence to the $350 from the cash box.

We couldn't believe it! The question "Why" stayed in our minds for over a year. Then one day while we were buying a new sofa, Sue and I found out why. The cashier recognized us and told us that she was one of the jurors. She said the judge told the jury exactly what they were to decide, and they couldn't do anything about it. She apologized and said she was very sorry for us. After putting her mind and heart at ease, I said,

"Justice belongs to the Judge of all judges, and He will surely recompense."

Such attacks from the enemy have a negative effect on some within the body, particularly those who only want a sweet "no problems" kind of church. These folks are usually the ones that aren't involved in the work of the ministry but are just there to attend the services and get blessed.

This will sound critical, but they want everything to be peaceful, without problems, and full of God's love, power, and anointing. But that's not reality, and any advancing work of God that is destroying the work of the devil will face opposition, just as it says in John 15:18–21.

Our inability to remain in a permanent place was problematic for the fellowship. The constant moving from place to place and the challenges and circumstances that went along with it was, to put it mildly, laborious. It was stressful for everyone, and we always lost a few members.

I would see some growth and then see some loss, and then see some more growth and then some more loss. As in sports, you win some distance toward your goal and then you lose a little, you win a little more back and you lose a little again. It may go on like this for some time until you reach your goal. The main thing is never to give up and to keep on pressing toward the goal.

No doubt, this can be hard on the team. Some quit and give

up and that's disheartening. But I had to constantly remind myself that every yard we gained in the battle, we were gaining for Jesus and that it wasn't really our battle at all, but His.

There was an almost invisible issue that plagued Pocatello. The city fathers were not enthusiastic at all about growth, and they held businesses, jobs, and housing at bay. Many big businesses wanted to come to Pocatello, but the city said no. They went to Idaho Falls or Boise sometimes, but usually they went to another State. The effect was that many of our members had to move to find better jobs.

With so little industry in Pocatello, not many people moved there. The population of Pocatello in 1975 was 45,000. Twenty-five years later it was 55,000, an annual growth rate of only 400. On top of that, most were Mormons. Pocatello was, and is, one of the slowest growing cities in the United States.

As hard as this was on me, it was even harder on Sue and children. Only they and the Lord knew just how much sacrifice they made to keep on truck'n. I'm not complaining, just stating the facts.

For a time, God graciously held off the enemy, and we were able to get things back in order and get on with the work of the Lord. Although we wanted to build our own facility, we were constantly looking for a building that would suit our purpose and have room for growth. After almost two years, finding nothing suitable, we decided to look for vacant land to build our church on.

We located eleven acres in Chubbuck. It was in an area of new growth and was properly zoned for a church. Chubbuck is right across the street from Pocatello, and everything about this property looked good. It was a nice large piece of flat fertile farm land, power and utilities in the street and right on a good road parallel to a main road in town.

We bought the property and started planning to divide it into six one-acre lots that we would sell and one five-acre parcel for the church. We applied for water and sewer hook-up from the City of Chubbuck and they refused us!

I called and asked why, and all they would tell me was that

they didn't have enough water to supply us. I knew this wasn't true and that there was more to it.

We hired a lawyer and requested a meeting with the city council. The Mayor, John Cotant was a super-staunch Mormon. He was not only in charge of the meeting but he did all the talking. His spirit was of that same kind that the apostle Jude wrote about in his letter to the church.

Our attorney, a non-Mormon, argued with Mr. Cotant for over thirty minutes, and got nowhere. Then he leaned over to me and whispered that he didn't believe we could do anything about it and we were wasting our time. Just then Mr. Cotant said that if we wanted to hook up to the sewer we would have to put in, at our expense, a quarter of a mile of sewer line down the street and two lift stations. The estimated cost was $100,000.

Mr. Cotant said sarcastically, that we might as well sell the property and look elsewhere. He said he was not going to allow us to build *our* church in *his* backyard, meaning Chubbuck, which he considered *his* city.

Then he had the gall to say that he, as a real estate broker, would be happy to take our listing and sell the property for us.

This had all the earmarks of *illegal* in big red letters, but our attorney advised us that we would just waste our time and money if we tried to fight it. He said to sell the property, cut our losses, and stay out of Chubbuck.

After much prayer we decided to divide the acreage into one and two-acre parcels and put it on the market to sell by owner. It sold quickly. We didn't make a bundle, but we didn't lose anything either.

If you're wondering why I've shared these lost battles, it's because I want you to know that not everything worked out perfectly. I have read many books about other ministers, and most of them only tell about their victories. That's not real life. If I can't share the failures with you, I have no right to share the victories either.

When I read about one success after another and no failures, it sometimes make me think there must be something wrong with me, for I have almost as many losses as wins.

When I planned this book, I made a decision to give you the whole story. If there is any consolation in it, God called us only to be faithful, not successful. However, in being faithful, we will see more triumphs than we would if our only goal is to seek success. In other words, with God, remaining faithful, is in itself a victory.

After losing a number of battles, God showed me something in the Spirit that I hadn't seen before: every battle that seemed lost in the eyes of man really wasn't lost after all. On the contrary, we won in the spirit realm, as long as we hadn't given up the fight or rebelled against God.

I began to see that all the while God was trying our faith and also testing our enemy; just as He had tested Pharaoh before Moses. But Moses and the people didn't understand what God was doing. They thought everything Moses did was unsuccessful. Because it brought them hardships, it must have been a failure.

This was the cup that God had given them to drink. We prayed that our cup would pass from us, but it was God's will that we drink it, and drink it we did.

We picked up the pieces, regrouped, and began to move forward. We found and purchased a building in Pocatello, thanks to my good Mormon friend Dean Funk. It had been a business and before that a residence, located right on a main street called Pole Line Road, which ran from Pocatello through the middle of Chubbuck. The address was 3607 Pole Line Road. We bought a house next to the church and used it for classrooms.

A few years earlier, I had applied for a Residential and Commercial Contractor License and became an official contractor. I named our company Alpha Omega Construction, and over the years we built about a dozen custom homes, a few duplexes, and a commercial building. We did a number of remodels as well.

I wanted to take some of the financial burden off the church and to be able to give more generously to the many mission ministries Sue and I were supporting. I also had in mind that as a contractor I could build our church building and save a lot of money.

We bought the property on Pole Line Road, did some

remodeling, and began holding services. It was tight, but it was ours. We had plans to expand, so we didn't mind squeezing in for now. Shortly after that we drew up our rough plans for expansion and began praying over them, all the while raising funds for the project. At this time President Carter was raising the interest rates every month or so and the bank refused our loan application when rates reached 16%.

Then we turned to the Assemblies of God (thank God for unity!) and joined their Omega Church Bond program, where they loan money to the church on the amount of bonds that the members buy. These bonds either pay yearly dividends or are held until maturity and then turned in for their maturity value, which includes the interest accumulated over the term of the bond.

After securing our loan I submitted our expansion plans and drawings to the Pocatello Building Department and waited to hear back from them. After about a week or so they called me into the department to discuss our project.

Jay, the Building Department Project Manager, was in charge and had three others with him. The more we discussed the project, the more I could see that they had no intention of granting us a building permit.

The first thing I thought of was that I was dealing with the same spirit as before with the eleven acres in Chubbuck. I had a holy anger about me, and this time I wasn't going to sit still for it. I started praying in my mind and didn't let up all through the whole meeting.

They said they wanted to change our address to the side street adjacent to our property and that they had plans to widen that street and take about fifteen feet of our property. They didn't say when they would widen, but of course they wanted their fifteen feet now.

This would mean that we wouldn't have the room to build an addition on the existing building. Then they said we couldn't continue to use the entrance from Pole Line Road any more and would have to enter from the side street.

Next, they wanted to widen Pole Line Road, again, some day, and for now, only in front of our property. We were to put in the curb and gutter, the ten-foot-wide utility and shrubbery area, and the sidewalk. I sat there thinking "If it ever came to all of this having to be done, we'd be dead in our tracks." A change such as this would be irreversible.

As a contractor, I knew that what they demanded was unethical and borderline illegal. I also knew that they could make anything legal if they wanted to.

As things progressed, I felt my old nature rise up within me. I desperately wanted to do verbal battle with them, but I forced myself to subdue my anger. I did my best to keep my cool and believe for a miracle. I challenged their requirements with respect—but not with timidity—and I prayed as the battle continued.

I reiterated my earnest concerns about how these changes would impact the neighborhood. The side street, as our new and only entrance and exit, would be so congested that the city would be inundated with complaints from the neighbors. Jay shrugged his shoulders and pooh-poohed the idea.

In frustration, I turned a little to the left, put my right elbow on the table and buried my forehead in my right hand. With closed eyes and pursed lips I contemplated releasing a torrent of rebukes at all four of them.

Then, I felt a definite quenching of the Holy Spirit within me, so I repented, took a deep breath, and muttered under my breath reverently "God, I need a miracle here, and I need it now!"

I looked up at the four men with nothing to say. Then I heard the door open behind me. When Jay and the others looked up, they stopped dead. I turned around to see who it was and saw Dean Funk, my Mormon friend. He had his left hand on the door-knob and his right hand on the door-jamb, barely looking into the room. He looked at me and said,

"Hi, Pastor Ford, Everything okay?"
I answered,
"Hello, Dean!"
I wanted to unload. I wanted to tell him exactly what was on my mind, but I had a check in my spirit and instead I said,
"Well ... sure, Dean, I think everything will be okay."
With that he said,

"Okay, Pastor Ford. If you ever need anything, just give me a call!"

He said goodbye and shut the door.

I turned back and saw the four men looking at each other questioningly. Jay said they needed a few minutes alone, and they went into an adjoining room. A couple of minutes later they came out and took their seats again.

Jay began to tell me that they had reconsidered things and I could pick up my building permit the next day. I asked about the restrictions and he said there would be none.

I was delighted, but remained calm. I wanted to shout praise to the Lord, but I didn't want to cast any pearls before swine, as the Scriptures say in Matthew 7:6.

God had done it again! When I got into my car I shouted, Hallelujah! Stomped my feet and clapped my hands. My body shook with excitement from head to toe.

I remembered God's promise in Proverbs 16:7 (Living Bible), "When a man is trying to please God, God makes even his worst enemies to be at peace with him." It says God *makes* them be at peace: they weren't willing to do right, so God applied pressure. I'll bet those guys were steaming about it from then on.

Sometimes it's hard to remember that our battle is not against flesh and blood but against evil spirits in the heavenly realm. These evil spirits manifest their power, influence, and will through humans here on earth. All this is recorded throughout the Bible, but I recommend reading Ephesians 2:2; 6:12, the entire book of Jude, and Revelation 2:20–23.

The four ruling spirits mentioned in Jude and Revelation (Cane, Balaam, Core, and Jezebel) are more than just names of people. They died many years before Jude and John wrote about them. Jude verses 17–18 says that these spirits will be manifest in the last days. These verses refer to the same thing in 2 Peter 3:3.

These Scriptures annihilate the false teaching that the demon spirits were cast into hell during the days of Jesus and the apostles. You won't find a single Scripture where any demon was cast into hell, not by Jesus or any of his disciples. Yes, they were cast out, but where did they go?

Matthew 12: 43–45 says, "When an unclean spirit goes out of a man, he goes through dry places, seeking rest, and finds none. Then he says, 'I will return to my house from which I came.' And when he comes, he finds it empty, swept, and put in order. Then he goes and takes with him seven other spirits more wicked than himself, and they enter and dwell there; and the last state of that man is worse than the first. So shall it also be with this wicked generation."

What hope do we have? Get rid of the evil spirit and fill the void with the Holy Spirit, and walk in the truth; for the truth will set you free. Hallelujah!

I found out later that Dean was going from room to room looking for someone when he stumbled upon our room. It was the look on the four men's faces that caused him to ask me if everything was okay, but I know it was God that orchestrated the whole thing. I thanked Dean; even though he had no clue God had used him for this miracle.

Here is a little background about Dean Funk. He was raised Christian but converted to Mormonism, I think for social and professional reasons. We often had spiritual discussions along with business related conversations, and we had lunch together occasionally.

He knew that meeting with me meant hearing about Jesus and salvation as a gift through faith and not works. Dean always had the right answers, and I felt confident that he had a personal relationship with Jesus.

He was a Real Estate agent and a City Council member. He had recently been the Mayor of Pocatello. He had a lot of clout in the city, and was a likeable guy. From the beginning he took a liking to me and showed respect for me at all times. He was supportive of what I was doing and helped me out whenever he could.

Psalms 23:5 says that "God will prepare a table for us in the midst of our enemies." At that table where I sat before these four men from the city planning department, I was truly in the midst of my enemies. Let me say it this way, God *turned* the tables on my enemies and made me the victor when He led Dean Funk to that room.

I called my good Lutheran friend, Erhardt Anderson, and asked him to meet with me about helping us with our church building addition. Erhardt had no other work at the time, which was perfect timing for us. We came to an agreement on an hourly wage, the elders accepted it, and our building program was off and running.

I would get to the site at 6:30 AM and Erhardt would arrive about 6:50. His shift started at 7 AM and ended at 3:30 PM with a half hour for lunch. Erhardt went home at 3:30, but I kept working until after 9:00, sometimes as late as 11:00.

Surely running on pure nervous energy, I kept up this schedule until the end of the project. The first month, down in the huge hole for the basement, I lost thirty-five pounds I could ill afford. It could reach a hundred and ten degrees down there, with very little air circulation.

Even with a number of others helping, setting up the panels and rebar for the ten-foot basement walls was a project in itself. One young gal came all the way from Idaho Falls just to cut rebar.

Charlie and Linda Lotshaw donated and delivered the heating and air conditioning materials for the entire building. We had forced-air gas heaters and two outside heat pumps. Everything was top notch. They even brought the ducting, wiring, thermostats, tools, and six or eight men to install it all. What a blessing these good people have been to us and to the body of Christ all these years.

There was a young man in his early twenties, Paul Kaufmann, who was strong physically as well as spiritually. He and his parents, Harold and Marie, were Spirit-Filled Baptists, and his mother would witness to almost anything that was breathing.

Paul was a licensed evangelist with the Baptist Church but felt limited in ministry due to doctrinal differences over the gifts of the Spirit, so he migrated our way and became a part of ICC.

Paul was there all through the building stage, and we became good friends. He was of high moral character and a likeable young man. I often thought I'd like to see him become interested in my daughter, Michelle, but I didn't feel comfortable talking about it.

I knew I wasn't called to be a matchmaker. I didn't find out until later that Paul's mother was working on this all along. One day she suggested to Paul, in the presence of Michelle, that he ought to date her. Now that could have been a disaster but, God is on the Throne in all things, and Paul asked her out.

Eventually he asked me for her hand in marriage. They now have three wonderful girls, Kriana, Ambriel, and Natasha. Paul became quite a Bible thumper and taught Bible studies in homes as well as the church.

Later we officially licensed him as a Spirit filled evangelist. He preached on a regular basis on Sunday evenings, as did all my trainees. Paul preached now and then on Sunday mornings when I was away. If it hadn't been for the building program and Marie, maybe Paul and Michelle would never have met. God does all things well. Amen!

With the building schedule I was keeping, I couldn't lead any Bible studies or conduct the mid-week service any more, so others I had trained carried the load. I still did the Sunday morning and evening services, and if it hadn't been for the grace of God I never could have done it all.

In the beginning we had lots of help constructing our building, especially with tear-down and clean-up. A number of the woman fixed lunches, snacks, and beverages for everyone. As time went on, though, people became weary or their schedules filled up, and they couldn't continue to help. Fewer workers had to carry the load.

The building did get finished. We settled in, and things found a new and better state of normalcy. The existing building that we added on to had a nice big kitchen, ample classrooms, and a secretary's office off the main entry.

I had a big office upstairs with windows looking out over the town in two directions. We installed a huge gold-colored cross lit from the rear with neon lighting on the front of the building. Man, was it a sight to see. It lit up the sky and almost spoke out loud of the love of Jesus.

Charlie and Linda Lotshaw, back in California, founded and maintained a ministry called Helping Hands (**www.lotshawhelpinghands.com**). They gathered overstock items from merchants and manufacturers such as food, clothing, school supplies, blankets, office supplies and more. They would distribute these things to needy people, churches, and nonprofit organizations in a number of states.

Once a month they would come to Pocatello with a semi trailer loaded full. From our parking lot at ICC we would, distribute to churches, missions, food banks, and the Salvation Army, to name a few.

This also spoke volumes to the churches and the entire city, about unity within the body of Christ. Up to fifteen organizations came on a regular basis. Then, in turn-around, they would pick up potatoes, wheat, and whatever the farmers offered and take it back home to distribute there.

What a blessing this was, and everyone was very thankful for the sacrifices that Charlie and Linda made in donating their time and equipment to help the needy.

We continued to see the signs and wonders that the Bible says will follow any true believer in miracles. Are you ready for this one? Hold onto your hat.

I got thinking that the fellowship needed some good old-fashioned time together at the local park for fun, games, and a picnic on a Saturday. I wanted to make a day of it, say about 10 AM to 3 PM.

We set a date and began announcing it at all the Bible studies and during the morning and evening services. We had people in charge of everything we could think of. Everyone was excited and willing to help out.

As the date drew closer, the weather forecast was looking grim and people were asking if we shouldn't change the date. But, you know me, Mr. man of faith, I wouldn't budge. I believed that the forecast would change for the better, and that there would be no rain that day even if the weatherman said there would be. I had said more than once that the weatherman can *predict* the weather, but we know the Man who *provides* the weather.

The forecast didn't improve as the week of the picnic arrived, and people were concerned about keeping our plans. But I continued to tell everyone we were going to stick to our date and have the picnic.

A few people told me to my face that I was being foolishly stubborn and that they wouldn't be there if the forecast didn't change. I actually began to think about changing my mind just to keep peace within the fellowship, but the more I prayed about it, the more I felt compelled to remain committed to the set date.

I really did have a strong, settled, peace in my heart about it. I felt that the Holy Spirit was the force behind my faith. I made no apologies and continued to say firmly that it wasn't going to rain on our picnic.

On Friday the weather forecast looked even worse, and a number of people called to say they wouldn't be coming. I understood their concern, for a number of them had small children and lived twenty, thirty, and even fifty miles away. But I refused to budge and I wouldn't entertain any more discussion. It wasn't going to rain on our picnic!

Saturday morning came and the sky didn't look good. It was dark and cloudy, and it looked like we were in for a downpour. I began to question myself about being stubborn; and I earnestly asked the Lord to check my heart, but, the more I prayed about it, the more peace I had that it would be all right.

I had Sue's full support. What a fantastic wife I have! She has always stuck by my side and supported me, even when she didn't agree with me. She always had a good attitude about it, too. We gathered all the things we had committed to taking, packed the car, and drove off to the park.

We were early, but a few others had already arrived. I'm not sure if they were there for the picnic or just to see if we were going to show up ourselves. At any rate, they asked if we were going to go ahead with it, and I said,

"Absolutely!"

While others were arriving we unpacked our things and

began setting up tables and games. Now and then another person or family would show up.

The sky was getting blacker, and it looked scary up there. It started to rain. We stood there looking up at the sky. Then we began to look at each other, blinking and wondering if we all were experiencing the same thing. Not one drop of rain had fallen on any of us. We held our hands out, palms up, checking for rain, but there was none.

We started walking around the park, and it was the same thing all over. No rain. We saw the rain splashing in the three streets that bordered park, but none fell on the park itself. God is absolutely fantastic, even when His people just want to have fun. I can hardly sit still over it. GLORY!

We had our picnic. We played our games throughout the day, and no rain landed on us as long as we didn't go out in the street. Neighbors near the park noticed we weren't getting wet, and some walked over to check it out for themselves.

It rained for about half the day, but no rain landed on the park all the time we were there. It wasn't a real downpour, but it wasn't a light sprinkle either. It was a constant moderate rain, and none of it fell on us.

God revealed His will to me by placing it in my heart. All He required of me was that I stand with Him by confessing it out of my mouth. I didn't control the weather, God did. All I did was plan the picnic. Did God put it in my head to plan the picnic? I don't know about that, but He put it in my heart that it wouldn't rain on us, and it didn't.

Once you know God's will, your words and actions will either make it happen or stop it its tracks. I have God's Word to back that up. Proverbs 18:21 says, "Death and life are in the power of the tongue, and they that love (believe) it shall eat the fruit thereof." This verse literally means that what you say out of your mouth and believe in your heart, you will have.

Jesus said the same thing in Mark 11:23: "whosoever shall say…and shall not doubt in his heart, but shall believe that the things which he says shall come to pass, he shall have whatsoever he says."

Because I believe with my whole heart that God's Word is true and that these verses are as much for me as they are for anyone, I've seen numerous miracles like this one.

One person standing strong in this kind of faith is a majority with God. In 2 Chronicles 16:9, God tells us He is on the constant lookout for even one person man, woman or child, with this kind of commitment and tenacity. He is looking for the opportunity to show himself strong, miraculous, on behalf of such people.

The next day, Sunday, after the song service, I made mention of the miracle that God had done at the picnic. I didn't want anyone to feel targeted or guilty for not attending, but I did want to give God the glory for such an over-the-top miracle as this. There was glorious praise to God, but there were sheepish looks on a few faces.

On the brighter side, as the people told their friends and neighbors of this and other miracles, people trickled in to check us out for themselves. Because of the people, the message of God's goodness was being spread all over town.

God was leading me to believe for bigger things. Bigger you say? Oh, yes. God always has something bigger up His sleeve for anyone who will believe for it. I dedicated myself to seek His leading and wisdom and set my elders and deacons to doing the same. Because there is so much more to tell of outright over-the-top miracles of God, as well as trials, and tribulations, I am writing a sequel to this book that should be available soon.

God bless you, and keep the faith.

Evangelistic Opportunities

Not everyone is called to be an Apostle, Prophet, Evangelist, Pastor, or Teacher, but all Christians are called to win souls for Christ. There are many ways to do this, but I want to suggest one in particular.

If my story has blessed you and you know of anyone who could use an encouraging word, why not start your own outreach ministry and send them a copy of this book. Perhaps a friend, workmate, your pastor, or even a missionary would benefit from my story. You never know, that person could be the instrument of God to start a revival somewhere. All praise to God, you would be the initiator.

Over the years I have used my life events as a witnessing tool to win hundreds to Christ. Now that my story is in book form, it can be an even more effective tool. It can be given to others, who will give it to others, and so on.

Wrongfully Accused has been presented, not only as a life story, but also as a how-to book to use in small group settings to win souls to Christ and to inspire hope, faith and courage. With the anointing of the Holy Spirit, you could even start a revival in your own community.

There are many men and women in the armed forces who put their lives on the line for all of us so that we can live in a free county. If you know of one of these courageous souls, why not send them a copy of this book?

If you don't know one and would like to be part of our missionary outreach to the military you may send your donation to us addressed to, His Grace Ministries, Inc., PO Box 707, Everson, WA 98247. Or you may use your credit card or PayPal account through our e-mail address or website. Please mark your gift, "books for soldiers," and all of it will be used for that purpose.

To schedule speaking engagements, miracle healing meetings, or seminars please e-mail us at **hgmin5@gmail.com**. If the Lord leads you to stand with us in this ministry with financial support, you my use your credit card or PayPal with our e-mail address, or our website at **www.hisgrace5.org.**

I would like to leave you with this word of promise from Jeremiah 29:11–13 (Living Bible).

For I know the plans I have for you, says the Lord. They are plans for good and not for evil, to give you a future and a hope. In those days when you pray, I will listen. You will find me when you seek me, if you look for me in earnest.